THE PSYCHOLOGY OF MISINFORMATION

King Charles III is Dracula's distant cousin. Governments are hiding information about UFOs. COVID-19 came from outer space. These sound like absurd statements, but some are true and others are misinformation. But what exactly is misinformation? Who believes and spreads things that aren't true, and why? What solutions do we have available, and how well do they work? This book answers all these questions and more. Tackling the science of misinformation from its evolutionary origins to its role in the internet era, this book translates rigorous research on misleading information into a comprehensive and jargon-free explanation. Whether you are a student, researcher, policymaker, or changemaker, you will discover an easy-to-read analysis on human belief in today's world and expert advice on how to prevent deception.

Jon Roozenbeek is an award-winning researcher from the University of Cambridge whose work straddles psychology, area studies, and computer science. He studies the psychology of misinformation and group identity in times of conflict and authored *Propaganda and Ideology in the Russian–Ukrainian War* (2024).

Sander van der Linden is Professor of Social Psychology in Society and Director of the Cambridge Social Decision-Making Lab at the University of Cambridge. He is ranked among the top 1 percent of highly cited social scientists worldwide.

Contemporary Social Issues

General Editor
Brian D. Christens,
Vanderbilt University

Contemporary Social Issues is the official book series of the Society for the Psychological Study of Social Issues (SPSSI). Since its founding in 1936, SPSSI has addressed the social issues of the times. Central to these efforts has been the Lewinian tradition of action-oriented research, in which psychological theories and methods guide research and action addressed to important societal problems. Grounded in their authors' programs of research, works in this series focus on social issues facing individuals, groups, communities, and/or society at large, with each volume written to speak to scholars, students, practitioners, and policymakers.

Other Books in the Series

Developing Critical Consciousness in Youth: Contexts and Settings
Erin Godfrey and Luke Rapa, editors

Critical Consciousness: Expanding Theory and Measurement
Erin Godfrey and Luke Rapa, editors

When Politics Becomes Personal: The Effect of Partisan Identity on Anti-Democratic Behavior
Alexa Bankert, author

Young Black Changemakers and the Road to Racial Justice
Laura Wray-Lake, Elan C. Hope, and Laura S. Abrams, authors

The Psychology of Misinformation

Jon Roozenbeek
University of Cambridge

Sander van der Linden
University of Cambridge

Shaftesbury Road, Cambridge CB2 8EA, United Kingdom

One Liberty Plaza, 20th Floor, New York, NY 10006, USA

477 Williamstown Road, Port Melbourne, VIC 3207, Australia

314–321, 3rd Floor, Plot 3, Splendor Forum, Jasola District Centre, New Delhi – 110025, India

103 Penang Road, #05–06/07, Visioncrest Commercial, Singapore 238467

Cambridge University Press is part of Cambridge University Press & Assessment, a department of the University of Cambridge.

We share the University's mission to contribute to society through the pursuit of education, learning and research at the highest international levels of excellence.

www.cambridge.org
Information on this title: www.cambridge.org/9781009214407

DOI: 10.1017/9781009214414

© Jon Roozenbeek and Sander van der Linden 2024

First published 2024

A catalogue record for this publication is available from the British Library

A Cataloging-in-Publication data record for this book is available from the Library of Congress

ISBN 978-1-009-21440-7 Hardback
ISBN 978-1-009-21436-0 Paperback

CONTENTS

FIGURES

ACKNOWLEDGMENTS

We are grateful to the many people whose help was instrumental for the research that went into this book. First, we would like to thank all the current and former members of the Cambridge Social Decision-Making Lab, whose excellent research and insights we've relied on a great deal. In no particular order: Melisa Basol, Rakoen Maertens, Cecilie Steenbuch Traberg, Claudia Schneider, Steve Rathje, James He, William (Patrick) McClanahan, Ahmed Izzidien, Christel van Eck, Cameron Brick, Anne Marthe van der Bles, Karly Drabot, Elif Naz Çoker, Kayla Pincus, Helena de Boer, Vivien Chopurian, Zsofia Szlamka, Ondřej Kácha, Amos Fong, Danielle Goldwert, Ana Sabherwal, Kristian Steensen Nielsen, Michael (Mikey) Biddlestone, Flávio Azevedo, Dongwon Lee, Fatih Uenal, Breanne Cryst, Charlotte Kukowski, Ramit Debnath, Aleksander Bjørge Gundersen, Carolin Ziemer, Hannah Logemann, Kayleigh Dawson, Georgia Capewell, Barbara Czekaj, Petra Georgoulis-Hluzova, Katie Barnes, Ceejay Hayes, Yara Kyrychenko, Sushmeena Parihar, and Trisha Harjani. Second, we want to thank our great colleagues at the (former) Winton Centre for Risk and Evidence Communication, including Alexandra Freeman, Sir David Spiegelhalter, Sir John Aston, John Kerr, and Aarushi Shah. Third, we are grateful to all our collaborators and fellow scientists from outside of Cambridge: Steve Lewandowsky, Jay Van Bavel, John Cook, Beth Goldberg (and the rest of the Jigsaw team, including Bomo Piri, Shira Almeleh, and Rachel Xu), Nabil Saleh, Fadi Makki, Lisa Fazio, Briony Swire-Thompson, Jane Suiter, Eileen Culloty, Jesper Rasmussen, Ruth Elisabeth Appel, Rebecca Rayburn-Reeves, Jonathan Corbin, Thomas Nygren, Carl-Anton Werner Axelsson, Joel Breakstone, Fabiana Zollo, Walter Quattrociocchi (and team), Stefan Herzog and Ralph Hertwig (and team), Sahil Loomba, Alex de Figueiredo, Ulrich Ecker, Kurt Braddock, Deen Freelon, Dolores Albarracín, Jana Lasser, David Garcia, Julian Neylan, Johannes Leder, Lukas Schellinger, Ariana Modirrousta-Galian, Phil Higham, David Rand, and Gordon Pennycook. Fourth, the anti-misinformation interventions we've helped design would not have been possible without the following people: Ruurd Oosterwoud, Rivka Otten, Lisa Poot, and Bram Alkema (DROG), Marije Arentze (Fontys Academy for Journalism), Martijn Gussekloo, Bas Breugelmans, and Bas Janson (Gusmanson), Christina Nemr (Becera), Tyler Golson and Paul Fischer (Global Engagement Center), TILT, and Luke Newbold and Sean Sears (Studio You London). Fifth, we want to thank our colleagues and funders from the IRIS Academic Research Group, JITSUVAX (and EU Horizon 2020), the UK Cabinet Office, the Global Engagement Center, the British Academy, the Economics and Social Research Council, the American Psychological Association, Jigsaw, Google, Meta, Omidyar Network India, and the Alfred Landecker Foundation. Sixth, we want to thank Janka Romero, Rowan Groat, Emily Watton, and Brian Christens (Cambridge University Press) for all their hard work commissioning, editing, proofreading, and helping revise this book. And finally, we owe a great deal of thanks to Sacha Altay, Martin Worthington, Jay Van Bavel, and Alexander Bor, who provided extensive and hugely useful input on various chapters in this book.

Prologue

Let's play a little game. Try to guess if the following statements are true or false (no peeking below for the answers!). The virus that causes COVID-19 came from outer space. King Charles III of Britain is Count Dracula's cousin. John Kellogg invented cornflakes to prevent people from having impure sexual thoughts. The US military hides information about UFOs from the public. The average person accidentally swallows about eight spiders per year in their sleep.

Are you ready? Let's see how well you did.

COVID-19 most likely didn't come from outer space. This may seem obvious, but in 2020 an apparently dead serious group of scientists claimed that the virus may have "arrived via a meteorite [...] that struck Northeast China on October 11, 2019" (E. J. Steele et al., 2020). Who knows if their claim will be proven true at some point, so let's put this one in the "maybe" pile. King Charles does indeed appear to be a distant relative of Vlad III of Wallachia, better known as Vlad the Impaler, who inspired Bram Stoker's Dracula (Beever, 2022; CBS News, 2011). The claim that John Kellogg invented cornflakes as an "anti-masturbatory morning meal" is widespread (Mayyasi, 2016; Soniak, 2023), but the fact-checking website Snopes rates it as "mostly false": Kellogg designed cornflakes to be easy to digest, pre-prepared, and healthy, although he did recommend a bland diet to discourage masturbation (it's just that there's not much evidence, apparently, that he invented cornflakes for this reason). It's a fact that the US military hides information about UFOs from the public (Hopkins & Snyder, 2022), but this statement is incomplete: UFOs (Unidentified Flying Objects or Unidentified Anomalous Phenomena, UAPs, as the military calls them nowadays) are commonly observed, but officials are wary of disclosing too much information about them for national security reasons (e.g., because they don't want the public know about secret military technology); the *implied* claim that was not made explicit in this statement, however, is unlikely to be true as of this writing.[1]

And finally, people don't accidentally swallow many spiders in their sleep, although this is a widespread myth.[2] This is actually a brilliant example of how easy it can be to spread misinformation, but not in the way you might think. In 2001 David Mikkelson of *Snopes* published an article debunking the spider myth (Mikkelson, 2001). He explained how unlikely it is for spiders to crawl into people's mouths by accident, and even found the myth's original source: a 1993 article in the magazine *PC Professional* by Lisa Birgit Holst about the dangers of internet misinformation. In turn, Holst had taken the claim from a 1954 book about insect folklore that listed a collection of common misbeliefs. Ironically, Mikkelson explained, Holst's article became so popular that the spider myth became one of the most widely circulated pieces of misinformation on the Internet. The Snopes article went viral, and other websites followed suit by publishing their own debunking articles. Not only the claim itself but also its correction became widespread. Many of these websites uncritically copied Mikkelson's explanation of the myth's origin, but there was a catch: it was completely made up. A Swedish YouTuber named LEMMiNO (2016) conducted an exhaustive investigation in search of Holst's article in *PC Professional*, but came up with nothing. He then realized that he'd been tricked: Lisa Birgit Holst is an anagram for "this is a big troll." Mikkelson had made her up to prove the point that many people uncritically accept information without fact-checking it (Snopes, 2023). The trolling worked brilliantly: in their eagerness to dispel what they thought was a commonly believed piece of misinformation, debunkers simply copied Mikkelson's explanation without doing any further research.

If you didn't know all of this, you're not alone: it can be very difficult to tell fact from fiction (Channel 4, 2017). Some lies are so well crafted that they're almost impossible to debunk, and some of the most cleverly designed misinformation contains a kernel of truth. Take the UFO claim from earlier: it's objectively correct, but phrased in such a way that it's easy to infer a wrong conclusion. Objective truths and the subjective interpretation of them can sometimes be hard to disentangle.

The above claims are all relatively benign, but misinformation isn't always harmless. The Protocols of the Elders of Zion, a conspiracy theory invented by the Russian secret service under Tsar Nicholas II, is still influential today as a justification for anti-Semitic beliefs (Bronner, 2007; Whitfield, 2020). The spread of vaccination myths has sometimes been associated with a drop in

---

[1]   **ALIENS!** Although some military officials have said publicly that "the U.S. has retrieved craft of non-human origin" (Gabbatt, 2023; Kean & Blumenthal, 2023), with one official testifying in front of Congress that he was informed of "a multi-decade UAP crash retrieval and reverse-engineering program" (Becket, 2023). So maybe we're wrong. Who knows.

[2]   We don't have numbers on how many spiders are swallowed on purpose.

vaccine uptake (Larson, 2020; Motta & Stecula, 2021). And false and misleading news stories about nuclear energy can influence people's risk perceptions around nuclear technology, which might hamper informed debate about how to combat climate change (Ho et al., 2022; Thakur & Ward, 2019). But what exactly *is* misinformation? To what extent does misinformation take on problematic proportions for society? Who believes and shares misinformation, and why? How does the rise of modern technology such as social media impact how misinformation is created and spread? And what solutions do we have available, how well do they work, and do these solutions themselves not pose potential risks? These are some of the questions that we tackle in this book.

Research on the spread of, belief in, and consequences of misinformation has long been popular (H. M. Johnson & Seifert, 1994; Lewandowsky et al., 2005; McGuire, 1961; Price & Hsu, 1992), but really took off around the 2016 US presidential elections. If you look up "misinformation" on Web of Science, you'll find that the number of publications on the topic rose from 43 per year in 2000 to 231 in 2015, and to a whopping 2,249 in 2022. While it's impossible to tackle the entirety of this sprawling research field on these pages, we've done our best to cover the most important scientific insights into various aspects of the misinformation problem. To do this, we've tried to incorporate as many viewpoints as possible. We of course have our own thoughts and ideas, and we discuss these where relevant, but we've tried to be as nuanced as we could when discussing the various perspectives and research approaches. For instance, Chapters 3 (which asks whether misinformation is a problem), 4 (which examines why people believe and share misinformation), and 5 (which tackles echo chambers and filter bubbles) explicitly discuss competing perspectives in detail. We hope we've done each of these perspectives justice.

We have divided this book into three parts. Part I (Chapters 1–3) sets the stage and covers the necessary background information. Chapter 1 delves into the complexities of defining misinformation: as the above examples showed, it's often difficult to know if a piece of information is objectively true or false. Instead, misinformation is oftentimes contextual: truth value might be absent altogether, a statement might leave out relevant information, or the framing might be such that a true claim is nonetheless misleading. We explain these complexities using illustrative examples, categorize the different definitions that researchers have used over the years, and present our own working definition of misinformation which we will use throughout this book. Chapter 2 is about the history of misinformation, starting with its evolutionary origins and deception in the animal kingdom. We then discuss how information was produced and spread throughout human history, focusing especially on the role of technological innovations. We begin this story in the time before Gutenberg's version of the printing press came about around 1440 AD, before moving on era of the printing press (until 1920 or so), the mass media era (1920–1990s), and finally the internet age (from when Al Gore invented the

Internet until the present day). Chapter 3 tackles whether the spread of misinformation poses a problem for society. The answer to this question might
sound intuitive (especially coming from two people who are writing a book
about it), but it's not: there are many nuances here that are worth exploring in
detail, and some scientists have argued that the misinformation problem is at
least somewhat overblown.

Part II (Chapters 4–5) covers the belief in and spread of misinformation.
Chapter 4 addresses these questions from a psychological perspective. It discusses the various theories that researchers have proposed and tested over the
years about why people believe things that aren't true, and why they might
share false or misleading information with others (e.g., on social media). We
discuss the belief in and sharing of misinformation separately. This is because,
although it might sound logical that people usually share misinformation
because they believe it, this isn't always the case. Rather, misinformation
belief and sharing are explained by somewhat (although not entirely) different
mechanisms. Chapter 5 is about digital technologies, and whether the arrival
of the Internet has ushered in an era in which it's uniquely easy for misinformation to proliferate. This chapter focuses on echo chambers and filter bubbles, and asks if social networks promote isolation from inconvenient ideas
and viewpoints (more so than was the case before the Internet).

Finally, Part III (Chapters 6–8) is concerned with how to counter misinformation. Chapter 6 looks at how misinformation is regulated by governments and other legislative entities. Misinformation has become of
increasing interest to lawmakers around the world (both in democratic and
not so democratic countries). How have countries such as the US and UK, and
supranational bodies such as the European Union, tried to regulate how misinformation (and related content such as hate speech) is consumed and spread
on social media platforms? How comprehensive is this new legislation? And,
importantly, what are the risks of creating new laws (on top of already existing
limits to speech such as libel, slander, and fraud), for example when it comes
to inspiring autocratic countries to crack down on political opposition under
the guise of fighting "fake news"? Chapter 7 explores anti-misinformation
measures that are targeted at individuals, focusing on interventions that either
tackle susceptibility to misinformation or seek to reduce the sharing of it. We
cover four different types of interventions: *boosts* (which aim to build new
skills and competences or foster existing ones, such as media literacy and critical thinking programs, as well as "prebunking"); *nudges* (subtle, nonintrusive interventions that incentivize positive behavior, for example reducing the
sharing of misinformation on social media); *debunking* (correcting misinformation after it has already spread, for example through fact-checking); and
the *(automated) labelling* of various kinds of problematic content. We discuss
the evidence behind of these interventions from lab and field studies, as well
as what we don't know (yet). And finally, Chapter 8 is about our own research

program, much of which has focused on "fake news" games and videos that are grounded in a framework from social psychology called "inoculation theory." The chapter details how this research program came about, as well as some of the insights we believe we've arrived at over the years. We also wanted to emphasize some of the shortcomings and nuances of this research, and discuss the (in our view) important implications of these nuances for researchers and policymakers seeking to understand and counter misinformation.

Each chapter is structured in a way that we're told is common in publishing, with an introduction, a main body, and a conclusion. Where relevant, we've added footnotes at the bottom of the page with additional information. To avoid burdening the reader with excessive footnotes, we've opted for what we believe is a unique approach in scientific writing: all information that is of critical importance for an accurate understanding of each chapter can be found in the footnotes, whereas any contextual and other nonessential information is provided in the main body. You can therefore safely read only the footnotes and nothing else.[3] However, we recommend reading the whole book including the main text, as we've worked pretty hard on it and would be disappointed if you skimmed it.[4]

Attentive readers might ask: "Hey Sander, didn't you just write a book about misinformation? Why do you need a new one?" To answer these questions: yes, Sander did publish a book called *FOOLPROOF: Why Misinformation Infects Our Minds and How to Build Immunity* (2023). As Jon was tasked with writing the initial draft of the chapters in the book you have in front of you, he has heroically avoided reading *FOOLPROOF* to prevent himself from being influenced by it. So although there is overlap between the two books, there are important differences in scope, topics of discussion, and especially the conclusions.[5] Most importantly, we've done our best to incorporate as many different perspectives as possible. Only in the last chapter (Chapter 8) do we address our own work in detail, but in a (what we hope to be) appropriately self-critical manner: over the years, some people have disagreed with our approach to misinformation intervention design. Much of this disagreement has been reasonable and well intended, although not all of it (for the last time: we're not lizard people[6]). Some of these critiques have prompted us to make substantial changes to how we conduct our research and design our interventions, which we hope will be informative for people looking to learn more about how misinformation works, and what to do about it.

---

[3] Just kidding, the main text is important too. The large print giveth and the small print taketh away (Waits, 1973).

[4] As a former colleague of ours (Elif Naz Çoker) likes to say: we're not *mad* scientists, just disappointed ones.

[5] An even more attentive reader might ask: "how do you know this, Jon, if you haven't read *FOOLPROOF*?" Point taken.

[6] Although that is what a lizard person would say, isn't it?

Finally, we wrote this book with an audience in mind that is interested in misinformation, but doesn't necessarily have a psychology, behavioral science, or political science degree (or maybe not yet). We've avoided scientific jargon as much as possible, and explain numerical information (e.g., in graphs) in nontechnical terms where relevant. However, we haven't compromised too much on complexity: some topics (such as how echo chambers work, see Chapter 5) are not always intuitive to grasp, but they're critical for a comprehensive understanding of misinformation. We've intended for this book to serve both as a textbook for students taking courses on mis- or disinformation at the undergraduate and postgraduate level, and as a resource for people outside of academia (e.g., policymakers, educators, or people who work for fact-checking organizations, but also interested nonexperts). We've done our best to incorporate the most recent and most robust scientific research in the field, and to represent it fairly and reasonably. Most of all, we hope you'll enjoy reading this book.

PART I

SETTING THE STAGE

1

Defining Misinformation

1.1 INTRODUCTION

Most people who regularly use the Internet will be familiar with words like "misinformation," "fake news," "disinformation," and maybe even "malinformation." It can appear as though these terms are used interchangeably, and they often are. However, they don't always refer to the same types of content, and just because a news story or social media post is false doesn't mean it's always problematic. To add to the confusion, not all misinformation researchers agree on the definition of the problem or employ a unified terminology. In this chapter, we discuss the terminology of misinformation, guided by illustrative examples of problematic news content. We also look at what misinformation *isn't*: What makes a piece of information "real" or "true"? Finally, we'll look at how researchers have defined misinformation and how these definitions can be categorized, before presenting our own definition. Rather than reinventing the wheel, we've relied on the excellent definitional work by other scholars. Our working definition is therefore hardly unique; we and many others have used it as a starting point for study designs and interventions. We do note that our views are not universally shared within the misinformation research community. We can therefore only recommend checking out other people's viewpoints with respect to how to define the problem of misinformation or related terms such as fake news, disinformation, and malinformation (Altay, Berriche, et al., 2022; Freelon & Wells, 2020; Kapantai et al., 2021; Krause et al., 2020; Lazer et al., 2018; Pennycook & Rand, 2021; Tandoc et al., 2018; Tay et al., 2021; Vraga & Bode, 2020; Wardle & Derakhshan, 2017).

1.2 FAKE NEWS, MISINFORMATION, DISINFORMATION, MALINFORMATION...

On the surface, "misinformation" seems easy to define. For instance, you might say that misinformation is "information that is false" or tautologically define

Kim Jong-Un Named *The Onion*'s Sexiest Man Alive For 2012 [UPDATE]

Published November 14, 2012

FIGURE 1.1   Example of a false but relatively harmless news headline (*The Onion*, 2012).

fake news as "news that is fake." Or, to use David Lazer's more comprehensive phrasing, fake news is "fabricated information that mimics news media content in form, but not in organisational process or intent" (Lazer et al., 2018, p. 1094). An example of a news story that would meet Lazer's definition is a hypothetical headline from www.fake.news that reads "President drop-kicks puppy into active volcano." This headline is false (that we know at least), and www.fake.news mimics news content but is not universally considered to be a trustworthy source of information (and presumably doesn't follow the ethical guidelines and editorial practices used in most newsrooms). Many would also agree that this headline may have been written with malicious intent in mind (assuming the authors weren't joking): If someone were to believe it, they would be left with an inaccurate perception of another person, in this case the president, which might inform their decision-making (e.g., leading them to vote for somebody else or disengage from the political process altogether). However, things aren't always this straightforward: Not only is it sometimes difficult to discern what is true or false, but true information can also be used in a malicious way, and false information can be benign and sometimes hilarious. Take, for example, the headline from Figure 1.1.

The Onion is an American satirical news site that publishes humorous but false stories which mimic regular news content. The rather wonderful part about this specific story is that the online version of the *People's Daily*, the Chinese Communist Party's official newspaper, apparently believed that it was real, and reposted the article along with a fifty-five-page photo reel of the

North Korean leader (BBC News, 2012). But despite the story being entirely false, it was benign, even though some people believed it (though we recognize some feelings may have been hurt when people found out that Kim Jong-Un *wasn't* named 2012's sexiest man alive). If anything, the ability to make fun of powerful people through satire is often seen as a sign of a healthy democracy (Holbert, 2013), and as far as satire goes the *Onion* story was rather mild.

At the same time, false information is not always benign, nor does it always try to mimic regular news content. Figure 1.2 shows an example of a Facebook post which got quite a bit of traction in 2014 and again in 2016.

The post is associated with #EndFathersDay, a fake hashtag movement started by members of the 4chan message board some time in 2014. Some 4chan users wanting to discredit feminist activists came up with a talking point that they thought would generate significant outrage and tried to get it trending on Twitter (Broderick, 2014). These kinds of artificial smear campaigns imitate the language and imagery of a group in order to bait real activists and harm their credibility. The image from Figure 1.2 was manipulated to make it look like there were women on the streets protesting for the abolition of Father's Day. But if you look closely, you'll see that the image was photoshopped. The demonstration where the original picture was taken was about something entirely unrelated. Nonetheless, this post is an example of how easy it is to manufacture outrage online using very simple manipulation tactics. Its creators didn't even have to bother setting up a "news" website to spread their content or mimic media content in form: All they had to do was photoshop a picture of a demonstration and spread it on social media.

To add another layer of complication, the *intent* behind the production of (mis)information also matters a great deal. It can happen that someone creates or spreads misinformation unintentionally (analogously to a virus spreading among asymptomatic people). For example, a journalist could write a news article fully believing it to be true at the time, only for the information in the article to later turn out false. Simple errors can and do happen to the best of us. Similarly, someone may share something on social media that they either erroneously believe to be true or don't believe but share anyway because they're distracted (Pennycook & Rand, 2021). Oftentimes, however, misinformation is produced intentionally. In February 2022, just after the start of the Russian invasion in Ukraine, Melody Schreiber at the *Guardian* noticed a drop-off in the activity of Twitter bots that were spreading misinformation about COVID-19 vaccines (Schreiber, 2022). The reasons behind this reduced activity were varied, but it appears that a significant number of Twitter bots that were spreading COVID-19 misinformation were run from within Russia. These bots went dormant for a while, but soon became active again to pivot their attention away from COVID-19 and toward the war in Ukraine. Building a Twitter bot and programming it to spread misinformation takes some time, effort, and money, and it's reasonable to assume that the people who created the bots intended for them to spread false and misleading

Quinn Cinco ▸ BUSHWICK,BROOKLYN 11237
March 24 at 2:28pm · 🌐

Me being a father i found this very wrong and disrespectful

FIGURE 1.2 Example of a false and malicious social media post (Snopes, 2016).

information. This type of deliberate, organized misinformation is often referred to as *disinformation* (Dan et al., 2021; Freelon & Wells, 2020). What this phenomenon also shows is that a substantial amount of misinformation on social media may be not only inorganic (spread by bots rather than real humans) but also *topic-agnostic*: The topics about which misinformation is spread can be contingent on what happens in the world (such as a pandemic or a war), rather than being driven by a public demand for misinformation content.

In the earlier examples, it's arguable that the producer's intent behind the misinformation was malicious: for example, by getting people to doubt the safety and efficacy of vaccines (Loomba et al., 2021). Similar to the Kim Jong-Un story from before, however, it is also possible for intentional misinformation to have benign motivations behind it. For instance, in the early days of the Russian invasion in Ukraine in February 2022, stories began to circulate about a mystical fighter pilot, the "Ghost of Kyiv," who was said to have single-handedly shot down six Russian planes during the first night of the invasion. The Ukrainian ministry of defense even tweeted a video in celebration of the pilot's alleged heroism. The "Ghost" thus became a symbol of Ukraine's heroic resistance against a much larger invading force. Later on, however, the Ukrainian Air Force Command admitted on Facebook that the story was nothing more than war propaganda: The "Ghost" was a "superhero-legend" who was "created by the Ukrainians." The Facebook post even urged Ukrainians to check their sources before spreading information (L. Peter, 2022). However, although the story was a deliberate lie, the motivations behind its creation are arguably defensible: It served as a rallying cry and morale booster during a time when it looked like Ukraine was about to be overrun and capitulation seemed imminent (Galey, 2022). This isn't to say there were no negative consequences. For example, the story may have increased distrust in the accuracy of Ukraine's reports about its performance on the battlefield (although we don't know this for sure). Also, people who don't support Ukraine are probably less likely to agree that the lie was benign, and even some pro-Ukrainian commentators might not find it all that defensible. Here, again, the complexities behind a seemingly straightforward question like "what is misinformation?" become visible: Intentional lies are often malicious, but not always, and the motivations behind the deliberate creation of misinformation can sometimes be understandable from a certain point of view. All of this leaves us with the following possibilities when it comes to false information:

	Intentional	Unintentional
Malicious	• Twitter bots spreading misinformation about COVID-19 • Intentional disinformation campaigns	• Accidental retweeting of misinformation • Unwittingly spreading propaganda or disinformation
Benign	• Satire (e.g., Kim Jong-Un being voted "sexiest man alive")	• Accidental retweeting of satirical or joke content (e.g., content found on the r/atetheonion subreddit)

This is already a complicated categorization, but it gets worse: Some types of content are *not* false but can nonetheless fall under a reasonable definition of "misinformation." We discuss this "real news problem" in the next section.

1.3 THE PROBLEM WITH "REAL NEWS"

Just like with misinformation, defining "real news" *seems* easy but isn't. After all, isn't real news simply "novel information that is true?" In many cases, this

FIGURE 1.3 Comparison between Trump's (2017, left) and Obama's (2009, right) inauguration attendance. Photos released by the US National Park Service (Leopold, 2017; National Park Service, 2017).

definition is reasonable: Statements such as "the earth is a sphere" and "birds exist" are seemingly uncontroversial and verifiable with a wealth of empirical evidence.[1] And indeed, many news headlines are unambiguous: "Parliament passes law lowering taxes on middle incomes," "Senator from Ohio supports Ohio sports team," "China–Taiwan tensions on the rise," and so on (we made these specific headlines up, but you get the point).

However, there are several considerations that offer nuance to such a seemingly simple problem. What counts as "true" is often contested, particularly in the context of politics (Coleman, 2018). Former White House Press Secretary Sean Spicer was widely mocked in early 2017 for asserting that US President Donald Trump's inauguration ceremony had "the largest audience ever to witness an inauguration, period, both in person and around the globe" (Hunt, 2017), despite footage clearly showing that more people were in attendance for Barack Obama's inauguration in 2009 (see Figure 1.3).

When pressed, Spicer stood by his claims, insisting that Trump's inauguration was the "most watched" in US history. He asserted that he had never meant to imply that the in-person ceremony had a higher attendance than Obama's, but rather that the overall audience (including television and online) was the largest ever (Gajanan, 2017). Whether Spicer was correct or incorrect in his original comments is therefore ambiguous: What does "witness" mean in this context? What did Spicer mean by "both in person and around the globe"? That *both* the number of people attending in person *and* the number of people watching the inauguration in some other way were the

[1] That said, can we really be sure that the earth isn't a cube and that birds aren't secretly government surveillance drones?

A 'healthy' doctor died two weeks after getting a COVID-19 vaccine; CDC is investigating why

by Andrew Boryga
South Florida Sun Sentinel • Last Updated: Apr 08, 2021 at 10:12 am

FIGURE 1.4   Example of a true but misleading headline that went viral (Boryga, 2021).

highest ever (which would mean his initial comments were incorrect), or was he talking about both numbers added together? And did Spicer already have both online and television audiences in mind when he made his original comments, or did he later realize he messed up and only afterward thought of it as a possible defense? In the absence of objective answers, what you believe to be true probably depends to some extent on your personal beliefs: It's safe to say that Spicer's political opponents are less likely to accept his explanation than his supporters. In other words, what counts as true can sometimes (but certainly not always) depend on your perspective;[2] this phenomenon of political or emotional considerations overriding a calculated assessment of the evidence is called *motivated reasoning* (Van Bavel et al., 2021), which we will get back to in Chapter 4.

A second problem with "real news" is that news that is factually correct can nonetheless be misleading. A famous example of this occurred in 2021, when the news story from Figure 1.4, originally by the *South Florida Sun Sentinel*, went viral and was shared millions of times on social media (Parks, 2021).

Every word in the headline is technically correct: The doctor did die, and the CDC (US Centers for Disease Control and Prevention) did investigate whether his death was related to the vaccine. However, the reason this article was shared so many times was presumably not because of the headline's factual content but rather because of what it implied: that the doctor died *because* he got vaccinated. However, as the *Chicago Tribune* now notes at the top of the article, "a medical examiner's report said there isn't enough evidence to rule out or confirm the vaccine was a contributing factor." You wouldn't know this just from reading the headline, however; it's fair to say that the headline is at the very least misleading (employing the correlation = causation fallacy) despite being factually correct and published by a legitimate news source. But while the *Chicago Tribune* story may have been accidentally misleading, this isn't always the case: *Malinformation* is information that is true or factual, but intentionally conveyed in such a way that it may cause harm or pose an imminent threat to a person, organization, or country (Wardle & Derakshan, 2017).

---

[2]   Or, in the fascinating words of a public relations executive we were once in a video call with, "what counts as disinformation depends on who your client is."

Another, perhaps more practical way to define "real news" is through source credibility: One can assume that a news story is true if it was published by a legitimate source. And indeed, some news outlets have (much) higher quality standards than others, so as a heuristic (a rule of thumb) it isn't a bad idea to rely on prior knowledge about the credibility and trustworthiness of the source of a story. However, even credible outlets sometimes publish information that's misleading (such as in the example from Figure 1.4) or outright false.[3] As we discuss in Chapters 2 and 3, misinformation coming from reliable or trusted sources can potentially have serious consequences. Also, an underlying assumption here is that traditional media operate independently from the government. This is the case (or tends to be) in democracies, but not so much in autocratic and semi-autocratic countries, where the most credible sources are often *not* part of the mainstream media.

Furthermore, in many cases you don't know a source's credibility. A lot of social media content is spread by individuals, not news outlets, and it's difficult to know whether any given person tends to share reliable information. Platforms such as YouTube also feature thousands of content creators who discuss politics and world events, and despite their non-status as traditional media outlets, they can (but don't always) produce high-quality news and opinion content. Dismissing such creators as untrustworthy simply because they aren't a television channel, newspaper, or news site is not entirely reasonable. You could argue that established media sources have editorial practices in place that make the source *generally* more reliable (and are often better than the alternative), but nonestablished media channels can also give a voice to people who are underrepresented in more traditional media, which can in some cases be problematic but in other cases enriches public debate.

To complicate matters *even* further, scientific research is generally speaking subject to rigorous peer review and many types of quality checks before publication, and scientists are trained to disregard their personal biases as much as possible. But at the same time, there are high-profile examples of scientific fraud and questionable research practices, and the "replication crisis" has cast doubt on quite a few findings that we used to believe were robust. Does this mean that science is therefore unreliable? The answer is no; healthy skepticism can be productive, and at the same time blind trust in *any* scientific finding is probably not too helpful. But the scientific method, with all its built-in checks and balances, remains an excellent way to arrive at robust conclusions that hold up to independent scrutiny, even if it isn't (and can never be) foolproof.[4]

---

[3] It's worth noting that high-quality outlets tend to issue corrections for erroneous information that they have published. For example, the *New York Times* publicly apologized for publishing misleading stories about the existence of weapons of mass destruction in the lead-up to the 2003 US war in Iraq (*New York Times*, 2004). We return to this matter in Chapters 2 and 3.

[4] Except for Sander's other book, which is tautologically *Foolproof* (Van der Linden, 2023).

1.4 DEFINING MISINFORMATION

Although misinformation and "real news" may sound easy to define, people often disagree over what's true and what isn't, true information can nonetheless be presented in a misleading way, and relying on source credibility is often helpful but certainly not always. To illustrate this further, see Figure 1.5, which shows a flowchart to help distinguish between misinformation and non-misinformation.

As the figure shows, classifying something as misinformation is easiest for information that is verifiably false. Most false information might be labelled "misinformation" (with some exceptions, as discussed earlier), but it can also have other cues of "misleadingness" such as missing context, conspiracist ideation, or a high degree of (negative) emotionality.[5] At the other end of the spectrum we have information that is both true and uncontroversial (such as the fictitious "Senator from Ohio supports Ohio sports team" headline from earlier). This can include simple facts, neutral statements, or factual news headlines from reliable sources. All relatively uncontroversial; so far, so good.

Our problems start when we look at the overlap between *misleading but partly true misinformation* and *true but ambiguous non-misinformation*. A

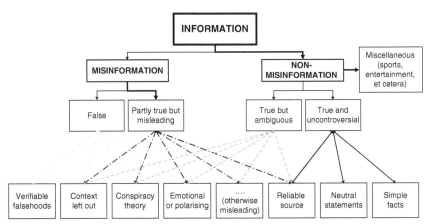

FIGURE 1.5 A flowchart for defining misinformation and non-misinformation. *Note:* Thicker arrows mean that type of content is likely to be more common: Non-misinformation is more common than misinformation, miscellaneous content is more common than news content, and misleading information is more common than information that is verifiably false (Allen et al., 2020; Grinberg et al., 2019). We recognize that the four categories of misinformation and non-misinformation shown here are not mutually exclusive, and it's not always clear which category best applies to a given piece of content. See also Chapter 8.

---

[5] We've also added an arrow from "false" to "reliable source" in Figure 1.5 because reliable sources sometimes publish false information.

good example is the headline from Figure 1.4 (about the doctor dying after receiving a COVID-19 vaccine). It's arguably misleading because many people (probably) inferred a wrong conclusion from the headline, but is it *misinformation*? Two reasonable people might give different answers to this question. As Figure 1.5 shows, misleading information and ambiguous non-misinformation can (but don't always) share features that can be seen as signs of manipulation or dubious argumentation, such as a (formal or informal) logical fallacy, a high degree of (negative) emotionality, a lack of context, a conspiracy theory, or a personal attack (Piskorski et al., 2023). This makes the distinction between (some kinds of) misinformation and non-misinformation fuzzy and subjective.

To give an example, moral-emotional language is a known driver of virality on social media (Brady et al., 2017), and emotional storytelling is often used by people who are seeking to spread doubts about vaccine safety (Kata, 2010, 2012). Does this therefore mean that any news headline that uses moral-emotional language is misinformation? Of course not: (Negative) emotions can be and often are leveraged to lead people to false conclusions, but they can also be used for benign purposes (think of charity drives or some political appeals). At the same time, you could argue that a claim that includes an emotional appeal (e.g., "Trump's racist policies have horribly devastated the USA") is of lower epistemic quality than the same claim phrased in a more neutral fashion (e.g., "Trump's policies have negatively impacted US race relations"), assuming that the goal is to inform but not necessarily persuade message receivers. But here we're talking about epistemic quality and not necessarily truth value, and so the label "real news" may not be very helpful.

The same goes for conspiratorial reasoning: Some conspiracy theories later turn out to be true, and in some cases it can be reasonable to suspect that a conspiracy might be happening even when not all of the facts about an event are known. However, true conspiracies tend to be uncovered via "normal" cognition and critical thinking (e.g., the mainstream media reporting on Watergate), whereas most popular conspiracy theories are not only statistically implausible (Grimes, 2016) but also fall prey to predictable patterns of paranoid suspicion and conspiratorial reasoning (Lewandowsky et al., 2018). Then again, it's also true that some conspiracies *are* misinformation even if their objective veracity can't be determined (like how you can't know *for sure* that psychologists didn't invent mental illness to sell self-help books – it's just that this is very likely to be false).

This discussion has substantial implications for when you want to start fighting misinformation: So do you only focus on "fake news" (as some scientists have done) or do you also include misleading information? If the latter, how do you define "misleading"? And how does your definition inform how you design your intervention? We return to this discussion in Chapters 6–8.

In the end, all of this might mean that an objective definition of misinformation that satisfies every observer is impossible, as there's an inevitable degree of subjectivity to what should and shouldn't be labelled as misinformation or "real news." However, this doesn't mean that we should simply give up: After all, some examples of misinformation are unambiguous, and as we will see later in this book, we don't need a universally agreed upon definition as a starting point for intervention.

So with that being said, we have to start somewhere. Over the years, many researchers have attempted to arrive at a definition of misinformation that takes into account the complexities described earlier (Freelon & Wells, 2020; Kapantai et al., 2021; Krause et al., 2020; Lazer et al., 2018; Roozenbeek & van der Linden, 2022; Tandoc et al., 2018). These definitions tend to fall under one of these four categories, or combine several of them:

- *Veracity-focused*: Content can be classified as misinformation if it has been fact-checked and rated false, or if it goes against established scientific or expert consensus (Lewandowsky & Oberauer, 2016; Pennycook & Rand, 2019; Tay et al., 2021).
- *Source-focused*: If a story or claim comes from a source that is known to be unreliable (e.g., www.fakenewsonline.com), it's more likely to be misinformation (Pennycook et al., 2021).
- *Intention-focused*: Misinformation is content is produced with a clear intention to manipulate or mislead, for example in the case of organized disinformation campaigns (Eady et al., 2023; Silva et al., 2023).
- *Epistemology-focused*: Content can be classified as misinformation if it is epistemologically dubious, for example by making use of a documented manipulation technique or logical fallacy (Cook et al., 2017; Piskorski et al., 2023; Van der Linden, 2023).

Each of these approaches has benefits and drawbacks. Veracity-focused definitions are more or less objective (because the veracity of a claim can sometimes be objectively established), but don't incorporate content that's misleading or otherwise manipulative (which is much more common than verifiable falsehoods). Source-focused definitions avoid the complications of establishing veracity but neglect the fact that unknown sources can provide high-quality information and high-quality sources can sometimes spread misinformation. Intention-focused definitions establish a clear motivation behind why content is produced but don't account for the fact that the intentions of content producers can be hard and sometimes impossible to discern. And finally, epistemology-focused definitions retain a degree of objectivity without the burden of having to establish veracity, but the boundaries of what counts as misinformation (and what doesn't) become fuzzy (see Figure 1.5). In practice, scientists are faced with constraints: for example, because they need to make choices about study design or what types of social media content they manage to get a hold of; sometimes the definition of misinformation used in a study depends on practical considerations more than theoretical ones.

Throughout this book, we will be talking about a range of news and social media content (along with other types of information) that we consider to fall under the "misinformation" umbrella, which requires us to establish what types of content we have in mind when we use this term. In our view, source-based and intention-based definitions are a bit too narrow. As we will see in Chapters 2 and 3, sources that are ostensibly of very high quality can sometimes become the source of highly impactful misinformation. Also, the intentions behind why a piece of misinformation was produced are often guesswork and can only be reliably discerned in relatively few cases. Finally, focusing on veracity alone fails to capture the (likely much larger) amount of problematic content that is not explicitly false. We will therefore use a definition that is both veracity- and epistemology-focused:

Misinformation is information that is false or misleading, irrespective of intention or source.

By "false or misleading" we mean that misinformation can be provably false as well as misleading (e.g., because important context is left out) or otherwise epistemologically dubious (by making use of a logical fallacy or other known manipulation technique). This allows us to incorporate both content that is verifiably false and content that is otherwise questionable (Piskorski et al., 2023); in our view, lying is but one way to mislead or manipulate people; clever misinformers often don't need to lie to get what they want. Importantly, we're careful to not only focus on *news* content or content that is produced by media outlets, but rather to include *any* form of communication through which misinformation might spread (including, for example, content produced by regular social media users). As we will see, this definition captures a wide range of problematic content, while not accidentally flagging too much legitimate content as misinformation. Our definition is also in line with much of the rest of the research field. One study in which 150 experts were asked how they define misinformation found that "false and misleading" information was the most popular definition among experts, followed by "false and misleading information spread unintentionally" (Altay et al., 2023). However, it also has several shortcomings. For instance, some statements are misleading even if no known manipulation technique is used. Without a comprehensive definition of "misleading" or "manipulative," our definition is therefore also imperfect.[6]

---

[6] Recent advances in the automated detection of persuasion and manipulation techniques can help shed light on how common these techniques are, and how much they drive engagement in the form of likes, comments, and clicks (G. Da San Martino et al., 2020; Piskorski et al., 2023). While this still wouldn't lead to a comprehensive definition of "misleading" content, it would help us better understand how people engage with various types of manipulation.

1.5 CONCLUSION

In this chapter we've given our perspective on how to define misinformation, drawing on the literature that has been published on this matter in recent years. False information can be created and shared for benign as well as malicious reasons, and shared both intentionally and unintentionally. Also, misinformation can sometimes be misleading but not outright false, but it can be very difficult to objectively determine whether information is misleading. We've therefore argued that defining misinformation is more complicated than focusing on whether a piece of information is true or false, and that the intent behind the creation of (mis)information matters but can't always be accurately discerned. We've also tried to tackle the problem of defining "real news": Whether something is true is often up for debate, particularly in the context of politics. With this discussion in mind, we have proposed our own definition of misinformation, which we will use throughout this book: *Misinformation is information that is false or misleading, irrespective of intention or source.* Of course, this definition kicks the can down the road a bit, as we, for example, haven't offered a comprehensive definition of "misleading"; there are quite a few different ways to mislead people, including cherry-picking data, posing false dilemmas, leaving out context, and so on, but this kind of bottom-up approach also has its limitations. We therefore acknowledge that a degree of subjectivity is inevitable here: *Not* including misleading content means excluding the most impactful and potentially harmful misinformation (see Chapter 3), but it also doesn't work to have an exhaustive list of all the different ways in which content can be presented in a misleading manner (there are simply too many). This is a difficult philosophical problem which we won't attempt to offer a solution to here. We instead invite the reader to put their philosopher's hat on for a while and think this matter through.[7] In the next chapter, we will discuss the history of misinformation: When did people start misleading each other? And how have technological inventions such as the printing press and the Internet affected this dynamic?

---

[7] Do let us know if you find a way out of this maze.

2

A History of Misinformation

2.1 INTRODUCTION

Misinformation has only recently seen a surge in research interest and public attention, but the concept itself is much older. Not only have humans manipulated and lied to each other since the dawn of language, but animals are also known to use manipulation to achieve certain goals. In this chapter, we provide a historical overview of misinformation. First, we look at some of its possible evolutionary origins. We then trace how false information has been used as a tool of persuasion throughout history, and discuss the role of technological innovations such as the printing press and mass communications. Finally, we look at the recent advent of the internet era, and what role misinformation plays in society today.

2.2 DO ANIMALS LIE?

Misinformation has existed (albeit in a different form) since well before humans were around. Animals are routinely observed manipulating each other at the sensory and perceptual level (Mokkonen & Lindstedt, 2016). Michael Bang Petersen, Mathias Osmundsen, and John Tooby (2022) mention the example of two male deer entering a conflict over access to a mating partner or a stretch of territory. For both animals, it's best not to have the conflict escalate into full-fledged combat (which can result in serious injury even for the winner). Their conflict therefore follows certain rituals, during which both animals try to persuade the other that they would win if they were to actually fight. For two animals belonging to the same species, the best predictors of fighting ability are relative size and strength. Loudness is correlated with size (in deer anyway), and so when two male deer engage in conflict, the first thing they do is bellow at each other from a distance. If there's a clear difference in loudness, the stag with the quieter bellow (likely to be significantly smaller than the other stag) tends to cut its losses and leave. If no clear winner can be determined, the two animals meet each other face to face, but they don't start fighting quite yet. Instead, they begin to parallel-walk next to each other, sizing up their opponent (from the side, because it's easier to see how big a deer is from the side than from the front) and trying to convince the other that they'd lose if a fight broke out. If there's a clear difference, the likely loser usually withdraws. Only when the parallel walking doesn't yield a clear outcome do the two stags engage in physical combat by locking their antlers together.

Petersen, Osmundsen, and Tooby argue that while it's important for both stags to be able to accurately determine their opponent's strength, they also benefit greatly from deceiving their opponent into thinking they're stronger than they actually are. In other words, it's extremely important to extract accurate *cues* about the opponent's fighting ability, but also to emit deceptive *signals* that exaggerate their own. After all, if two animals are of about equal actual strength, but one of them is tricked into thinking the other is stronger and withdraws, then the other wins the conflict without having to engage in costly physical combat. Petersen, Osmundsen, and Tooby, following a theory put forward by John Krebs and Richard Dawkins (1978), argue that natural selection therefore rewards strategies that seek to instill false beliefs in one's opponents. Examples of these strategies are everywhere: cats raise the hairs in their fur in order to look bigger (known as "piloerection"), and animals such as snakes and possums are known to play dead to trick predators. Squirrels pretend to hide food to fool their competitors and reduce the chances of their stash being stolen (M. A. Steele et al., 2008). Professor of Comparative Cognition Nicola Clayton, a colleague of ours in Cambridge, has done research showing that intelligent birds such as jays and ravens often hide their food using misdirection techniques that resemble those used by professional magicians (N. S. Clayton et al., 2007; Garcia-Pelegrin et al., 2021). Of course, this dynamic runs in two directions: not only is it beneficial to deceive, but also to not be deceived. Animals therefore also develop strategies to detect whether the signals omitted by an opponent are accurate, leading to a kind of coevolutionary "arms race" in which both deception ability and deception detection tools constantly evolve.

While this reasoning may apply to animals, it doesn't have to hold for humans as well. In his book *Not Born Yesterday: The Science of Who We Trust and What We Believe* (2020, Chapter 4), Hugo Mercier departs from the "arms race" analogy, and instead likens the evolution of human communication to the evolution of omnivorous diets. Many animals have very specific diets (e.g., pandas eat only bamboo), and therefore don't usually have to worry about their food choices (e.g., because the food they eat is almost always fresh). This also means that they don't evolve mechanisms for learning how to avoid "bad" or toxic food, because they don't encounter this in their natural environment very often. Omnivores, on the other hand, are happy eating many different types of food, which increases both their versatility and adaptability as well as their vulnerability to disease. This leads to both higher openness (a higher willingness than other animals to consider new types of food) and higher vigilance, and the emergence of strategies that help them avoid food that is likely toxic. These strategies can require quite a bit of sophistication, for example, because animals need to remember what they ate a few hours ago that might have made them sick. Mercier argues that the difference between humans and other primates in terms of their communication ability is similar to the difference between specialist and omnivorous animals. Where nonhuman primates communicate mostly using specific signals, humans can communicate about anything and everything if they want to. Humans are therefore much more open to different forms of communication, and with that also more vigilant. So rather than evolving from a state of gullibility to one of vigilance, as the "arms race" analogy would suggest, Mercier says that the reverse is the case: humans evolved from a situation of conservatism (with only a limited set of communicative signals being able to affect us) to one of vigilance *and* openness. In other words, vigilance (against being manipulated) and openness (to different forms of communication, including manipulation) go hand in hand; people, in Mercier's view, are therefore not nearly as vulnerable to manipulation as many believe. Then again, as is often the problem with how evolutionary psychology approaches the study of modern-day human behavior, Mercier's argument is difficult to test experimentally; it may well be the case that some forms of manipulation are highly effective (see Chapters 3 and 4, for example), even if the evolutionary process that underlies them isn't clear.

2.3 MISINFORMATION THROUGH THE AGES

It's fairly safe to assume that before we had writing systems, early humans engaged in plenty of attempts to manipulate and deceive one another, but we don't have a lot of evidence available to know for sure. However, with the invention of writing also came historiography and record-keeping, and ever since then plenty of societies have recorded examples of successful and not so successful misinformation. Joanna Burkhardt, in her report *Combating Fake News in the Digital Age* (2017), divides the history of misinformation into four separate eras: (1) before, and (2) after the invention of the Gutenberg printing press; (3) the era of mass media; and (4) the internet age. We'll discuss the role of misinformation in each of these time periods and explore how technological innovations have influenced the creation and spread of misinformation throughout the ages.

2.3.1 Before the Printing Press

Perhaps the earliest known example of misinformation can be found in the Babylonian epic of Gilgamesh (written about 2100–1200 BC). In his book *Ea's*

Duplicity in the Gilgamesh Flood Story (2019), Martin Worthington, a professor of Middle Eastern Studies at Trinity College Dublin, claims to have found
an example of "fake news" in the ancient Mesopotamian poem the *Epic of
Gilgamesh*. In 1872, the Assyriologist George Smith discovered that the eleventh tablet of the *Epic* (produced in the seventh century BC) contained a passage very similar to the Flood story from the Book of Genesis. In the story,
the God Ea (known as the "trickster god") warns Uta-napišti, the Babylonian
version of Noah, that a huge flood is coming, and instructs him to build a boat
and take in birds and beasts of every stripe. Once the boat was finished and
Uta-napišti shut its doors, rain began to fall, and all the rest of mankind per-
ished. After six days the rain stopped, and on the seventh day Uta-napišti sent
out birds to go find land. The third bird, a raven, didn't return, indicating that
it had found land and that the waters were receding (British Museum, 2022;
University of Cambridge, 2019).

　　Worthington argues that Ea's warning to Uta-napišti about the oncom-
ing flood was a verbal trick, designed to be understood in multiple ways. One
interpretation of Ea's message to Uta-napišti is that of a promise of abundant
food if humans would help him build the Ark. Another translation of the
same words, however, warns Uta-napišti of impending disaster. The words
"ina šēr(-)kukkī, ina lilâti ušaznanakkunūši šamūt kibāti" can be interpreted
both as "At dawn there will be *kukku*-cakes, in the evening he will rain down
upon you a shower of wheat," and "By means of incantations, by means of
wind-demons, he will rain down upon you rain as thick as (grains of) wheat"
(taken verbatim from University of Cambridge, 2019).[1] In other words, Ea
manipulates Uta-napišti by making him believe that building the Ark will
bring him great rewards, even though his words could just as easily mean that
disaster is afoot. Why exactly Ea decided to be this duplicitous is a matter of
debate. Worthington (2019, pp. 325–327) offers several explanations. For one,
Ea was bound by an oath to the other Babylonian gods not to reveal the flood
to humans. By being ambiguous to Uta-napišti, he didn't technically violate
his oath while still helping mankind survive the deluge. Another possibility is
that Ea was acting out of self-interest. In Babylonian theology, the gods relied
on humans to feed them. If all of mankind died in a flood, all the gods would
starve. Tricking Uta-napišti into building an ark that would allow him to survive would therefore not only be beneficial to Uta-napišti and all the others on
the Ark, but also to himself.

　　During the last war of the Roman Republic (32–30 BC), right after the
death of Julius Caesar, his potential successors, Mark Antony and Octavian
(Augustus), both made use of common misinformation techniques to win
over the hearts and minds of the public. These are sometimes referred to as
the "Info-wars of Rome" (Kaminska, 2017). Octavian claimed that Antony was

---

[1]　Our ancient Babylonian is a bit rustier than it once was, sadly.

"bewitched" by his new wife, Cleopatra (then queen of Egypt). To undermine Antony's campaign, Octavian allegedly produced a fake document claiming to be Antony's final will, which revealed his true commitment to Cleopatra and Egypt rather than Rome (MacDonald, 2017). As depicted in Shakespeare's famous rendition of the story, Antony and Cleopatra both died by suicide. Octavian is often regarded as a true master of manipulation: he even had coins minted with catchy slogans to help spread his propaganda (Sifuentes, 2019).

Skipping ahead a few years, misinformation and harmful rumors were common throughout medieval Europe, often with negative consequences. For example, think of the many witch trials (Boudry & Hofhuis, 2018) and the persecution of minorities based on false information (Terrell, 1904). In 1475, rumors began to spread around Trento, Italy, about a missing boy who had supposedly been abducted and killed by some of the city's Jews, who were said to have drunk his blood as part of their Passover celebration. The Prince-Bishop of Trento, Johannes IV Hinderbach, called for the arrest and torture of all of Trento's Jews and had several of them burned at the stake (Hsia, 1992). The Pope in Rome tried briefly to intervene through a mediator (apparently aware that the stories were false), but Hinderbach refused to back down, and tried to have the boy canonized as Saint Simon of Trento (Soll, 2016). Anti-Semitic stories of "blood libel" and the supposed ritualistic killing of Christian children by Jewish communities have been common throughout Europe since at least 1144, with the death of a twelve-year-old boy from Norwich, England. As recently as 2014, the Anti-Defamation League petitioned to have a Facebook page called "Jewish Ritual Murder" taken down (Teter, 2020).

2.3.2 After the Gutenberg Printing Press

There's little doubt that Johannes Gutenberg of Mainz, Germany, brought about a revolution in mass communication with the creation of his "movable type" printing press (the use of movable blocks, such as pictographic or alphabetic characters, to reproduce a document), around 1440 AD. However, Gutenberg probably shouldn't be called the "inventor" of the printing press. There is evidence of printing (with large wooden blocks rather than individual metal ones) being used in Zhejiang, China, as early as 800 AD (Newman, 2019). Bi Sheng, a Song dynasty engineer, invented the earliest known movable type technology (using Chinese porcelain) somewhere between 1039 and 1048 AD (He, 1994). The first movable type that used metal (the type that Gutenberg perfected) probably originates from Korea: some accounts claim that a thirteenth-century Korean civil minister named Choe Yun-ui invented movable metal type printing to print a lengthy Buddhist text (Newman, 2019), and the oldest surviving book that was printed using this type is the *Buljo-Jikji-Simche-Yojeol* (or *Jikji* for short), which dates back to 1377 (Park & Yoon, 2009).

In an interesting example of misinformation, the Dutch city of Haarlem once also claimed to be the cradle of the printing press. Laurens Janszoon Coster, a sexton (or parish clerk) who supposedly lived in the city in the late fourteenth and early fifteenth century, was long said to have invented metal movable type printing and run a successful printing company in the 1420s, about twenty years before Gutenberg (van der Linde, 1870). However, the only source for this claim is the book *Batavia* by Hadrianus Junius, published in 1588, and no contemporary records of Coster's invention appear to exist. Junius is said to have made this claim "not to convey facts, but to deliver a deliberate mythologization of an already well-established legend about the invention of printing in Haarlem" (Robbe, 2010). In other words, he made it up for clout. Tragically, the city of Haarlem remained devoid of further noteworthy achievements until a New York City neighborhood was named after it in the year 1660.

Nonetheless, Gutenberg's printing press undoubtedly made reading materials much more accessible to the masses. This had several important consequences both in Europe and worldwide. For example, Jeremiah Dittmar (2011) argues that European cities where printing presses were established grew about 60 percent faster between 1500 and 1600 than similar cities without a printing press. In the first few hundred years after Gutenberg's innovation, Europe and then the rest of the world witnessed the rise of mass-printed books, novellas, essays, pamphlets, and newspapers. Writing and publishing, previously beholden mostly to religious institutions (Copeland, 2006), soon became widely available as tools designed to not only inform but also to persuade, frighten, and mislead. The famous Anglo-Irish satirist Jonathan Swift, frustrated with the fraught political climate of his time, published an essay called *The Art of Political Lying* (1710). He writes:

Few lies carry the inventor's mark, and the most prostitute enemy to truth may spread a thousand, without being known for the author: besides, as the vilest writer hath his readers, so the greatest liar hath his believers: and it often happens, that if a lie be believed only for an hour, it hath done its work, and there is no further occasion for it. Falsehood flies, and truth comes limping after it.[2]

Swift, for his part, was no stranger to publishing works that veer into misinformation territory, although, like the example of Kim Jong-Un from the previous chapter, these works were satirical. He's best known for *Gulliver's Travels* (1726), a famous work of satire that lampooned popular adventure books such as Daniel Defoe's *Robinson Crusoe* and whose first edition was published as if it were a factual account of the author's travels under the pseudonym Lemuel Gulliver, "first a surgeon, and then a captain of several ships." Another example is *A Modest Proposal* (1729), in which Swift ironically

---

[2]   Incidentally, the last line is possibly the original source for the well-known expression "a lie is halfway around the world before the truth has got its boots on," variously and erroneously attributed to Winston Churchill, Mark Twain, and Oscar Wilde (Tearle, 2021).

suggests that poor Irish people could sell their children as food to the rich to earn some extra cash (even going so far as to suggest different ways the children may be prepared and served).[3]

In some countries, the widespread availability of printing gave rise to the development of mass media and a free press. In his book *The Idea of a Free Press: The Enlightenment and Its Unruly Legacy*, David Copeland argues that in early seventeenth-century England and eighteenth-century America, the first printed newssheets were "published by authority," and fit the needs of people who held political power. Alongside such government-directed publications, a public desire for information and competition among political and religious actors opened up the way for a press that printed *despite* authority (Copeland, 2006, p. 8). Eventually, this process (along with the increasing popularity of Enlightenment ideas about freedom of expression and liberty of conscience) led to the establishment of the free press as we know it today.

There soon came a period where journalists and other media content producers tried to test the limits of the media landscape. Sensationalist stories became hugely popular, often at the expense of accuracy. The nineteenth and early twentieth centuries featured a series of famous hoaxes and journalistic pranks. A good example is the Great Moon Hoax of 1835, when *The Sun*, a New York-based newspaper, published a set of articles describing a series of alleged discoveries on the moon, such as moon bison, trees, oceans, and even a new species called "vespertilio homo" or "man-bats." So many people are said to have believed the story that religious groups were starting to prepare for missionary work on the moon, although it's very difficult to find independent verification of this (Matthias, 2022). The author of the hoax articles, Richard Adam Locke, later said that it wasn't his goal to fool anyone but that he had "underestimated the gullibility of the public" (Zielinski, 2015). The well-known writer and poet Edgar Allan Poe also wasn't happy with the story, not only because he knew it was made up but also because he believed that Locke had plagiarized a previous story of his about a man who travels to the moon in a hot air balloon. Poe later retracted this accusation, but he did publish a hoax article of his own a few years later (and in the same newspaper), about a man who had crossed the Atlantic Ocean in a hot air balloon (Goodman, 2008).

Another amusing example of how heated early journalism could get is that of two competing newspapers from West Virginia, the *Clarksburg Daily Telegram* and the *Clarksburg Daily News*. Suspicious that *Daily News* editors were stealing their stories, the *Telegram* published an article in 1903 about a man with the unlikely name of Mejk Swenekafew, who had been shot after a fight with a friend of his over a pet dog. The next day, the same article appeared

---

[3] Cameron Brick, a professor at the University of Amsterdam, wrote a "modest proposal for restoration ecology" (2019), which involved a "radical culling" of an invasive non-native species (i.e., humans) in California.

in the *Daily News* as well, after which the *Telegram* revealed that they'd made the story up and that Swenekafew's name spelled backwards read "we fake news." The *Daily News* was forced to publicly admit their wrongdoing (Starmans, 2019).

The hilarity of these hoaxes and pranks notwithstanding, the rise of modern journalism was not without hurdles. Misinformation has been rife throughout its existence, sometimes with serious consequences. Throughout the nineteenth century, US national media often painted lynchings of black Americans in a positive light, and portrayed racist lynch mobs as "chivalrous knights who were defending the honor of their race" (Wasserman, 1998). These lynchings were often triggered by false stories of African-Americans committing crimes such as rape and murder against white people (Terrell, 1904).

Perhaps one of the most consequential examples of deliberate misinformation is the forgery known as the *Protocols of the Learned Elders of Zion* (original title: *Программа завоевания мира евреями*, or "the Jewish program for conquering the world"). This document, created in 1903 by the Russian secret service under Tsar Nicholas II, alleges a massive Jewish conspiracy to control the global economy, the press, and international politics (Whitfield, 2020). It was based on a variety of anti-Semitic sources, such as the 1868 novel *Biarritz* by the Prussian postal worker and agent provocateur Hermann Goedsche. One chapter in the book describes a nightly meeting in a cemetery in Prague where Jewish leaders discuss their plans for world domination (Cohn, 1966). Despite being exposed as a forgery as early as 1921, the *Protocols* found massive uptake especially after World War I and the Russian revolutions of 1917 (Bronner, 2007). The *Protocols* continue to influence conspiracy theorists even today (Whitfield, 2020), which shows the limitations of debunking misinformation after it has spread, something we will get back to in Chapter 7.

2.3.3 The Mass Media Era

It's difficult to pinpoint exactly when the mass media era started: was this after printed materials became available to large audiences in the sixteenth century, after the emergence of newspapers in the seventeenth century, after photography and the telegraph were invented in the early nineteenth century, or even with the rise of the newspaper industry in the late nineteenth century? For the sake of clarity, we'll put the starting point of the mass media era around 1920, when nonprint media such as radio and later television became broadly available (at least to audiences in industrialized countries). The first commercial radio program in the US was broadcast from Pittsburgh in 1920 (Federal Communications Commission, 2020), and the BBC started broadcasting from London in 1922. Soon, most people who could afford a radio had one in their home.

Orson Welles' *War of the Worlds*, broadcast on CBS on October 30, 1938, is now widely known as a powerful example of the persuasive power of the mass media. Being the Halloween episode of a longer radio series, its premise was to make an invasion of Earth by Martians sound as realistic as possible, with newsreaders describing the horrors inflicted by the invaders' heat ray in gruesome detail. People who tuned in during the broadcast had missed the introduction explaining that the show was a fiction, and media outlets reported that so many of them had fallen for the hoax that it evoked "mass hysteria" (Schwartz, 2015). However, there doesn't appear to be much evidence for this: investigations by Jefferson Pooley and Michael Socolow at *Slate* (2013) and David Emery at *Snopes* (2016) showed not only that very few people had listened to the broadcast (because it aired at the same time as a much more popular program), but also that reports of mass hysteria were greatly exaggerated. What did happen, according to author A. Brad Schwartz (2015), is that *The War of the Worlds* provoked a nationwide debate about the power of the radio as a tool to mislead people, a debate amplified by the rise of the Nazis in Europe and Joseph Goebbels' use of radio for propaganda purposes.

Speaking of Goebbels, the Nazi regime was the first to make extensive use of modern media technologies to spread propaganda. Goebbels believed that propaganda should serve as the "background music" to government policy (Goebbels, 1934). In service of this, he made sure that almost every German had a radio in their home to listen to Hitler's speeches, and directors such as Leni Riefenstahl further popularized the regime through propaganda films such as *Triumph des Willens*. This policy appears to have had long-term consequences. Nico Voigtländer and Hans-Joachim Voth (2015) conducted a study in which they found that Germans who had grown up in the 1920s and '30s were two to three times more likely to espouse extreme anti-Semitic beliefs (and generally had more negative attitudes about Jews) than people born earlier or later who hadn't been exposed to Nazi propaganda in schools, through the media, and in the Hitler Youth. This effect was especially pronounced for people born in regions of Germany that had stronger anti-Semitic attitudes before the Nazis came to power, indicating that indoctrination may be particularly effective when it exploits preexisting prejudices (see Chapter 4).

After World War II came the Cold War between the US and the USSR, which was rife with propaganda and misinformation. Both America and the Soviet Union set up propaganda programs aimed at destabilizing countries in each other's sphere of influence (Sussman, 2021). Famous are US Senator Joseph McCarthy's unproven accusations of Communist subversion in the government, media, and entertainment industries. The Soviets, for their part, jammed foreign radio broadcasts, arrested citizens for allegedly listening to them, and tried to spread pro-Soviet narratives through arts and literature, a phenomenon known as Agitprop (Magnúsdóttir, 2018). The Cold War came to an end in 1991, when the Soviet Union dissolved into numerous independent states and the Warsaw Pact, the collective defense treaty of many Socialist countries, ceased to exist. This also put a temporary damper on political disinformation, as Russia and the West became uneasy allies for a while.

The first years after the Cold War marked one of the most notorious examples of misinformation, at least in the Western world. In 1998, Andrew Wakefield, a British medical doctor, published an article in the prestigious journal *The Lancet* alleging a link between the MMR (measles, mumps, rubella) vaccine and autism in young children. The study caused a worldwide media uproar, and a significant and immediate increase in vaccine skepticism (Motta & Stecula, 2021). However, the study soon turned out to not just be a scientific mistake but a deliberate fraud (Rao & Andrade, 2011): an investigation by journalist Brian Deer (2004) revealed that Wakefield and his lead coauthor John Walker-Smith had misrepresented their data to fit their preconceived conclusions. *The Lancet* later retracted the publication in its entirety, and most of Wakefield's coauthors renounced their affiliations with the paper and himself. The *BMJ* later noted that "the [...] paper has received so much media attention, with such potential to damage public health, that it is hard to find a parallel in the history of medical science" (Godlee, 2011).

2.3.4 The Internet Era

It is an uncontroversial fact that the Internet was invented by former US presidential candidate and Nobel Peace Prize winner Al Gore. In a 1999 interview with CNN anchor Wolf Blitzer, Gore claimed that he "took the initiative in creating the Internet." His political rivals and the media were quick to exploit Gore's statement as fodder for ridicule, linking it to previous gaffes and crediting Gore with various other important discoveries such as the :-) emoji and opposable thumbs. Not to be outdone, Gore later also (jokingly) claimed to have invented the environment. Gore's gaffe is an example of an imprecise statement being taken out of context and beginning to live a life of its own, which is something that often happens in the context of misinformation. Although "taking the initiative in creating the Internet" may be taking things a bit too far, Gore (as a Congressman and later as Senator) had been heavily involved in promoting high-speed telecommunications technology and national network initiatives since the 1970s (Kahn & Cerf, 2000). In 1986, he was also the chairman of a senatorial subcommittee that fostered the creation of a series of supercomputer centers which were key in the emergence of the commercial Internet a few years later. All in all, Gore may have been a victim of his own tendency to exaggerate his accomplishments, but it's difficult to dismiss his claim as false (Wiggins, 2000). Nonetheless, the meme abides.

As with the Gutenberg printing press, who gets to claim credit for the Internet's invention is less important than the effects it may have had on the spread of (mis)information. We don't know exactly when the first person started lying on the Internet, but it's fairly safe to assume that this happened soon after it became widely available in the mid-1990s. One of the first known examples of email spam is an email titled "Global Alert for All: Jesus is Coming Soon" (1994) by someone named Clarence L. Thomas IV.[4] Phishing scams, emails made to look like they were sent by a reputable organization with the intent of extracting money from recipients, date back to about 1995 (San Martino & Perramon, 2010). *The Onion* began publishing satirical news in 1998, and their articles were regularly mistaken for real news and reposted by non-satirical news outlets, as we saw in the previous chapter (Posetti & Matthews, 2018).

A hugely influential example of harmful misinformation in the internet era came from one of the world's foremost media outlets, the *New York Times*. In the run-up to the 2003 US invasion of Iraq, journalist Judith Miller published a series of articles alleging the existence of an Iraqi site said to be producing biological weapons. Miller's accounts, however, were never independently verified (Posetti & Matthews, 2018). After the United States invaded Iraq, the US government was forced to admit that the "weapons of mass destruction" that the Iraqi government was said to harbor (a major pretext for the invasion) didn't exist (Borger, 2004). The *New York Times* later issued an apology, stating that Miller's reporting had been inaccurate and that its editors had failed to weigh the available evidence against their desire to have Saddam Hussein removed from power (*New York Times*, 2004). Some argue that Miller's reporting directly influenced the US government's decision to invade, highlighting the potential for misinformation to have real-world consequences (Posetti & Matthews, 2018). Moreover, research by Stephan Lewandowsky, a professor of cognitive science at Bristol University, and his colleagues showed that the false claims of weapons of mass destruction continued to influence people's reasoning despite the later retractions (Lewandowsky et al., 2005).

The internet era also ushered in a time of information warfare. Leveraging the Internet and social media to spread certain narratives during violent conflict became an increasingly important part of warring parties' strategies. The goal of such information campaigns is to influence public opinion among target audiences (domestically or internationally): for example, to reduce popular support for a government's economic sanctions against another country (Jankowicz, 2020; Van Niekerk, 2015). Well-known examples of conflicts where information warfare plays a key role are the war in Syria and the Russia–Ukraine conflict, the latter of which we discuss in detail in Chapter 3.

Throughout the 2000s and 2010s, politicians began to make increasing use of the Internet for their election campaigns. However, social media also proved to be a useful vehicle for political misinformation. This topic became especially salient in 2015 and 2016, when misinformation was said to play an

---

4   Unlikely to be the same person as US Supreme Court Justice Clarence Thomas, as far as we can tell.

important role in the US presidential elections and the Brexit referendum in the United Kingdom. Although there currently doesn't seem to be convincing evidence that misinformation directly influenced these elections' results (Allcott & Gentzkow, 2017; Bovet & Makse, 2019; de Waal, 2018; Eady et al., 2023; Guess et al., 2019), there has been widespread concern that the spread of misinformation may adversely influence the democratic process (Mackey, 2016). For instance, the Russian government mounted a disinformation campaign during the 2016 US presidential elections, which was primarily aimed at increasing support for the Republican candidate, Donald Trump, and reducing support for his Democratic rival, Hillary Clinton, as well as to undermine Americans' trust in the electoral system (Ferrara, 2017; Keller et al., 2020; Timberg & Romm, 2018). To what extent this was successful is up for debate (considering the billions of dollars in campaign expenditures by both major parties and external donors), but there is some evidence that the impact of disinformation campaigns was low (Eady et al., 2023). Others saw political misinformation as a lucrative business. For example, a group of teenagers from the Macedonian town of Veles ran a network of "fake news" websites pushing out nonsense articles about the US elections. Their goal wasn't to influence politics but rather to make money: the web traffic they managed to attract resulted in significant income from advertising revenue (Kirby, 2016).

Nonetheless, the widespread use of bots and other automated methods to spread misinformation has become cause for concern (Starbird, 2019). One study estimated that around 17 percent of the Twitter user base was made up of bots (Varol et al., 2017). Social media platforms such as Facebook and Reddit regularly find and remove bot networks, many of which appear to be run by governments (Marineau, 2020). These bot networks do not create misinformation from scratch; rather, they identify narratives that suit a particular political purpose, and amplify them (Badawy et al., 2019; Broniatowski et al., 2018; McKew, 2018).

Of course, no history of misinformation would be complete without mentioning the COVID-19 pandemic. In the early days of the pandemic, when there was a lot of uncertainty about the origins, causes, and spread of the virus, as well as about how to treat it, there was plenty of room for misinformation to proliferate widely. The World Health Organization (WHO) went so far as to declare this problem an "infodemic" (Zarocostas, 2020). COVID-19 misinformation ranged from false information about how to cure the disease to speculation about the virus having escaped from a research lab in Wuhan and, later on, conspiracy theories about COVID-19 vaccines (Brennen et al., 2020; Loomba et al., 2021).[5] In Iran, hundreds of people died after drinking poisonous

---

[5] The idea of the COVID virus having escaped from a research lab is plausible enough to have been taken seriously by a host of respected scientists (Horton, 2021), and pressure by Chinese officials on WHO investigators to dismiss the theory has raised suspicion (Dyer, 2021a, 2021b). However, a large-scale investigation later determined that the outbreak very likely

methanol in an attempt to cure the disease (Delirrad & Mohammadi, 2020). In Great Britain, people set mobile phone masts on fire, believing that 5G radiation was somehow linked to COVID infections (Jolley & Paterson, 2020). More amusingly, a group of researchers published an ostensibly serious article claiming that "COVID-19 arrived via a meteorite, a presumed relatively fragile and loose carbonaceous meteorite that struck Northeast China on October 11, 2019" (Steele et al., 2020). We return to the topic of COVID-19 misinformation in Chapter 3.

2.4 CONCLUSION

In this chapter, we have discussed the history of misinformation, from its possible evolutionary origins to the advent of the digital age. We have shown that lying and manipulation are common strategies for survival and procreation in the animal kingdom. We have also seen that malicious rumors have been common throughout the ages, which can be used as a coordination device to incite deadly interethnic riots (Horowitz, 2000). Deliberate propaganda has also been part of human politics for millennia. The Gutenberg printing press enabled the rapid dissemination of printed materials to audiences everywhere, leading not only to the rise of the free press and modern journalism but also to hoaxes, low-quality tabloids, and organized disinformation. In the internet era, misinformation is a more salient topic of discussion than ever before. Whether Al Gore's invention has materially affected the spread and proliferation of misinformation isn't easy to say (see Chapter 5): rumors and half-truths were known to spread even before the Internet, and there are plenty of examples of harmful misinformation throughout history. At the same time, this is the first period in history where misinformation can be automated, shared with others within the blink of an eye, and easily targeted at both massive audiences and specific subgroups. That said, although it's easy to point at individual examples of misinformation likely having had adverse consequences, this doesn't necessarily mean that the problem is pervasive enough to wreak havoc at the societal level. We discuss this question in the next chapter.

originated in the Huanan seafood wholesale market in Wuhan, and was thus of natural origin (Worobey et al., 2022). That said, the former head of the Chinese Center for Disease Control said in May 2023 that a lab leak "shouldn't be ruled out" as a possibility (Camut, 2023), so some uncertainty remains.

3

Do We Have a Misinformation Problem?

3.1 INTRODUCTION

In the previous two chapters, we have looked at how to define misinformation and explored the role it has played throughout history. Examples of misinformation having real-world consequences aren't exactly hard to find (BBC News, 2018; Debies-Carl, 2017; Phartiyal et al., 2018), and misinformation has been a hugely important topic of discussion in popular media, among politicians, and in scientific research. In this chapter, we discuss an important and rather fundamental question: Is misinformation a problem? We will show that there are reasonable arguments on both sides. Our goal isn't to persuade our readers that one perspective is better than the other, preferring instead to explain the arguments each side has put forward and leave it up to the reader to form their own opinion. We divide this chapter into three parts. We first discuss the arguments behind why misinformation might not be as big a problem as we think. Next, we discuss the evidence for why misinformation *does* pose a significant problem.[1] We conclude with a case study: information warfare in the Russia–Ukraine war.

3.2 PERSPECTIVE #1: THIS IS (BASICALLY) FINE

Hugo Mercier, Sacha Altay, Manon Berriche, and Alberto Acerbi have published a series of papers in which they argue that the scope of the misinformation problem may be seriously overstated, and that societal concerns over the spread and malicious influence of misinformation constitute more of a "moral panic" than a problem that requires immediate and invasive action (Altay, 2022; Altay, Berriche, et al., 2022; Mercier & Altay, 2022). They therefore caution that attempts to reduce misinformation consumption and sharing may be

---

[1] We realize that this order of presentation may inadvertently bias our readers (Miller & Campbell, 1959). We humbly ask the reader to deactivate this bias while reading this chapter.

missing the mark. They put forward the following arguments: that exposure to misinformation is uncommon compared to entertainment content and harmless memes (at least in Western countries); that misinformation is mostly spread by a small number of powerful individuals; that misinformation is a symptom of deep-rooted sociopolitical and economic problems; that studies aimed at assessing people's belief in misinformation suffer from important conceptual challenges that cause us to draw the wrong conclusions about how susceptible people are to believing misinformation; and finally that concerns about the influence of misinformation on people's behavior are severely overstated. We will discuss each of these arguments in turn.

First, exposure to misinformation online may be less common than is often assumed. In one of the first large-scale exploratory studies of "fake news" sharing behavior during the 2016 US presidential election campaign, Andrew Guess and colleagues (2019) found that, although the sharing of news links on social media was commonplace, 91.5 percent of people in their sample of Facebook users never shared fake news with others, and only a small fraction shared two or more links to fake news websites. Those that did share fake news tended to be conservative, older (over sixty), and pro-Trump (although the authors note we shouldn't put too much weight on this finding due to a possible sampling bias). The authors speculate that the age finding is due to a possible lack of digital literacy among older Americans, although Mathias Osmundsen and colleagues (2021) find no correlation between media literacy and misinformation sharing. Also, in a large study on older Americans' engagement with dubious political news, Benjamin Lyons and colleagues (2023) argue that "the existing literature overemphasizes the importance of factors like digital literacy relative to standard political variables such as political interest and partisanship." In their view, it's not a lack of literacy skills but rather "calcified partisanship" that explains why older Americans are more likely to engage with highly partisan news content.

In another study, Jennifer Allen and colleagues (2020) evaluated the scale of the "fake news" problem at the level of the information ecosystem, which includes not only social media but also television and other forms of media. They found that news content made up only about 14 percent of Americans' daily media diet, and that this news came overwhelmingly from television (which outweighed online news consumption by a factor of about five). Importantly, the authors also showed that "fake news" comprised about 0.15 percent of people's daily media consumption. They therefore argue that "the origins of public misinformedness and polarization are more likely to lie in the content of ordinary news or the avoidance of news altogether as they are in overt fakery." And even then, Altay and colleagues (2022) caution that *engagement* with misinformation shouldn't be conflated with *belief*: people may share misinformation mockingly, to warn others, or for any number of reasons other than in order to express genuine belief and agreement.

Instead of misinformation, people appear to predominantly consume so-called "phatic" content, which contains no practical information but does perform a social function (such as "I love you sister!" or "good news, everyone!"). In a large-scale investigation conducted on the popular French Facebook page Santé + Mag, Manon Berriche and Sacha Altay (2020) found that such phatic posts were the strongest predictors of engagement, followed by content conveying positive emotions. Conversely, "only 28% [of posts in the dataset] consisted of health misinformation." Berriche and Altay therefore argue that Facebook (and by extension other social networks) are predominantly *social*, in the sense that they are mostly used to foster relations between people (rather than serving as a conduit for false or misleading content).

Second, rather than people sharing dodgy content among themselves, it appears that only a small number of individuals are responsible for spreading a disproportionate amount of misinformation. For instance, the Center for Countering Digital Hate (2021) identified twelve individuals who produced a whopping 65 percent of the shares of anti-vaccine misinformation on social media, the so-called "Disinformation Dozen." A study by Nir Grinberg and colleagues in the journal *Science* (2019) looked at the proliferation of fake news on Twitter during the 2016 US presidential election and found evidence of so-called "superspreaders" and "superconsumers": 0.1 percent of users were responsible for sharing 80 percent of the fake news (in turn, about 1 percent of users were exposed to about 80 percent of all misinformation). In the realm of politics, examples of elected officials and other elites spreading misinformation are so common that we won't detail them here. While this doesn't necessarily negate the notion that misinformation can pose a problem, Altay (2022) argues that it should influence our considerations around how to tackle misinformation. After all, interventions that empower individuals to better identify problematic content are likely to be far less effective than targeting these powerful "super-spreaders."

Third, misinformation spreads more widely and has more persuasive power in times of high polarization, inter-group tensions, and economic malaise. Altay (2022) argues that misinformation is therefore a *symptom* of underlying, much deeper problems. Trying to tackle misinformation often becomes a game of "whack-a-mole," doomed to continue indefinitely if these root causes are left unaddressed. In other words, it's not *misinformation* that's the problem, but rather the hardships and policy failures that give rise to environments in which misinformation can thrive. Addressing misinformation therefore requires systemic solutions rather than focusing on individual attitudes and behavior (Chater & Loewenstein, 2022); we return to this discussion in Chapters 7 and 8.

Fourth, studies that seek to determine how likely individuals are to believe misinformation may suffer from significant methodological problems and therefore arrive at conclusions that are overly alarmist. One important study

by Soroush Vosoughi and colleagues (2018) was widely reported as showing that "false news spreads faster than the truth" (Dizikes, 2018; Fox, 2018;
Greenemeier, 2018). However, Altay and colleagues (2022, p. 8) argue that
Vosoughi's study "did not examine the spread of true and false news online
but of *'contested news'* that fact-checkers classified as either true or false, leaving out a large portion of uncontested news that is extremely viral." By this,
they mean that the study compared news that was fact-checked and rated
false to fact-checked news that was rated true, not *all* false news and *all* true
news: an example of sampling bias. However, this criticism is not entirely
correct as Vosoughi and colleagues did replicate their findings even on non-
fact-checked news. Nonetheless, some journalists overgeneralized their findings and important nuance was lost.[2] Later studies, for instance by Matteo
Cinelli and colleagues (2020), revealed that such findings might be platform
or topic-dependent, instead observing that true and false news (at least about
COVID-19) appear to exhibit very similar spreading patterns. Similarly, misinformation does not appear to always spread faster than factual information
on other platforms such as Reddit (Bond & Garrett, 2023).

Another potential shortcoming of misinformation research has to do
with the design of the surveys used to test the prevalence of misinformation
belief. Most survey studies have people rate a series of items (such as social
media posts or news headlines) that either do or do not contain misinformation on a scale, usually a binary (true/false), four-point, six-point, or seven-
point scale: for instance, people may be asked, "To the best of your knowledge,
is this headline accurate?" or "How reliable do you find this social media
post?" (Roozenbeek, Maertens, et al., 2022). However, this approach may be
problematic as it doesn't allow participants to indicate that they're not sure,
which invites random guessing. Altay and colleagues (2022, p. 13) cite an as
yet unpublished article by Luskin and colleagues (2018), in which the authors
show that not including a "don't know" option significantly overestimated the
proportion of participants professing belief in misinformation; in other words,
many people who studies assume are misinformed may in fact be *uninformed*.

Finally, despite alarmist narratives that exposure to and belief in misinformation have real-world adverse consequences (such as affecting the outcome of an election or lowering vaccination rates), the evidence of a direct
causal link between misinformation and behavior isn't always clear-cut. For
instance, although several studies show a link between belief in misinformation about COVID-19 and self-reported vaccination intentions (Loomba
et al., 2021; Roozenbeek, Schneider, et al., 2020), it is possible that both factors
(COVID-19 misinformation belief and vaccine hesitancy) are explained by a
latent variable such as (lack of) trust in institutions or the medical community.

---

[2]   Sinan Aral, one of the co-authors of the Vosoughi study, wrote an article on Medium
      addressing this discussion, which is well worth a read (Aral, 2022).

There is also a distinct lack of studies that investigate the causal links between misinformation and behavior (Schmid et al., 2023): it is possible that this link, if it exists at all, is weak, particularly when it comes to behaviors with important implications for democracy and society, such as how people vote (Ecker et al., 2022).

Overall, it's possible that concerns over misinformation constitute more of a "techno-panic" than a societal issue that requires immediate action. Amy Orben, a researcher at the University of Cambridge, has argued that technology panics occur in what she calls "Sisyphean cycles" (Orben, 2020b). In her article, she traces how widespread societal concerns over new technologies (radio, television, smartphones, and so on), including from prominent scientists, repeat themselves each time these technologies emerge. Through a variety of pressures and incentives, scientists (and especially psychologists) are encouraged to investigate how these technologies affect people, particularly children. However, Orben argues that these efforts are often fruitless because we do not learn from past technological panics, and the study of technologies and the phenomena they supposedly evoke starts from scratch each time around.

Concerns about misinformation may therefore be a consequence of the currently ongoing social media "techno-panic." For instance, many people have expressed concern over (especially young girls') mental health being negatively affected by social media. In a series of studies (Ghai et al., 2022; Orben, 2020a; Orben et al., 2020; Vuorre et al., 2021), Orben and her colleagues tried to quantify the strength of this relationship, and concluded that "the association between digital technology use, or social media use in particular, and psychological well-being is – on average – negative but very small" (Orben, 2020a). In other words, social media appears to negatively affect our well-being, but not to such an extent that it is time to panic. If this is the case, isn't it also possible that the adverse effects of misinformation on society and democracy are overblown? After all, if so few people actively consume and believe misinformation to begin with (Allen et al., 2020), if new and potentially dangerous misinformation technologies such as "deepfakes" continue to be vanishingly rare and mostly unimpactful (Brennen et al., 2020), and if the real-world evidence of how misinformation affects important societal phenomena is inconclusive (Marineau, 2020; Roozenbeek, Culloty, et al., 2023), then what justifies the massive investments that go into solving the problem and the enormous amount of attention paid to it by journalists, scientists, and policymakers?

3.3 PERSPECTIVE #2: THIS IS *NOT* FINE

Some scientists don't (fully) agree with the arguments mentioned above, and consider misinformation to be a problem that warrants substantial attention. Their arguments can be broadly summarized as follows: misperceptions are commonly held and a successful democracy relies in part on an accurately informed populace; despite methodological challenges, there are some studies that identify a plausible association – and sometimes even causation – between misinformation belief and behaviors such as vaccine uptake and medical treatment seeking; and some people and organizations have been known to successfully use misinformation to achieve their goals (such as the passing or delaying of legislation). As above, we will discuss each of these points in turn.

First, although numerous studies show that the sharing of explicitly false information in online networks is relatively rare (Allen et al., 2020; Guess et al., 2019), inaccurate beliefs are common, sometimes to a problematic degree. Surveys show that small percentages of people surveyed believe in patent absurdities such as "the earth is flat" (Foster & Branch, 2018), but this could be due to people giving random responses to survey questions (King et al., 2019) or trolling (Lopez & Hillygus, 2018).[3] We'll therefore focus on examples of beliefs that are not only false but also held by a substantial share of the population, in a way that can't be explained by statistical or methodological artifact alone.

In a study we conducted in 2020, we found that around 43 percent of people surveyed across five different countries believed that the virus that causes COVID-19 was bioengineered in a military lab in Wuhan (Roozenbeek, Schneider, et al., 2020).[4] Substantial numbers of Americans continued to believe that the 2020 US presidential elections were fraudulent two years after they were held (around 40 percent as of November 2022; see Carbonaro, 2022), and a poll conducted in seventeen countries found that around 15 percent of people believed that the US government, not Al-Qaeda, carried out the 9/11 attacks (WorldPublicOpinion.org, 2008). As Jennifer Allen and colleagues (2020) argue, it's unlikely that so many people acquire these false beliefs through exposure to "fake news" alone, but this doesn't mean that news and other media content don't play an important role.

Some argue that this prevalence of false beliefs isn't consequence-free, but can lead to undesirable outcomes for democracy and society. For example, at least some protesters who entered the US Capitol on January 6, 2021, were relying in part on the false belief that the election was fraudulent; this was documented by the fact-checker Politifact, which examined hundreds of court files noting many defendants mentioned that they acted upon false

---

[3] Adam Berinsky (2018) investigated whether endorsement of political rumors in surveys represents genuine beliefs or expressive responses (e.g., people expressing opposition to policies or politicians rather than their actual belief in the rumor). He found that the proportion of excessive responses is very small. In other words, surveys measuring belief in political rumors are likely to be a pretty accurate measure of people's real beliefs.

[4] While a natural lab leak was certainly a feasible (albeit low-confidence) hypothesis at one point in time (Dyer, 2021b), with the US government launching an investigation into the virus' origins (BBC News, 2021), the latest evidence shows that COVID-19 is likely to have been natural in origin (Worobey et al., 2022). Moreover, although lab accidents do happen, this is still very different from the conspiracy theory that COVID-19 was somehow engineered as a bioweapon.

information (McCarthy, 2021). Also, although complex ethnic tensions in India undoubtedly played an important role (Arun, 2019), hundreds of mob lynchings leading to injury and even death occurred because people ultimately acted upon false rumors (Goel et al., 2019; see also Van der Linden, 2023, Chapter 5). Similarly, although there is a baseline level for alcohol poisonings, harmful alcohol-related incidents reached an all-time high in Iran during the pandemic around the time fake cures about ingesting methanol and other cleaning products went viral on social media, suggesting a plausible association (Delirrad & Mohammadi, 2020).

The larger argument from Altay and colleagues (2022) that other deeper social, political, and religious motivations play an important role in explaining societal misconceptions is difficult to causally disentangle from the influence of misinformation. For example, if people acquire incorrect beliefs about science or politics vicariously via others in their social network, that still implies the information they receive or act upon is incorrect. Similarly, people who deeply distrust the mainstream media may still be basing their judgments on incorrect or misleading information. It's thus possible that this disconnect between the low overall prevalence of false news stories and the high incidence of false beliefs in many populations is explained by the high volume of polarizing, misleading, and speculative content produced by legacy media (such as opinion programs on television) and online and offline discussions that don't fall under the banner of "news." At the very least, it seems reasonable to presume that people acquire false beliefs in part through some kind of media consumption.

More broadly, James Kuklinski and colleagues (2000) argue that widespread belief in misinformation (in their case about welfare) can lead to public preferences being different than they would have been if more people had been accurately informed. This, in turn, could affect how salient voters perceive certain issues to be, how these issues are debated in the media and among politicians, and so on. Although a subjective claim, the "normative thrust" of public opinion research has long been the assumption that democracy relies on an accurately informed citizenry (Kuklinski et al., 2000, p. 790).

Second, there are numerous studies that establish a plausible relationship between misinformation belief and people's behavior. For instance, Skyler Johnson and colleagues (2017) investigated the efficacy of alternative medicine on cancer patients' chances of survival. They found that patients who chose alternative therapy as the primary treatment for their (curable) cancer were much more likely to die from the disease than people who opted for conventional treatment. While this study doesn't establish a causal link between misinformation belief and adverse health outcomes (i.e., death), it seems reasonable to assume that a substantial number of cancer patients who opted for alternative therapies did so because they (falsely) believed them to be as or more effective than mainstream treatments. Another more recent example is the prevalence of crypto scams: in the unregulated crypto market, huge numbers of people lost vast amounts of money to pyramid schemes, Ponzi schemes, and so-called "rug pulls." These scam artists make clever use of manipulation techniques and misinformation to convince their audiences to invest, sometimes with disastrous consequences.[5]

In her book *Stuck: How Vaccine Rumors Start – and Why They Don't Go Away* (2020), Heidi Larson lists several examples of vaccine rumors being associated with a drop in vaccination rates. She mentions a 1974 article published in the UK, which described thirty-six cases of children with neurological complications after receiving the DPT (diphtheria/pertussis/tetanus) vaccine. TV channels and newspapers quickly picked up on the publication, which led to the establishment of the "Association of Parents of Vaccine-Damaged Children." Several additional studies were conducted to reassess the safety and efficacy of the vaccine, finding that it was safe enough to use, but this did little to assuage people's fears. Larson notes that DPT vaccination rates dropped from 81 percent in 1974 to 31 percent in 1980 (Larson, 2020, pp. xx–xxi). Another example is the impact of Andrew Wakefield's MMR vaccine paper on Somali immigrant communities in the US, UK, and Sweden. Larson (2020, pp. 10–11) writes that in part thanks to Wakefield making inroads with Somali communities in Minnesota and reinforcing existing seeds of doubt about the links between vaccines and autism, MMR vaccination rates dropped from 91 percent in 2004 to 54 percent in 2010. Interestingly, Somali communities worldwide have high confidence in vaccines in general, but have been highly skeptical specifically of the MMR vaccine (Motta & Stecula, 2021). Studies conducted in Sweden and the UK found that Somali parents' main concerns were that their child might stop speaking or walking after the vaccination (Jama et al., 2018; Tomlinson & Redwood, 2013).

The above examples are correlational and don't establish if belief in misinformation *in general* is linked to people's decisions to get vaccinated (but see Loomba et al., 2021, which is one of the few studies to establish causal evidence of the effects of misinformation exposure on intentions to get vaccinated, and also S. L. Wilson & Wiysonge, 2020). In one of our studies, led by Sahil Loomba, we looked at how misinformation belief relates to COVID-19 vaccine uptake (Loomba et al., 2023). We administered a psychometrically validated instrument (the Misinformation Susceptibility Test or MIST, see Maertens, Götz, et al., 2023) to about 16,400 people from around the United Kingdom. This large sample allowed us to identify regional variations in how good people are at identifying misinformation. We then correlated this regional variation in misinformation susceptibility with COVID-19 vaccination rates in these regions, and found that there was a positive and meaningful association

[5] YouTubers such as Coffeezilla (www.youtube.com/@Coffeezilla), Patrick Boyle (www.youtube.com/@PBoyle), and münecat (www.youtube.com/@Munecat) do a great job of explaining how these kinds of scams work and how crypto scammers manipulate their audience.

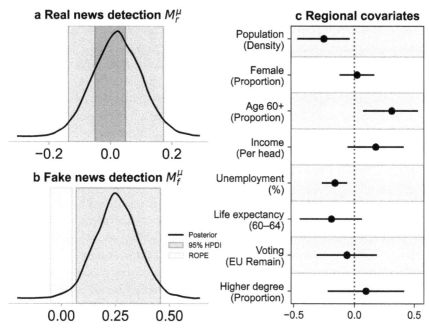

FIGURE 3.1 Fake news detection ability scores are positively associated with regional COVID-19 vaccination rates in England and Scotland. The figure shows the standardized coefficients for the relationship between real news detection ability (panel a) and fake news detection ability (panel b) and COVID-19 vaccination rates. For fake news detection ability, the coefficient is around 0.25, or significantly above 0, indicating that there is a meaningful association between how good people are at detecting fake news and COVID-19 vaccine uptake in the UK; for real news detection the coefficient is around 0, indicating no effect. The model controls for regional variation as well as a set of regional covariates such as age, gender, income, and how people voted in the 2016 Brexit referendum (panel c): for instance, the proportion of people in a region of the UK that are over sixty years old is also positively associated with higher COVID-19 vaccine uptake. Adapted from Loomba et al. (2023) and Loomba (2023).

between the two: in regions where people were generally more susceptible to believing misinformation, vaccination rates were usually lower. On the other hand, people's ability to correctly identify "real news" (or true information) was not associated with vaccine uptake. See Figure 3.1.

It's very difficult to know if people decide to not vaccinate their child, fall for a crypto scam, or seek alternative treatment for cancer *because* they saw and believed misinformation. However, it's reasonable to argue that the link is *plausible*: while there may be some other reason why, for example, vaccination rates drop pretty consistently after an anti-vaccine rumor goes viral, or alcohol poisonings go up at a time when rumors about methanol as a cure for disease abound, the hypothesis that misinformation plays a role is worth our attention. Misinformation may be most effective when it resonates with people, and *why* it resonates with people is a complex topic to untangle (see Chapter 4), but at a very basic level, it seems clear that some people make decisions based on false information, and that they acquired this information from somewhere (be it the media, their peers, or someone else).

Third, coordinated mis- and disinformation campaigns can be effective at delaying and softening legislation, and thus affect the political process (Oreskes & Conway, 2010). For example, the negative effects of tobacco consumption on people's health have been well-established scientific knowledge since at least the 1950s. As public opinion turned against tobacco, lawmakers began to look for ways to curb cigarette smoking. In response, tobacco companies such as Philip Morris and Brown & Williamson mounted a sophisticated influence campaign aimed at both policymakers and the wider public.

In 1994, a whistleblower known as "Mr. Butts" sent about 4,000 internal tobacco industry documents to Stanton Glantz, a professor at the University of California, exposing more than thirty years of deliberate disinformation. In their book *The Cigarette Papers* (1996), Glantz and his colleagues describe in great detail how tobacco companies tried to mislead public officials and the wider public. In August 1969, John W. Burgard, then the Executive Vice President of Sales and Public Relations at Brown & Williamson, requested senior marketing supervisor R. A. Pittman to run a marketing campaign that would "bring the industry side of the smoking and health controversy to the attention of the general public" (Glantz et al., 1996, p. 187). This campaign consisted of six objectives (taken verbatim from Glantz et al., 1996, pp. 188–189):

1. To set aside in the minds of millions the false conviction that cigarette smoking causes lung cancer and other diseases; a conviction based on fanatical assumptions, fallacious rumors, unsupported claims and the unscientific statements and conjectures of publicity-seeking opportunists.
2. To lift the cigarette from the cancer identification as quickly as possible and restore it to its proper place of dignity and acceptance in the minds of men and women in the marketplace of American free enterprise.
3. To expose the incredible, unprecedented and nefarious attack against the cigarette, constituting the greatest libel and slander ever perpetrated against any product in the history of free enterprise; a criminal libel of such major proportions and implications that one wonders how such a crusade of calumny can be reconciled under the Constitution can be so flouted and violated.
4. To unveil the insidious and developing pattern of attack against the American free enterprise system, a sinister formula that is slowly eroding American business with the cigarette obviously selected as one of the trial targets.
5. To prove that the cigarette has been brought to trial by lynch law, engineered and fostered by uninformed and irresponsible people and organizations in order to induce and incite fear.
6. To establish – once and for all – that no scientific evidence has ever been produced, presented or submitted to prove conclusively that cigarette smoking causes cancer.

One of the ways in which tobacco companies sought to sow this doubt was by publishing misleading "fact-checks" such as this one (Glantz et al., 1996, p. 173):

ASSERTION: "All doctors are convinced that smoking is dangerous."

FACT: Doctors are by no means unanimous in condemning smoking. There are many who have expressed publicly their unwillingness to accept statistical evidence as scientific proof of a causal relationship between cigarette smoking and human disease. For example, some of the country's most eminent men of medicine and science – from such renowned institutions as Bellevue Hospital, Columbia University Medical School, Yale University Medical School, and New York Medical College – have testified before the U.S. Congress that the charges against tobacco remain unproved.

Of course, this "fact-check" is based on a false premise (there doesn't have to be unanimity for there to be consensus), and moreover the dissenting scientists were often sponsored by the tobacco industry itself, which might have biased their opinions. Nonetheless, without this background the "fact-check" *looks* pretty convincing.

In another memo, most likely written around the same time as the Burgard memo above and in reference to the same campaign, two other Brown & Williamson employees noted that "Congress and federal agencies are already being dealt with" (by the Tobacco Institute, an industry trade and lobbying group). With respect to the campaign aimed at the wider public, they said the following:

Doubt is our product since it is the best means of competing with the "body of fact" that exists in the mind of the general public. It is also the means of establishing a controversy. Within the business we recognize that a controversy exists. However, with the general public the consensus is that cigarettes are in some way harmful to the health. If we are successful in establishing a controversy at the public level, then there is an opportunity to put across the real facts about smoking and health. Doubt is also the limit of our "product." Unfortunately, we cannot take a position directly opposing the anti-cigarette forces and say that cigarettes are a contributor to good health. No information that we have supports such a claim. **Truth is our message because of its power to withstand a conflict and sustain a controversy**. If in our pro-cigarette efforts we stick to well documented fact, we can dominate a controversy and operate with the confidence of justifiable self-interest. (Glantz et al., 1996, pp. 190–191; emphasis added)

In other words, to challenge the widely held (and correct) belief that cigarettes are bad for your health, tobacco companies didn't try to persuade anyone that the *reverse* was true, but rather they tried to persuade them that there was reasonable doubt about the claim. They realized that spreading outright lies would be detrimental to their goals, but they didn't need to: instead, they exploited the fact that science is imperfect and that proving something beyond all doubt is almost impossible. As long as they could assert that claims were "unproven," they could continue to fight legislation and regulation. See Figure 3.2. And indeed, Allan Brandt (2012) notes that "looking back at the half-century that followed the path-breaking science clearly linking cigarettes

According to repeated nationwide surveys,

More Doctors Smoke CAMELS than any other cigarette!

FIGURE 3.2 A tobacco advertisement (Stanford Research into the Impact of Tobacco Advertising, 2021).

to disease and premature death, it is striking to note the utter lack of serious and effective regulatory action on the part of the federal government." Put differently, there is a good case to be made that the tobacco industry's years-long disinformation campaign was highly effective in achieving its goals by manipulating regulators and the public at large.[6]

Another example which follows a very similar playbook is the ongoing campaign to undermine action against climate change (Bonneuil et al., 2021; Franta, 2018).[7] Coan et al. (2021) conducted a complicated and hugely impressive study into the prevalence of so-called "super-claims" about climate change in publications by climate-skeptical think tanks and blogs over a period of twenty years (2000–2020). By "super-claims" the authors mean the most common overarching arguments that are used to counter the scientific consensus about climate change: "climate change is not happening," "it's not us," "it's not bad," "the science is unreliable," and "solutions won't work." See Figure 3.3.

---

[6] As a counterargument, the percentage of smokers (in the US) has steadily declined over the past decades, from 40 percent in 1974 to 11 percent in 2022 (Gallup, 2022). In other words, despite tobacco companies' influence campaigns, fewer and fewer people have taken up smoking ever since it became widely known that cigarettes cause cancer. Smoking rates might have declined quicker had it not been for these campaigns (we don't know), but the decline has been slow and steady regardless. We thank Alexander Bor for drawing our attention to this point.

[7] A Dutch punk band, Hang Youth, summarized this problem as follows: *Shell is een prima bedrijf, als ik de website mag geloven.* This translates to "Shell is a fine company, if I'm to believe the website."

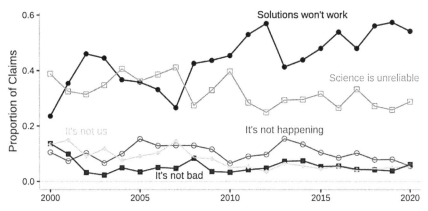

FIGURE 3.3 Prevalence of "super-claims" about climate change in climate change think tank publications, 2000–2020. Taken from Coan et al. (2021).

From the figure we can identify a general trend away from explicit climate denial and toward a focus on the costs of climate mitigation. Since around 2010, the claim that climate solutions won't work has become by far the most common argument against the scientific climate consensus. Before then, claims that climate change doesn't exist at all, isn't caused by humans, or cannot be reliably measured through scientific inquiry were more common than they are today. In other words, the argumentation strategies used by climate-skeptic people and organizations evolve over time. The overarching goal, however, remains the same: to "keep the controversy alive" after a scientific consensus has been reached (Oreskes & Conway, 2010). Doing so allows the campaigners to stave off or soften unwanted rules and legislation, at least for a time. The use of misinformation is instrumental in achieving this: although provable falsehoods are relatively uncommon, there is a clear element of manipulation that can be discerned in these kinds of communications (Bonneuil et al., 2021).

3.4 CASE STUDY: INFORMATION WARFARE IN THE RUSSIA–UKRAINE WAR

To better understand the role that misinformation can play in society, it's useful to look at a specific context in detail: the Russia–Ukraine war. We choose to focus on this conflict for both intellectual and practical reasons: one of us (Jon) wrote his Ph.D. dissertation about media discourse and social identities in eastern Ukraine between 2014 and 2018. We're therefore quite familiar with the conflict's historical context, and the role that the media have played in it. The below summary lacks a lot of detail and nuance. For the sake of brevity, we will focus on the information war as it played out on the Russian side, although there is much to be said about how Ukraine has positioned itself on this information battlefield (see our discussion of the "Ghost of Kyiv" from Chapter 1). For more information, we therefore refer to Jon's Ph.D. thesis (Roozenbeek, 2020b) and his book about propaganda and ideology in the Russia–Ukraine war (Roozenbeek, 2024).

In November 2013, protests broke out throughout Ukraine against then president Viktor Yanukovych, after he suddenly withdrew from an association agreement between Ukraine and the European Union. These protests concentrated on Kyiv's Independence Square (*Maidan Nezalezhnosti* in Ukrainian), and soon became known as the Euromaidan movement. Over the following months, the protests gradually escalated, culminating in the death of more than 100 protesters at the hands of snipers (A. Wilson, 2014). Yanukovych was removed from power in February 2014, and a new, pro-European government was sworn in. Not long after, soldiers without insignias began to occupy strategic military and administrative locations throughout Crimea, a peninsula in the south of Ukraine. After a contested referendum, Russia annexed Crimea in March 2014, in contravention of international law (Grant, 2015). In the meantime, demonstrations also began to pop up in the eastern Ukrainian *oblasts* (provinces) of Donetsk and Luhansk, ostensibly against the new government in Kyiv. These demonstrations soon turned violent, leading to a set of paramilitary groups (supported by the Russian army) declaring independence from Ukraine through yet another series of illegal referenda, and establishing the separatist "People's Republics" of Donetsk and Luhansk (Roozenbeek, 2020b, Chapter 1).[8] This provoked a prolonged military conflict between the Ukrainian army and the insurgents in Donetsk and Luhansk, who received funding, weapons, and training from Russia. After a bit more than a year of skirmishes and territorial exchanges, the conflict, which became known as the Donbas War, reached a relative lull in late 2015, although the conflict was never exactly frozen.

On February 24, 2022, after months of military buildup on Ukraine's borders, Russia launched a full-scale invasion of Ukraine from the north (through Belarus) and east. Russia's initial goal was to quickly reach Kyiv from the north and northeast, establish control over key cities such as Kharkiv, Mariupol, and Odesa, depose the Ukrainian government (led by President Volodymyr Zelensky), and install a Russia-friendly regime (Jones, 2022). Figure 3.4 shows a map of the military situation in Ukraine as it was after November 2022 and throughout the first half of 2023.

Russia was mostly unable to achieve these goals: the assault on Kyiv quickly stalled as Russian special forces failed to take control of strategic

---

[8]   Whether the Donbas insurgents declared formal independence or something more akin to self-rule isn't exactly clear; the key word on the referendum ballot (in Russian) was *samostoiatelnost*, which can mean both outright independence and self-rule. The more commonly used Russian word for "independence" is *nezavisimost*.

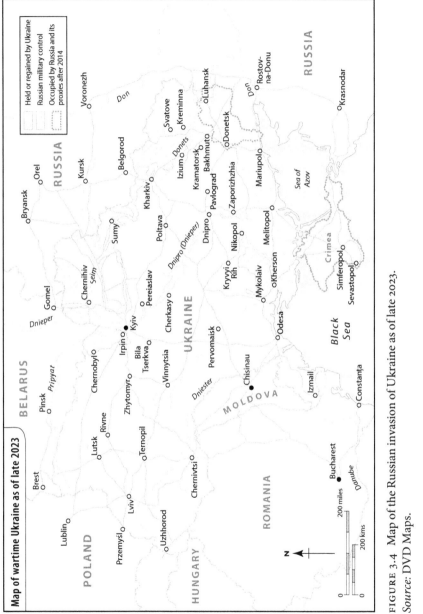

FIGURE 3.4 Map of the Russian invasion of Ukraine as of late 2023.
Source: DVD Maps.

airfields around the city, and Ukraine proved effective at disrupting Russian supply lines and preventing Russia from establishing air superiority. By April, Russia had abandoned its attempts to take Kyiv altogether and shifted its focus to the southern and eastern parts of Ukraine instead. However, although Russian forces managed to take control over key cities such as Kherson (just northwest of Crimea) and Mariupol (in the southeast) and lay siege to Kharkiv (Ukraine's second-largest city, located just twenty-six miles from the Russian border), the offensive stalled over the spring and summer of 2022. Instead, Ukraine managed a series of effective counteroffensives, reconquering all of Kharkiv *oblast* by September 2022 and taking back control of the city of Kherson in November (Institute for the Study of War, 2023). As of this writing, violent conflict is still ongoing (with Russia continuing to control significant swaths of Ukrainian territory), and how the war will play out in future is impossible to predict. Nonetheless, looking back at about a decade of conflict, we can analyze the role that information warfare, misinformation, and propaganda have played in the lead-up to the 2022 invasion.

The term "information warfare" is not easy to define. The *Oxford Essential Dictionary of the US Military* (2002) defines it as "a form of conflict in which the objective is to capture, degrade, or destroy the enemy's means of gathering, analyzing, and distributing data, particularly data regarding the enemy's armed forces." However, this definition is from 2002, before the advent of social media, and doesn't include influence operations that seek to manipulate, persuade, or dissuade the wider public. The European Center for Populism Studies (2022) therefore defines information warfare as a "concept involving the battlespace use and management of information and communication technology (ICT) in pursuit of a competitive advantage over an opponent." We will use the latter definition here, as we're interested specifically in the role of misinformation and propaganda in the conflict.

It's clear that control over the information space was hugely important right from the start of the insurgency in March 2014. The so-called Gerasimov Doctrine (named after Valery Gerasimov, Chief of the General Staff of the Russian armed forces) includes "information conflict" as a core component of Russia's approach to modern warfare (Gerasimov, 2016). Immediately after establishing control over parts of Donetsk and Luhansk *oblasts*, the newly minted authorities in the "People's Republics" shut down all Ukrainian television channels, fired and exiled journalists unwilling to support the insurgents (Roozenbeek, 2020a), and passed legislation aimed at censoring countervailing opinions and promoting pro-insurgency and pro-Russian narratives (Roozenbeek, 2020b, Chapters 1 and 2). They quickly set up a sprawling media landscape, dedicated not so much to persuading locals that the separatist republics posed an attractive alternative to Ukrainian nationhood but rather that Ukraine (and especially the new Ukrainian government) was a threat to Russian-speaking Ukrainians and sympathetic to Nazism (Roozenbeek,

2020b, 2022). This marked the beginning of a years-long, global information warfare campaign aimed at fostering the narrative that Ukraine was ruled by Nazis and far-right extremists, and that its government was illegally installed through a Western-backed coup, against the will of the people (Mateo, 2018). This campaign culminated in Russian president Vladimir Putin's speech on the eve of the war, in which he said that the goal of the "special operation" was to "demilitarize and denazify" Ukraine (Putin, 2022).

Although Ukraine (like most European countries) has been a host to far-right and anti-Semitic movements such as Pravyi Sektor ("Right Sector") and Svoboda ("Freedom"), these kinds of parties have existed on the periphery of Ukrainian politics since the country's independence from the Soviet Union in 1991. For instance, in the first parliamentary elections after the 2014 revolution, Pravyi Sektor received 1.8 percent of the votes, and Svoboda 4.7 percent (Central Election Commission of Ukraine, 2014). This isn't to say that Ukraine doesn't have a problem with extremism; for example, in 2015, an attack on an LGBT pride parade in Kyiv resulted in ten injuries, despite the presence of around 1,500 police and national guard soldiers (Amnesty International, 2015). However, these problems appear to be in proportion with other (eastern) European countries, with similar levels of anti-LGBT and anti-Jewish attitudes being reported in countries such as Poland, Hungary, and Russia (Anti-Defamation League, 2019; Pew Research Center, 2017).

Nonetheless, a large chunk of Russia's information war was dedicated to pushing the narrative that Ukraine and its government were exceptionally pro-Nazi. In Ukraine, this effort targeted two different audiences: Russian citizens and Russian-speaking Ukrainians (Roozenbeek, 2020b, Chapters 4 and 5).[9] The campaign's effectiveness (in terms of fostering the desired attitudes, sow doubt, and so on) differed across these groups. Domestically, the highly centralized and coordinated Russian state media presented a unified and mostly coherent message about Ukraine (Hutchings & Szostek, 2015; Tolz & Teper, 2018). The result was that a substantial share of Russians came to hold a much more negative opinion about Ukraine and Ukrainians after 2014; this shift from a mostly positive general attitude to a mostly negative one was sustained over a period of several years. See Figure 3.5.

As a result, a large percentage of Russians (around 46 percent in mid- to late 2022) "fully support" Russia's war in Ukraine (Volkov & Kolesnikov, 2022). When prompted, supporters echo dominant state media narratives about Ukraine: "It's not like we are taking anything [that isn't ours, referring to parts of Ukraine that Russia claims are part of Russia]"; "We're liberating [Ukraine]

---

[9] Media outlets such as RT (formerly Russia Today) and Sputnik are examples of Russian state media channels with an *international* scope; there is so much to be said about the purpose behind these channels and how effective they are at agenda-setting and influencing public opinion around the world that we unfortunately cannot go into too much detail here; for further reading, we refer to work by Ilya Yablokov (2015), Joanna Szostek (2017), and Vera Tolz and Yuri Teper (2018).

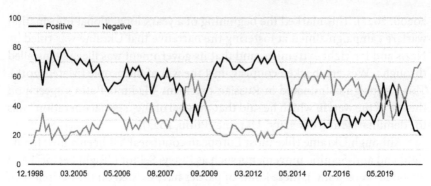

FIGURE 3.5 Russians' attitudes toward Ukraine over time. Note the shift from a generally positive to a negative attitude after 2014 (the Euromaidan revolution) and again in late 2021 (the lead-up to the 2022 invasion).
Source: Levada-Center (2022).

from Nazis and fascists"; and "what other choice was there? [...] Negotiate with [the Ukrainians]? It was too late!" In other words, for Russian audiences, the years-long effort to discredit Ukraine and fuel animosity toward Ukrainians appears to have been successful: Russians went from having very positive feelings about Ukraine to having very negative ones, to the point where a substantial percentage of them felt that a full-scale military invasion was justified. This also speaks to the mobilizing role of misinformation (Horowitz, 2000): people who support certain viewpoints (such as the invasion of Ukraine being justified, or the 2020 US elections being "stolen") might be extra-motivated by misinformation to take action: for example, attending a demonstration, committing an act of violence, or actively or passively support a military conflict. So while misinformation might be unlikely to motivate or persuade skeptics, it could have a substantial behavioral influence on partisans and people on the extremes.

With respect to Russian-speaking Ukrainians, the story is different (Mazepus et al., 2023): the Kremlin appears to have assumed throughout the eight years of its information war that Russian-speaking Ukrainians were Ukrainian only by accident of history (Putin, 2022), and longed to return to the Russian fold. A large chunk of media content produced within the "People's Republics" of Donetsk and Luhansk after 2014 therefore tapped into this assumed sentiment: for example, by hearkening back to the Red Army's victory over Nazi Germany in World War II (Roozenbeek, 2020b, Chapter 4). However, the Kremlin's assumption turned out to be mostly false. Gwendolyn Sasse and Alice Lackner conducted a series of high-quality opinion polls in Donbas and other predominantly Russian-speaking parts of Ukraine, and found that support for joining Russia in any capacity was extremely low in areas under Ukrainian control (around 4 percent in 2019) but higher (albeit still a minority) in separatist-held areas (Sasse, 2019; Sasse & Lackner, 2019). Thus, despite the onslaught of information aimed at Russian-speaking Ukrainians with respect to the alleged links between

Ukrainian nationalism and Nazism, tapping into World War II and Soviet nostalgia, and riffing on the historical ties between Donbas (and the rest of Ukraine) and Russia (O'Loughlin et al., 2017), Russia's information war mostly failed to convince Ukrainians that Russia posed an alternative to Ukrainian identity (Roozenbeek, 2022). This may help explain why invading Russian soldiers were met with derision and ridicule, rather than enthusiasm, in many parts of eastern and southern Ukraine (Jones, 2022).[10]

Russia's information war and promotion of misinformation and propaganda were therefore a partial success: years of sustained effort by state media to portray Ukraine as a pro-fascist country with a US-installed puppet government appear to have been successful at fostering stronger anti-Ukrainian sentiments within Russia itself. However, it was much less successful at reaching Russian-speaking Ukrainians, particularly those living outside separatist-held territories.[11] This analysis echoes the findings by Nico Voigtländer and Hans-Joachim Voth (2015) about anti-Semitic attitudes in Germany after World War II, which we mentioned in Chapter 2. Similar to the way many people who grew up under the Nazi regime continued to hold anti-Jewish attitudes decades after Hitler's death, many Russians (especially those who were already supportive of Putin) acquired misinformed beliefs to the point where some considered the invasion an appropriate response to perceived threats. Doing so, however, required sustained effort over multiple years; so while the persuasive power of individual examples of misinformation is not clear, the cumulative effect of misinformation exposure can be substantial. At the same time, there is less evidence that this strategy worked for people who were less positively inclined toward Russia or its government. In other words, rather than changing people's minds entirely, misinformation appears to have been most successful when tapping into preexisting attitudes.

3.5 CONCLUSION

In this chapter, we have discussed whether misinformation is a significant problem for society. There are reasonable arguments on both sides of this debate. On the one hand, we know from numerous studies that exposure to narrowly defined "fake news" is low, especially on social media. In addition, misinformation is disproportionately spread by a very small number of people, and many studies that look at the prevalence of misinformed beliefs and people's propensity to share misinformation with others suffer from

---

[10] To give an example, an elderly resident of the (predominantly Russian-speaking) city of Kherson, which was under Russian occupation at the time, was recorded yelling at a Russian soldier: "we will deal with our authorities [i.e., the government in Kyiv] on our own. We did not call you here!" (RTÉ News, 2022).

[11] Or people from the US, for that matter: a study by Eady and colleagues (2023) found that exposure to content produced by the Russian Internet Research Agency (the "troll factory") on Twitter was negligible: it appears to have had next to zero influence on people's attitudes and voting behavior around the 2016 US elections.

significant conceptual and methodological shortcomings, which may bias our conclusions. Most people continue to consume news from reliable sources, and misinformation may be a symptom (rather than a cause) of much deeper societal problems, though this relationship is likely to be dynamic, complex, and bi-directional. There is also little to no evidence that the prevalence of news content or the rise of social media have made the misinformation problem worse than it was before. Finally, concerns about the powerful influence of misinformation on people's opinions and behavior might be overstated. For example, misinformation is unlikely to convince people if they're already skeptical about the source or topic of the misinformation.

On the other hand, false beliefs are a common occurrence (even if these beliefs likely don't directly arise from exposure to "fake news" on social media). Some studies also identify an association between misinformation belief and behaviors such as alternative treatment seeking and vaccine refusal (although it's important to note that very few studies establish a direct causal link). Also, there are examples of misinformation campaigns (e.g., about tobacco and climate change) that didn't seek to persuade as much as to sow doubt and uncertainty, and in so doing were possibly effective at postponing or averting unwanted actions (such as the passing of legislation). There is also some evidence that misinformation can serve as a motivator to take action for people who already hold strong beliefs.

Finally, we looked at the role of misinformation in the Russia–Ukraine war, and see the same complexities emerge that we described above. We have seen how the prevalence of explicitly *false* information surrounding the war is dwarfed by misleading narratives that seek to evoke strong, negative emotions about groups of people. Individual examples of misinformation may not have been impactful (or at least, it's extremely difficult to establish this), but it's possible if not probable that prolonged exposure to Russian state media's coordinated efforts to discredit Ukraine and its government became associated with more pro-war attitudes among some members of the public.

Overall, we arrive at a nuanced picture of misinformation and its consequences for society: the scale of the problem is in part definition- and timescale-dependent, and relates to deeper socio-economic and political factors. It's possible that the apparent paradox of exposure to misinformation being low despite evidence of adverse consequences of misinformation depends on how you define misinformation: some types of misinformation are not very common (provably false news headlines, for instance), whereas the problem increases in scope when employing a broader definition that includes scams, junk news, propaganda, and clickbait (Altay, Berriche, et al., 2022, p. 2). Unfortunately, there continues to be a lack of experimental studies that would allow us to better explore the mechanisms behind misinformation exposure and belief, and how they causally relate to people's behavior.

PART II

MISINFORMATION BELIEF AND SPREAD

4

Why Do People Believe and Share Misinformation?

4.1 INTRODUCTION

In this chapter, we examine the psychological factors that underlie why people might believe misinformation and share it with others. As is usually the case in psychology, this is a question that has many different answers and interpretations and diverging schools of thought.[1] Also, a wealth of research shows that believing and sharing misinformation are not the same thing. Rather, the two seem to be relatively disconnected: just because someone believes a false claim to be true doesn't mean they'll share it on social media, and someone sharing a piece of misinformation doesn't always mean they also believe it. To avoid confusing the reader, whose presumed goal it is to be more rather than less informed after reading this chapter, we will therefore discuss misinformation belief and sharing separately. There are numerous publications that provide their own perspectives on what we discuss below, and offer nuance and additional elaboration that we're unable to provide here. We highly recommend checking them out (Ecker et al., 2022; Greifeneder et al., 2020; Lewandowsky & van der Linden, 2021; Pennycook & Rand, 2021; Tandoc et al., 2018; Van Bavel et al., 2021; Van der Linden, 2023).

4.2 WHY DO PEOPLE *BELIEVE* MISINFORMATION?

Most researchers agree that a combination of individual- and societal-level factors play a role in whether an individual believes a false or misleading claim, statement, news headline, or social media post (Hornsey et al., 2022). Individual-level factors include analytical thinking skills, cognitive reflectivity, but also thinking styles (such as a willingness to evaluate viewpoints you disagree with on their merits rather than dismiss them without further consideration), group

---

[1] Which is weird because it should go without saying that we're 100 percent right about everything. After all, why would we *want* to believe something that isn't true?

membership, and partisanship. Examples of societal-level factors include trust (such as in the mainstream media, governments, and other institutions), political polarization, quality of the media ecosystem, corruption, and inequality.

4.2.1 Individual-Level Factors

Individual-level factors can be broken up into cognitive and identity-based predictors of misinformation belief. In terms of cognition, several studies have identified numeracy skills (how good you are at solving math puzzles) as a good predictor of misinformation belief (Bronstein et al., 2019; Matchanova et al., 2023; Roozenbeek, Maertens, et al., 2022; Roozenbeek, Schneider, et al., 2020). This finding has prompted some researchers to posit that higher analytical thinking ability is strongly associated with lower misinformation susceptibility. Relatedly, researchers have proposed that an intuitive thinking style (as opposed to a reflective one) plays an important role (Pennycook & Rand, 2019, 2020). To illustrate what this means, consider the following question: in a lake, there is a patch of lily pads. Every day, the patch doubles in size. If it takes 48 days for the patch to cover the entire lake, how long would it take for the patch to cover *half* of the lake?

If you answered 47, you are correct! However, people who tend to rely on a more intuitive thinking style might say 24 (as 24 is half of 48). The Cognitive Reflection Test (Frederick, 2005) consists of a series of questions similar to the one above, and provides a measure of the extent to which people rely on either an intuitive or a reflective thinking style (people who answer more questions correctly are said to engage in more reflective thinking). The idea behind the "classical reasoning" account of misinformation belief (Bronstein et al., 2019; Pennycook & Rand, 2019, 2020, 2021) is that people who perform poorly on the Cognitive Reflection Test, and thus fail to sufficiently engage in analytical thinking (or deliberation), are more likely to fall for misinformation. This is not because they are *unable* to correctly identify a claim as being false (much like most people aren't *unable* to understand the lily pad problem), but rather because they don't make use of their analytical thinking ability: for example, because they're distracted by the whistles and bells of social media. In other words, people are "lazy, not biased" (Pennycook & Rand, 2019).

Another cognitive factor known to play an important role in misinformation belief is a concept called actively open-minded thinking (AOT). Jon Baron, who led a lot of the research on the development of the AOT concept and the scales used to measure it, describes AOT as "a set of dispositions aimed at avoiding 'myside bias', the tendency to think in ways that strengthen whatever possible conclusions are already strong" (Baron et al., 2015, p. 267; see also Stanovich & Toplak, 2023). However, Stanovich and Toplak (2023) argue that AOT doesn't actually correlate very well with myside bias but instead with *belief* bias, the difference being that "belief bias occurs when real-world knowledge interferes with reasoning performance, [whereas] myside bias is a bias toward searching and interpreting evidence in a manner that tends to favor the hypothesis we want to be true" (p. 23; see also Mercier, 2017; Stanovich et al., 2013). There is thus a spirited debate about what exactly AOT measures and what being high in actively open-minded thinking means in practice.

Nonetheless, the scale was shown to be strongly associated with misinformation belief in a variety of studies (Mirhoseini et al., 2023; Roozenbeek, Maertens, et al., 2022; Saltor et al., 2023). More specifically, these studies show that people who are more likely to agree with statements such as "willingness to be convinced by opposing arguments is a sign of good character" and "there is nothing wrong with being undecided about many issues," and *disagree* with statements such as "changing your mind is a sign of weakness" also tend to perform well on tests aimed at assessing their ability to spot misinformation. The more actively open-minded people claimed to be, the less susceptible they were to believing misinformation.[2]

The final cognitive factor that we will discuss here is the "illusory truth effect," which states that people are more likely to believe and share repeated information than information they receive only once (Fazio et al., 2015; Hassan & Barber, 2021; Henderson et al., 2021; Vellani et al., 2023). Lisa Fazio, a professor at Vanderbilt University, together with her Ph.D. student Raunak Pillai, conducted a study where they texted their study participants a series of true and false trivia statements over the course of several weeks (Fazio et al., 2022). Participants saw statements either once, twice, four times, eight times, or sixteen times. After this, they were asked to rate the accuracy of each statement. The researchers not only found clear evidence that repetition increases belief of both true and false statements, but also that the impact of initial repetitions (the first or second time something is repeated) was much larger than for later repetitions (see also Hassan & Barber, 2021). This implies that seeing misinformation multiple times can lead people to believe it more, but only so many times: seeing a claim twenty times doesn't necessarily mean you'll believe it more strongly than if you see it nineteen times. The illusory truth effect also extends to implausible statements such as "the earth is a perfect square" (Fazio et al., 2019) and has been found in children from as young as five years old (Fazio & Sherry, 2020).

With respect to identity-based factors, political partisanship is known to play a role in some countries (but not so much in others). In the United States, for instance, conservatives (or Republicans) tend to perform worse than liberals (or Democrats) on misinformation susceptibility tests (Baptista & Gradim, 2022; Garrett & Bond, 2021). There is some evidence of cross-cultural

---

[2]   Although all of these constructs are about "reflective thinking" and share some conceptual overlap (for example, numeracy skills and performance on the cognitive reflection test are both essentially math puzzles), actively open-minded thinking (AOT) taps more into metacognitive awareness about what constitutes "good thinking" (Baron, 2019).

consistency for this finding: for instance, in a study we published in 2020 on susceptibility to COVID-19 misinformation across five different countries, we found that identifying as more politically right-wing was a predictor of higher belief in misinformation about COVID-19 in Ireland, Spain, and Mexico, but not in the United Kingdom (Roozenbeek, Schneider, et al., 2020). Interestingly, this effect was also not significant for the United States, even though a lot of research contradicts this finding (Guess et al., 2019; Pennycook & Rand, 2019; Roozenbeek, Maertens, et al., 2022).

However, several studies conducted in Hungary and Ukraine have offered nuance to this finding. In Hungary, it wasn't so much liberal (versus conservative) ideology that predicted misinformation susceptibility, but rather opposition to versus support for the ruling government, with government supporters generally being more susceptible to misinformation than people who opposed it (Faragó et al., 2023; Szebeni et al., 2021). In the context of the war in Ukraine, Honorata Mazepus and colleagues (2023) found that, among Ukrainians, higher perceived conflict between Ukrainians and Russians made people less likely to endorse misinformation about the European Union, but *more* likely to endorse misinformation about Russia and/or Russians. This finding remained robust when controlling for group identity and political knowledge, which indicates that the degree to which Ukrainians perceived themselves to be in conflict with Russians, and not just their group identity (e.g., identifying as Ukrainian), was associated with the likelihood of believing misinformation about other groups.

Overall, social identity thus appears to play a role in misinformation belief. New York University professor Jay Van Bavel and his colleagues (2021) argue that "information is often interpreted in a biased manner that reinforces original predispositions," which they call partisan bias.[3] As an example of such bias, they mention that someone who believes in the death penalty might give less weight to the argument that the death penalty doesn't deter crime than someone who doesn't believe in the death penalty. The key element here is group identity: Van Bavel and colleagues claim that when people encounter misinformation that is identity-congruent (meaning: misinformation that is *positive* about groups that they identify with, the ingroup, or *negative* about groups that we don't identify with, the outgroup), it can happen that their identity-based motivations (the desire to believe information that is positive about our ingroup) conflict with accuracy-based motivations (the desire to hold accurate beliefs) (see also Pereira et al., 2021; Van Bavel & Pereira, 2018). Although Van Bavel and colleagues focus mostly on *political* identities, their

---

[3]   There is some discussion in the field about exactly what "partisan bias" means. Van Bavel's definition is different from others', who (for example) take partisan bias to mean asymmetry across partisan lines in the updating of prior beliefs (Tappin et al., 2020). This is a rather technical discussion that, while relevant, is complex to untangle and distracts somewhat from more basic discussions over whether identity-based motivations can affect people's judgments of (mis)information.

point is that *any* strongly held sense of identity can potentially interfere with accuracy motivations.

For example, let's imagine that you're part of a ragtag group of the last remaining fans of the New York Yankees baseball team.[4] And let's say that you see a news story on your Facebook feed that reads "Aliens have landed on Earth and are investing $50 billion in a new Yankees stadium," your motivation to hold accurate beliefs might compel you to dismiss this story as false.[5] However, your social identity goals (wanting the Yankees and your ragtag group of friends to do well) might motivate you to think that it's true (because it's a positive story about your ingroup). Which of the two ends up happening, according to Van Bavel and colleagues (2021), depends on which of them is more salient or "valued" to you at that time (as well as the general persuasiveness of the misinformation, as not all misinformation is as plausible and logical as the above headline).

While there seems to be some level of consensus that identity-based motivations can influence (mis)information judgments, *why* this is the case is still an ongoing debate. Some have argued that (at least in the United States) conservatives may be more psychologically vulnerable to misinformation for a variety of reasons: for example, a greater need to identify with the ingroup (Jost et al., 2018; Pereira et al., 2021; van der Linden et al., 2020). Another perspective is that conservatives in the United States, at least in the present moment, are more heavily targeted with misinformation than liberals. Because of this, they may be more exposed to information from less than reliable sources such as *www.fakenewsonline.com* or *www.aliens4yankees.gov*, which in turn fuels misinformation belief. And indeed, there's quite a bit of evidence to suggest that US conservatives are more exposed to misinformation than liberals (Garrett, 2019; Garrett & Bond, 2021; Guess et al., 2019), hinting at a possible link between what types of (news) media people consume and their levels of misinformation belief.

To explore this phenomenon further, Cecilie Steenbuch Traberg, a Ph.D. candidate at the University of Cambridge, led a series of studies to see if source credibility impacted misinformation belief (Traberg et al., 2023; Traberg & van der Linden, 2022). She showed both left-wing and right-wing study participants from the US a series of tweets containing some form of misinformation that they were asked to evaluate in terms of their accuracy. Cecilie manipulated the news source for each tweet such that the headlines appeared to originate from either left (e.g., the *New York Times*) or right-leaning (e.g., *Fox News*) news outlets. The content of the tweets was kept the same for all participants. She found that there was a clear asymmetry in how accurate people believed the misinformation to be, depending on whether the source was congruent with

---

[4] We are aware that New York Yankees fans have tragically gone extinct after languishing for years on the endangered sports fans list, but please bear with us for the sake of argument.
[5] If your reaction to reading this was "bah, humbug! Facebook is for boomers," age will one day catch up with you as well.

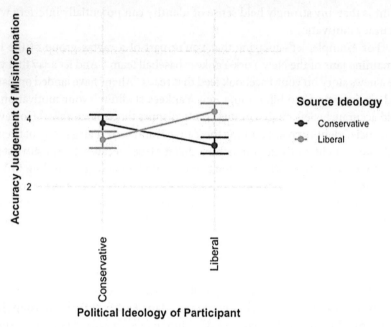

FIGURE 4.1 Belief in misinformation from conservative and liberal sources. The figure shows that conservative study participants rated misinformation published by a conservative source as more accurate than the same misinformation published by a liberal source; this effect is even larger for liberal participants.
Source: Reprinted from Traberg, C. S., & van der Linden, S. (2022). Birds of a feather are persuaded together: Perceived source credibility mediates the effect of political bias on misinformation susceptibility. *Personality and Individual Differences*, 185(111269). With permission from Elsevier.

their identity: liberal participants rated misinformation from liberal sources as more accurate than from conservative sources, and vice versa. Participants also indicated finding politically congenial sources more credible. This effect was especially pronounced for liberals. In other words, source credibility and how much we believe our news sources to be supportive of our (political) views can interfere with our judgments of (mis)information (see also Harff et al., 2022; Kumkale & Albarracín, 2004; Pornpitakpan, 2006). See Figure 4.1.

In a study we conducted in 2022 together with a team of researchers at the Max Planck Institute for Human Development in Berlin, we had the opportunity to compare the above-mentioned cognitive and identity-based predictors of misinformation belief with one another (Roozenbeek, Maertens, et al., 2022). To do this, we used a standardized instrument developed by a team led by our former Ph.D. student Rakoen Maertens (now at the University of Oxford) and Friedrich Götz (University of British Columbia), the Misinformation Susceptibility Test or MIST. The MIST consists of a series of twenty headlines (without source information): ten true and ten false (Maertens, Götz, et al., 2023). People taking the MIST indicate for each headline whether they think it's real or fake. Simplifying a little bit, their "veracity discernment ability" (i.e., their ability to tell apart true and false news) is calculated by taking the sum of all correct answers (with the maximum score being 20/20 correct). The advantage of the MIST is that the twenty headlines aren't random but were selected through a series of rigorous psychometric tests, starting out with 400 possible candidate headlines and whittling them down to the twenty best-performing ones.[6] This way, the MIST provides a standardized assessment of misinformation susceptibility, which is useful if you want to compare different predictors against each other.

In this study, we first wanted to see if varying how people are asked to respond to each headline affects the average scores. For instance, in the standard MIST people indicate whether each headline is real or fake. But what if you use a different question framing and ask whether each headline is reliable or unreliable, or trustworthy or untrustworthy? And what happens if you vary the response mode, that is, how many scale points you use? Does it matter if you use a binary (real or fake), six-point or seven-point scale (with six or seven being "fake" and one being "real")? Briefly put, varying either the question framing or the response mode didn't matter *too* much, which is nice because this makes it somewhat easier to compare different studies to one another. More relevant for this chapter, however, is that this result also meant that we had a high-quality dataset to test which of the above predictors of misinformation belief (cognitive reflection test performance, numeracy skills, actively open-minded thinking, and political partisanship) were most strongly related to veracity discernment ability (meaning people's performance on the MIST). The results are shown in Figure 4.2.[7]

The figure shows that the "hierarchy" of predictors of misinformation belief appears to be as follows: first, actively open-minded thinking (with people who are higher in open-minded thinking generally having higher veracity discernment ability), then numeracy skills (where higher numeracy is linked to higher veracity discernment) and political partisanship (with liberals having higher scores than conservatives), and finally cognitive reflection test performance, which is only weakly related to veracity discernment. Overall, we take this to mean that belief in misinformation is determined by a variety of identity-related and cognitive factors: while analytical thinking ability (by which we mean problem-solving skills here) may not be as important a factor, thinking style and a disposition toward considering incongruent or uncomfortable viewpoints and information, as well as partisan bias, appear to matter a lot.

Van Bavel and colleagues have formalized these findings into what they call the "integrative" model of misinformation belief (Van Bavel et al., 2021).

---

[6] The false headlines were generated by an AI (GPT-2) to ensure people hadn't come across them before (and yes, everything is done better by AI nowadays; what do you need humans for anyway?). Unrelatedly, did you know ChatGPT will write whole books for you if you prompt it enough times?

[7] "Regression is progress" (Bezimeni, 2011).

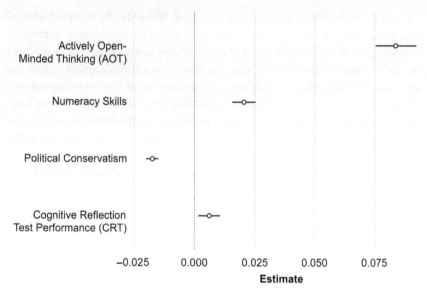

FIGURE 4.2 A visualization of a regression model, showing the relationship between veracity discernment ability (the ability to distinguish true information from false information), and actively open-minded thinking score (AOT), numeracy skills, political conservatism, and cognitive reflection test performance (CRT).

Note: The further away from 0, the stronger the relationship between a variable and veracity discernment ability; for example, political conservatism shows a negative association with veracity discernment, indicating that more conservative individuals are likely to have lower discernment scores.

Source: Adapted from data by Roozenbeek, Maertens et al. (2022).

This model incorporates identity-based as well as accuracy-based motivations to arrive at an account that combines insights from different strands of research. A summary of this "integrative" model is shown in Figure 4.3. Exposure to misinformation increases belief (Path 1) which can increase sharing (Path 2). Exposure to misinformation can increase sharing directly (Path 3) even if it doesn't increase belief (e.g., if someone shares misinformation by accident). Psychological risk factors (which can be identity- or accuracy-based) can increase exposure to misinformation (Path A) and influence both misinformation belief (Path B) and sharing (Path C).

Subsequent research has found that the predictions of this "integrative" model are well supported by experimental studies (Borukhson et al., 2022; Faragó et al., 2020; Rathje et al., 2023). David Borukhson and colleagues (2022), for instance, compared the predictions of different models of misinformation belief: not only the "integrative" model but also the "classical reasoning" model mentioned above (Pennycook & Rand, 2019, 2021) and the "motivated reasoning" model by Dan Kahan, which proposes that people who are better at analytical thinking believe *more* in identity-congruent misinformation than co-partisans who are not as good at this (in other words, people use their analytical thinking

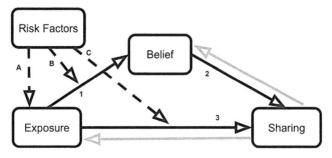

FIGURE 4.3 The "integrative" model of misinformation belief and sharing.
Source: Reprinted from Van Bavel, J., Harris, E., Pärnamets, P., Rathje, S., Doell, K. C., & Tucker, J. A. (2021). Political psychology in the digital (mis)information age: A model of news belief and sharing. *Social Issues and Policy Review, 15*(1), 84–113. With permission from John Wiley and Sons.

ability to defend their partisan identity rather than arriving at the truth; see Kahan, 2013). Borukhson and colleagues found that the integrative model outperformed all other models, providing yet further support that both accuracy-based and identity-based motivations matter for whether an individual accepts a false claim as true. In a scoping review of twenty-six published studies, Kirill Bryanov and Viktoria Vziatysheva (2021) conclude that "message characteristics – such as belief consistency and presentation cues – […] as well as […] individual factors including people's cognitive styles, predispositions, and differences in news and information literacy" all contribute to misinformation belief. This provides consistent evidence that misinformation belief is best explained by taking into account a variety of cognitive as well as identity-based individual-level factors.

4.2.2 Societal-Level Factors

There are numerous societal factors that can impact belief in misinformation. The first is trust: higher trust in scientists was found to be related to lower belief in misinformation about COVID-19 in five different countries (Roozenbeek, Schneider, et al., 2020); a similar relationship was found between COVID-19 misinformation and trust in information from the government (Melki et al., 2021). Conversely, exposure to unsubstantiated claims about voter fraud in the United States was shown to reduce trust in the electoral process, and specifically electoral integrity (although not support for democracy; Berlinski et al., 2023). Another study showed that exposure to misinformation on social media (which the authors cleverly measured by asking their study participants to install a browser plugin that would track their online behavior for a period of time) was linked to *higher* trust in government among those whose preferred political party was in power, but the reverse was true for government opponents: for Republicans, misinformation exposure was linked to higher trust in the Trump administration, but for Democrats the relationship was the reverse (Ognyanova et al., 2020).

On the other hand, Boulianne and Humprecht (2023) conducted a multiwave panel study in the UK, the US, France, and Canada to investigate the relationship between self-reported misinformation exposure and various measures of trust. They found that "when people are exposed to what they think is misinformation, they do not express more negative views about media and government. People do not easily change their views about these long-standing institutions [...] Most important, the pandemic did not dramatically alter the relationship between misinformation and trust in institutions" (p. 2041). These apparently contradictory findings between studies may be in part related to a difference in outcome measures: Ognyanova and colleagues measured *actual* exposure to misinformation, whereas Boulianne and Humprecht measured *self-reported* exposure (how much people *think* they see misinformation). It's possible that the two are somewhat disconnected: people who think they're exposed to a lot of misinformation might not see it very often in real life, or perhaps people who don't believe they see a lot of misinformation are actually exposed quite a bit.

Another societal factor impacting misinformation susceptibility is polarization. Libby Jenke, a professor at the University of Houston, conducted a study in which she looked at how affective polarization (i.e., how positively or negatively members of one group feel about members of another group) impacts misinformation belief (Jenke, 2023). She found that people with higher levels of affective polarization were more likely to believe in-group congruent misinformation (misinformation that is positive for their group, in this case their political party) and *less* likely to believe out-group congruent misinformation (misinformation that is positive for the other party). Jenke also provided evidence that this relationship can be causal: polarization *causes* misinformation belief. Importantly, these effects were stronger for people with higher levels of political sophistication. Jenke therefore argues that "education will not solve the issue," and discusses several implications of her findings: because the US is becoming increasingly polarized, we can expect "more rancor" in discussions between highly polarized groups of people over time. Citing Markus Wagner (2021), Jenke also notes that affectively polarized people are more likely to turn up to vote than people who are less polarized. Because polarized individuals are more likely to believe in-group congruent misinformation, their opinions about political issues and candidates may also become increasingly influenced by false information.

4.3 WHY DO PEOPLE *SHARE* MISINFORMATION?

The idea that believing and sharing misinformation are strongly correlated is pretty intuitive: after all, why would someone share something on social media if they don't at least believe it to be plausible (if not true)? However, it turns out that believing and sharing are not the same thing. Studies have noted a distinct disconnect between how accurate people perceive misinformation to be and how likely they are to share it (Pennycook et al., 2021; Pennycook & Rand, 2020). Cornell University professor Gordon Pennycook and colleagues (2021) note that, even though the veracity of news headlines has a large effect on accuracy judgments (meaning there is a large difference between the perceived accuracy of true and false headlines, in the sense that people tend to rate true headlines as far more accurate than false ones), this is not the case for sharing intentions. Instead, this effect is far smaller: people's intentions to share true and false headlines are approximately equal (and generally pretty low: most people appear to be relatively unwilling to share any news, real or fake). Pennycook and his colleague David Rand at MIT (2019, 2020, 2021) have therefore proposed that a large percentage of misinformation sharing on social networks occurs because social media users' "attention is focused on factors other than accuracy" (Pennycook et al., 2021). In other words, social media environments can distract people's attention away from accuracy and toward other factors (such as what gets you clicks and engagement), leading to misinformation being shared not purposefully but by accident. This is often referred to as the "inattention account" of misinformation sharing.

Other research has offered nuance to this explanation. For instance, Sacha Altay and colleagues (whose work we discussed in Chapter 3) conducted a study in which they showed that people are reluctant to share "fake news" because it hurts their reputation: study participants indicated that they would have to be paid to share fake news, and people's trust in both people and organizations who shared even one fake news story and otherwise only real news decreased substantially (Altay, Hacquin, et al., 2022). In a second study, Altay and Mercier (2021) showed that there might be a "positivity bias" to the sharing of epistemically suspect beliefs and misinformation: people were consistently more willing to share happier beliefs, even if these beliefs were of questionable veracity. And in yet another study, Altay and colleagues (2022) identify an "interesting-if-true" effect: study participants were more willing to share false news stories that they thought were interesting if they would turn out to be true. They therefore argue that people may not share questionable content by mistake, but rather because it has qualities that make up for its lack of reliability or veracity. In a similar vein, Alberto Acerbi (2019) argues that "cognitive attraction" plays an important role in misinformation sharing: the most successful misinformation is shared because it taps into people's cognitive preferences, such as negativity, sexuality, disgust, or how counterintuitive or interesting something is. The truthfulness of the information, he argues, is less relevant than its psychological appeal. This idea was corroborated by a study that evaluated how unverified information spreads on Twitter, which noted that such content is more likely to be novel and contains more negative emotions such as disgust (Vosoughi et al., 2018).

As with misinformation belief, political partisanship (and identity-based motivations more broadly) also appears to be important for misinformation

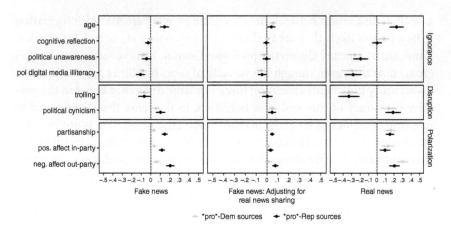

FIGURE 4.4 Psychological factors in fake and real news sharing. The figure shows the change in odds of sharing one more story from fake news and real news sources, set against different psychological factors, for both pro-Democratic (*pro*-Dem) and pro-Republican (*pro*-Rep) sources.

Source: Reprinted from Osmundsen, M., Bor, A., Bjerregaard Vahlstrup, P., Bechmann, A., & Bang Petersen, M. (2021). Partisan polarization is the primary psychological motivation behind political fake news sharing on Twitter. *American Political Science Review, 115*(3), 999–1015. With permission from Cambridge University Press.

sharing. Mathias Osmundsen, Alexander Bor, Peter Bjerregaard Vahlstrup, Anja Bechmann, and Michael Bang Pedersen from the University of Aarhus in Denmark conducted a study (2021) where they mapped the psychological profiles of about 2,300 American Twitter users. They then matched this data to the links to fake news websites (and other news sites publishing low-quality content) that each of these users shared, and tested which psychological factors were most strongly associated with the sharing of fake news. An important thing to note here is that Osmundsen and colleagues found that fake news sharing overall was incredibly rare (a fraction of a percentage of the Tweets in their dataset contained links to fake news or other low-quality websites); this is commonly observed across numerous studies, as we discussed in Chapter 3 (González-Bailón et al., 2023; Grinberg et al., 2019; Guess et al., 2019). They also weren't able to look at the sharing of false or misleading *claims*, only at links to websites that are known to publish dubious content.

With these limitations in mind, the researchers tested three different accounts of misinformation sharing against each other: the "ignorance" account (people share misinformation due to a lack of knowledge as to how to tell apart true and false news, or a failure to engage in analytical thinking), the "disruption" account (sharing occurs because people are trolling or out of political cynicism), and the "polarization" account (sharing happens because of partisan or other identity-based motivations). The results are shown in Figure 4.4.

Looking at Figure 4.4, it appears that the "ignorance" account isn't very well supported: age matters somewhat, in the sense that older people tend to share more fake news than younger people, but cognitive reflection (the measure of reflective versus intuitive thinking from the previous section) is uncorrelated with fake news sharing. Perhaps even more interestingly, people who are *more* politically unaware and *less* digitally media literate also tend to share *less* fake news. In other words, there appears to be no evidence that a tendency to engage in intuitive (as opposed to reflective) thinking, having better knowledge of what's going on in politics, or knowing a lot about how the Internet and social media work are related to whether people end up sharing misinformation.

The authors also report some (not very strong) evidence for the "disruption" account: people who are more cynical about politics also tend to share more fake news. Then again, trolling (sharing fake news for the fun of it or to get a rise out of people) was, if anything, *negatively* correlated with fake news sharing. It's worth noting here that these same patterns held for the sharing of *real* news, in the sense that trolls appear to share less news in general (not just fake news), whereas political cynics tend to share more news overall (real as well as fake).

Lastly, Osmundsen and colleagues discuss the "polarization" account, for which they find more support: sharing fake news correlates well with measures of political partisanship. Measures of positive affect for one's own party (how positively Democrats feel about Democrats and Republicans about Republicans) and especially negative affect for the other party (how negatively Republicans feel about Democrats and vice versa) were also good predictors of fake news sharing, especially for Republicans. However, all three measures also correlated with the likelihood of sharing real news, indicating that stronger polarization relates to higher news sharing overall (not just fake news or misinformation).

The content and phrasing of (mis)information also matter for whether people choose to share it. In a large and influential study, William Brady and colleagues (2017) showed that emotion plays a huge role in the diffusion of online content in social networks. They found that tweets about highly polarized debates (gun control, climate change, and same-sex marriage) tend to get more engagement (likes, retweets etc.) if they use more moral-emotional language: that is, language that expresses a particular moral emotion (words such as "greed," "punish," or "evil"). While Brady and colleagues didn't look specifically at misinformation, Soroush Vosoughi and colleagues (2018) found much the same result for false news: not only the novelty of misinformation but also the emotional reactions that false news evoked among its recipients may have been responsible for their finding that false news spreads faster than true news on Twitter. With respect to conspiracy theories, Jan-Willem van Prooijen and colleagues (2022) conducted a series of studies to show that belief in conspiracy theories is influenced by how entertaining people perceive them to be. However, this effect occurred irrespective of emotional valence, so some conspiracies might be simply entertaining to people regardless of whether emotionally evocative language is used to describe them.

Similarly, Steve Rathje, then a Ph.D. student with us in Cambridge and now at New York University, ran a large study on Facebook and Twitter to see if outgroup language (language about other groups of people) predicts social media engagement (Rathje et al., 2021). He found that in the US, aside from negative, positive, and moral-emotional language, partisan outgroup language in particular (Republicans talking about Democrats and vice versa) predicted engagement on both platforms significantly better than ingroup language (Democrats talking about Democrats etc.). This suggests that misinformation may be particularly effective if it taps into partisan or between-group animosity. This view is supported by Molly Crockett (2017), who argues that social media may reinforce the expression and sharing of "moral outrage," in part because the risk of backlash is lower if you can express this outrage anonymously and to like-minded individuals who share the same echo chamber (see Chapter 5).

Yara Kyrychenko, also a Ph.D. student in Cambridge, replicated Steve's findings in the context of pre-invasion Ukraine (Kyrychenko et al., 2023): here, too, outgroup language outperformed ingroup language in terms of driving engagement. Building on Steve's work, Yara also explored whether the drivers of social media engagement were impacted by the outbreak of the full-scale invasion of Ukraine by Russia in February 2022. What she found was extremely interesting: while outgroup language (and to an extent also outgroup hostility, that is, negative language about other groups) was a significant driver of engagement before February 2022, this stopped being the case after the invasion. Instead, ingroup solidarity became the most important predictor of engagement after the full-scale invasion: social media posts expressing positive sentiments about Ukraine, such as Слава Україні! ("glory to Ukraine!"), became hugely popular compared to posts expressing negative sentiments about Russia or Russians. This effect remained detectable for at least six months. This implies that the drivers of social media engagement are not stable over time, but can instead be influenced by events that impact people's perceptions of group identity (such as the outbreak of a military conflict). While there is some other work available that explores how news events can affect social media engagement (Garcia & Rimé, 2019), there doesn't seem to be a comprehensive theory as yet. How this phenomenon affects the spread of misinformation online is therefore not yet known.

4.4 CONCLUSION

In this chapter, we have discussed why people might believe misinformation and share it with others. We've covered a variety of individual- and societal-level factors, including analytical and open-minded thinking, political partisanship, trust, polarization, psychological appeal, repetition, emotion, and intergroup sentiment. There seems to be an emerging consensus within the field of misinformation research that no one factor is dominant in explaining why people believe or share misinformation, and that the best models of information belief and sharing allow for different predictors to interact with each other and vary according to circumstance, time, and context. A shortcoming of a lot of the research that we've discussed in this chapter is that much of it has focused on *false* information, which, as we explained in Chapters 1 and 3, isn't all too common compared to *misleading, hyperpartisan* or *manipulative* information. This is partially a methodological problem: it's simply difficult to classify misleading content objectively, especially on social media, and there can be much more disagreement than over whether a claim is misleading than if it's demonstrably false. In the next chapter, we therefore focus on how different kinds of content spread through social media networks: even if "fake news" is relatively rare, other kinds of potentially problematic content certainly aren't.

5

Echo Chambers and Filter Bubbles

5.1 INTRODUCTION

This chapter looks at if and how the consumption and sharing of (mis)information are shaped by the environments that we use to communicate. Most readers will have heard of terms such as "echo chambers" and "filter bubbles," but what are they exactly? And more importantly, how prevalent and problematic are they in our internet-addled times? As in Chapter 3, where we discussed the scale of the misinformation problem, the question of whether of echo chambers and filter bubbles have contributed to the spread and prevalence of misinformation is not at all obvious. This debate is ongoing, and where you land on this spectrum may affect what solutions you believe are required, something which we discuss in Chapters 6 through 8. Because we enjoyed writing Chapter 3, we figured we'd recycle its general structure here. We will try to offer a balanced perspective, and separately discuss the arguments for and against the notion that echo chambers have serious implications for the spread of misinformation, polarization, and democracy. In the interest of fairness and balance, we will flip the order of presentation from Chapter 3: after some definitional groundwork, we first address the arguments that say that echo chambers and filter bubbles are a serious problem, and then the arguments that oppose this idea. Finally, we will discuss some relevant nuances and attempt to bring together these disparate strands of scholarship. For this chapter, we've relied heavily on several books, reviews, and meta-analyses that have been published in recent years. It's unfortunately not possible to cover all the different nuances and perspectives in a chapter of a few thousand words; we therefore highly recommend interested readers to check out other researchers' work (Bruns, 2019; Guess et al., 2018; Hall Jamieson & Capella, 2008; Levy & Razin, 2019; Löblich & Venema, 2021; Pariser, 2011; Ross Arguedas et al., 2022; Sunstein, 2017; Terren & Borge-Bravo, 2021).

5.2 WHAT ARE ECHO CHAMBERS
AND FILTER BUBBLES?

When talking about echo chambers and filter bubbles, it's helpful to first define what these terms mean. Various definitions make the rounds. Toby Pilditch and Jens Madsen define echo chambers as "enclosed epistemic circles where like-minded people communicate and reinforce pre-existing beliefs" (Madsen et al., 2018). Mateo Cinelli and colleagues (2021) go with "environments in which the opinion, political leaning, or belief of users about a topic gets reinforced due to repeated interactions with peers or sources having similar tendencies and attitudes." Kathleen Hall Jamieson and Joseph Capella (2008, p. 76; see also Ross Arguedas et al., 2022) prefer "a bounded, enclosed media space that has the potential to both magnify the messages delivered within it and insulate them from rebuttal." Elaborating on this last definition, Amy Ross Arguedas and colleagues (2022, p. 10) write that "magnification" tends to refer to a reinforcing effect of attitude-consistent information (e.g., left-wing people receiving news mostly from left-leaning sources), whereas "insulation" refers to reduced exposure (or no exposure altogether) to counter-attitudinal information (e.g., if people avoid information that challenges their preexisting beliefs).

The terms echo chamber and filter bubble are often used interchangeably, but they're not the same. Filter bubbles refer to how social media platforms and search engines allow for (and even encourage) a high degree of personalization in terms of what users see. This, according to Eli Pariser, who coined the term in his book *Filter Bubble: What the Internet Is Hiding from You* (2011), may "erode the possibility of a relatively common ground" (Ross Arguedas et al., 2022, p. 10) as people self-select into seeing only information they like, while things they don't like are hidden from them. Pariser (2011, p. 10; see also Ross Arguedas et al., 2022, p. 10) refers to this as "a unique universe of information for each of us." The key difference between echo chambers and filter bubbles is that echo chambers aren't necessarily a consequence of algorithms or choices made by curators of media environments. Filter bubbles, on the other hand, are the result of ranking algorithm design choices, and imply a degree of intentionality (Ross Arguedas et al., 2022, p. 11): for instance, Facebook might personalize your timeline and show you posts that it thinks you will be most likely to act on. Another difference is that people may end up in echo chambers voluntarily, whereas filter bubbles require no active participation from those who are in them, but are instead curated from the top.

5.3 PERSPECTIVE #1: ECHO CHAMBERS ARE A PROBLEM

The earliest high-profile pessimistic view of the Internet and its potential to wreak havoc on deliberative democracy came from legal scholar Cass Sunstein of Harvard University. In his book *Republic.com* (2001), Sunstein argues that free speech is a necessary element of successful democracies, but that for free speech to work,

> people should be exposed to materials that they would not have chosen in advance. Unplanned, unanticipated encounters are central to democracy itself [...] Many or most citizens should have a range of common experiences. Without shared experiences, a heterogeneous society will have a much more difficult time in addressing social problems. People may even find it harder to understand one another. (quoted in Holbrook, 2001, p. 754; Sunstein, 2001, pp. 8–9)

Throughout *Republic.com*, Sunstein argues that the Internet's endless potential for personalization, and with it the option to exclude uncongenial viewpoints and ideas from one's day-to-day life, leads to self-insulation, which in turn may reinforce polarization and "cultural balkanization" (Davis, 2010). Sunstein acknowledges that the Internet can be a highly social environment, in which people with shared interests may come into contact where they otherwise never would have due to limitations of geography, language, and so on. However, he expresses concern that the Internet can be used by people of particular political persuasions to short-circuit what he calls "general interest intermediaries" (such as large newspapers and widely viewed news shows on national television channels), which are necessary to ensure chance encounters with unfamiliar or uncongenial views and build shared experiences (Holbrook, 2001, p. 756; Sunstein, 2001, Chapter 3).

Sunstein warns that this process will lead to increased polarization. He argues that people are much more likely to respond to arguments that they already agree with. When talking to people of a similar ideological ilk, such arguments will be much more common than arguments they don't find very convincing. Also, people tend to adjust their opinions toward the prevailing position in the group: for example, to make a positive impression on other group members. So if the Internet encourages people to sort themselves into groups where exposure to countervailing (political) arguments is highly uncommon, they might end up with more extreme opinions than they would have if they had been regularly exposed to other viewpoints; Sunstein calls this the "limited argument pool" (Holbrook, 2001, p. 757; Sunstein, 2001, Chapter 4).

Republic.com was published in 2001, when the Internet was dominated by chatrooms, email lists, and ancient memes now sadly lost to history. However, the passage of time and the coming of age of the Internet did little to assuage Sunstein's concerns. In *Republic.com 2.0* (2007) and again in *#republic: Divided Democracy in the Age of Social Media* (2017), Sunstein expressed his worries about the potential harm of the Internet for deliberative democracy. Partisan weblogs and especially social media platforms, according to Sunstein, may fuel not only polarization but also extremism and even terrorism. However, in *#republic*, Sunstein admits that the "Daily Me," the highly personalized information environment that he first warned about in 2001, had not yet come about (Martin, 2018).

Nonetheless, a great deal of research conducted using social media data has since shed light on echo chamber formation. In a systematic review of echo chamber studies, Ludovic Terren and Rosa Borge Bravo (2021) found that only five out of fifty-five included studies showed no evidence of echo chambers, and another twenty-five reported mixed results. Toby Pilditch (University College London) and Jens Madsen (London School of Economics), two colleagues of ours, ran a study to see if echo chambers come about even if people behave in a perfectly rational way and don't have any cognitive or social biases (Madsen et al., 2018). To test this, they used an approach called agent-based modelling, where you simulate the behavior of "agents" (in their case social media users) in a network under certain assumptions. In Toby's and Jens' study, agents updated their beliefs without biases, communicated honestly, and had perfect memory. Of course, this is not how people act in the real world: *some* people forget their good friend Jon's birthday (you know who you are), and much of this book is about how and why people aren't always honest to each other, but that's beside the point. The goal of the study was to see if echo chambers form even if humans behave in an error-free way, and this is exactly what Toby and Jens found: after some time, the agents in their model started to cluster together with other agents with similar beliefs, and became less exposed to agents with opposing beliefs. Interestingly, this effect was stronger as the network became larger, suggesting that the network *itself* (and not the people in it) contributes to echo chamber formation. In the same study, they also looked at whether educational solutions (providing agents with truthful information rather than information that reinforces their emerging biases) could ameliorate the echo chamber effect, and found that this reduced echo chamber formation, but didn't eliminate it entirely.

While agent-based modelling can yield useful insights, the approach is theoretical. Other research teams have therefore explored how echo chamber formation works using real-world social media data. In a seminal paper, Pablo Barberá (2015) looked at how Twitter networks can be a source of information about people's political ideology. Using a sample of millions of Twitter users from six countries (the US, the UK, Spain, Italy, Germany, and the Netherlands), he showed not only that studying user clusters on Twitter (who people follow and retweet) can accurately predict how people identify politically, but also that discussions on Twitter are highly polarized. In a case study about the 2012 US presidential elections (between Barack Obama and Mitt Romney), Barberá found that Twitter discussions are dominated by people with strong political views, whereas moderates don't contribute much to the discussion at all. He estimated that 85 percent of retweet interactions about the 2012 elections took place among like-minded individuals. This was especially the case for conservatives, who exhibited a larger degree of polarization than liberals.

In a study into the news consumption of about 10 million Facebook users, Eytan Bakshy and colleagues (2015), who were employed by Facebook, compared the role of individual choices and ranking algorithms in how much cross-cutting content (news content that cuts across political/ideological lines) people were exposed to and clicked on. They found that both individual users' choice to disengage from cross-cutting content and the Facebook News Feed algorithm limited how much people saw ideologically discordant information. According to the top line of the publication, Facebook's algorithm ensured that people encountered such information around 15 percent less often, and clicked on discordant news links about 70 percent less. However, the authors also found that individual choices matter more: the composition of people's friend networks was a more important factor in how much people consumed cross-cutting content than the algorithm alone. A limitation of this study is that the authors could only include active Facebook users who indicated their political preferences in their profile (which was about 4 percent of users at the time); this makes it difficult to generalize the findings to all Facebook (or social media) users, who might react in different ways to ideologically challenging information (Guess et al., 2018, p. 11).

Another influential study by Mateo Cinelli and colleagues (2021) compared the echo chamber effect across social media platforms (Facebook, Twitter, Reddit, and Gab Social, a US-based, predominantly right-leaning micro-blogging service). They specifically looked at how much the users of these platforms are polarized when discussing controversial topics (such as Obamacare, gun control, vaccines, and abortion). They observed a clear echo chamber effect on Twitter and Facebook, with users clustering into separate communities with highly similar leanings. Importantly, they found almost no communities that had no average leaning, meaning that the communities on these platforms are strongly polarized: when discussing controversial topics, Twitter and Facebook users cluster together into communities with strong opinions. Furthermore, users with a particular leaning on a given topic were much more likely to be reached by other users with a similar leaning, indicating that Twitter and Facebook users tend to be exposed to content from like-minded individuals when it comes to discussing controversial topics. However, Cinelli and colleagues found a very different pattern for Gab and Reddit, which showed little to no polarization at the user level. Instead, the *network as a whole* leaned one way or the other (to the left for Reddit and to the right for Gab), meaning that users on these platforms are mostly left- or right-wing, and thus form a single large and polarized community. These results are broadly in line with the aforementioned study by Madsen et al. (2018), which found that echo chamber effects are likely to be stronger in larger social networks. Reddit and Gab are small compared to Facebook and Twitter, which may make community formation and polarization less likely to occur.

Aside from social media users strongly preferring content that agrees with their preexisting beliefs, there is some evidence that partisans react negatively to counter-attitudinal information. Analyzing over four years of Twitter data from a random sample of 1.5 million Twitter users, focusing on the sharing of content posted by political elites (such as politicians and pundits), Magdalena Wojcieszak and colleagues (2022) found that people shared ingroup messages about thirteen times more often than outgroup messages. Importantly, they also showed that people often commented negatively on outgroup content. In the authors' words, "ordinary users not only actively create, but also further reinforce, online echo chambers by not only adding comments when sharing out-group elites but also adding negative comments to these shares." This pattern was not only present for the most politically extreme Twitter users: the authors note that their findings weren't driven by a small subset of partisans, but hold up across the political spectrum and even for moderates.

With respect to the spread of misinformation, a study by Michela Del Vicario and colleagues (2016) examined how reliable and unreliable information spread through Facebook. They found that *network homogeneity*, the degree to which users in the network exhibit similar levels of polarization, is the primary driver of content diffusion: rumors and unverified information spread faster in more homogeneous networks, particularly those that are already predisposed to such content. In the authors' words, "[social media] users tend to aggregate in communities of interest, which causes reinforcement and fosters confirmation bias, segregation, and polarization. This comes at the expense of the quality of the information and leads to proliferation of biased narratives fomented by unsubstantiated rumors, mistrust, and paranoia" (Del Vicario et al., 2016, p. 558). In a different study, Petter Törnberg (2018) notes that polarization can occur at the *opinion* and at the *network* level and contribute to the potential virality of misinformation. In particular, the presence of opinion- and network-polarized clusters can contribute to the diffusion of so-called "complex contagions," such as a piece of misinformation that requires repeated exposure from close trusted neighbors before people buy into it, which is more likely to happen in echo chambers. Carlos Diaz Ruiz and Tomas Nilsson (2023) argue that misinformation can circulate especially well as "identity-based grievances": controversies that are driven by identity-based differences can be weaponized by disinformation producers to exacerbate tensions, which works particularly well in cases of closed-off network structures. We mentioned some examples of this happening in Chapter 1 (e.g., the #EndFathersDay controversy).

Echo chamber formation may have other real-world consequences as well. In a study we conducted (led by the aforementioned Steve Rathje), we looked at how people's behavior on social media related to their attitude toward the COVID-19 vaccine (Rathje et al., 2022). To do this, we first ran two surveys where we asked participants from the US and the UK about their trust in vaccines as

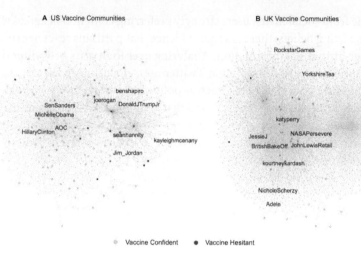

FIGURE 5.1 High and low vaccine confidence communities on Twitter, in the US (left panel) and UK (right panel).
Source: Taken from Rathje et al. (2022).

well as a series of other questions (such as about their political preferences). We also asked for their Twitter handle. We then analyzed who these users followed on Twitter, and correlated this data with how much they trusted the COVID-19 vaccine. We found that, in the United States, people with high and low levels of vaccine confidence clustered into separate communities, and that the likelihood of getting vaccinated against COVID-19 was associated with following low-quality news accounts on Twitter. Also, there was a clear political divide: people with high confidence in the COVID-19 vaccine were more likely to follow left-wing politicians and media outlets, and people with low confidence tended to follow right-wing political figures. However, in the UK, we didn't find this at all: Twitter communities weren't divided by different levels of trust in the COVID-19 vaccine, and there was no association between vaccine confidence and following news from low-quality sources. This shows the interplay between the social and technical factors that underlie echo chamber formation (see also Bastos et al., 2018, which showed that online and offline echo chambers can interact): Twitter (and other social networks) *can* enable echo chamber formation, but whether this ends up happening is in part dependent on the topic of discussion, as well as how polarized the network's users are. See Figure 5.1, which shows a clustering of high- and low-vaccine confidence communities, with high-confidence Twitter users following left-leaning Twitter accounts such as Hillary Clinton and Alexandria Ocasio-Cortez, and low-confidence Twitter users following right-wing influencers such as Sean Hannity and Ben Shapiro. In the UK, no clear clustering takes place, with most users having comparatively high levels of vaccine confidence. UK Twitter users also tend to follow less political accounts such as Katy Perry, Adele, and Yorkshire Tea.

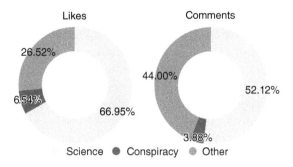

Science ● Conspiracy ● Other

FIGURE 5.2 Pie chart of engagements with fact-checking posts on Facebook for the "science" and "conspiracy" communities.
Source: Taken from Zollo et al. (2017).

From a practical standpoint, echo chamber formation may complicate the effectiveness of efforts to reduce the spread of misinformation. Fabiana Zollo, a professor at Ca' Foscari University in Venice, led a study in which she looked at how echo chamber formation relates to exposure to fact-checks (Zollo et al., 2017). Using a dataset of 54 million Facebook users from the United States, she first identified two communities on Facebook, one in which people predominantly consume scientific information, and one where they mostly consume unsubstantiated (conspiracy-like) information. She then looked at how both communities interacted with about 50,000 fact-checks that were posted on the platform. The results are shown in Figure 5.2.

Figure 5.2 shows that the conspiracy-oriented Facebook community barely interacts with fact-checks on the platform. Comparatively, Facebook users who already mostly consume scientific content are much more likely to like or comment on a fact-checking post. This shows that it can be very difficult for fact-checks to penetrate echo chambers. In a more general sense, the echo chamber effect may limit our ability to reach communities with many kinds of information: not only fact-checks but also potentially information about, for example, when and where to vote, or emergencies and disasters.

5.4 PERSPECTIVE #2: THE PROBLEM OF ECHO CHAMBERS IS OVERSTATED

A growing body of literature argues that initial concerns about echo chamber formation and its consequences for society were overstated. Several arguments support this case: people in general don't consume all that much political news and aren't as partisan as is often assumed; there's not much evidence that people actively avoid information they disagree with; and a lot of echo chamber research looks only at social media but ignores offline news consumption. Overall, the idea that echo chambers have measurable adverse consequences is also not backed up too well by the data.

First, many people don't seem to care all that much about politics. In their (non-peer-reviewed) report *Avoiding the echo chamber about echo chambers: Why selective exposure to like-minded political news is less prevalent than you think*, Andrew Guess and colleagues (2018, p. 8) note that at a general level, highly partisan news sources aren't very popular. At the time the report was published, the most popular political news shows on Fox News (right-leaning) and MSNBC (left-leaning) peaked at about 2 to 3 million viewers, compared to about 24 million for news broadcasts on less partisan channels such as ABC and NBC. Also, news shows in general aren't too popular compared to entertainment programs (such as TV series and sports). Online, strongly partisan sources such as Breitbart are far less popular than mainstream news outlets such as the *New York Times* and *The Guardian*, which are in turn dwarfed by websites dedicated to entertainment and shopping. This indicates that while most people have at least a passing interest in keeping abreast of the news, the majority of them are not extreme in their political convictions. In other words, while political discourse on social media may look vitriolic on the surface, most people don't appear to participate in it.

Second, there is some disagreement as to whether echo chambers exist in the first place. Some studies mentioned in the abovementioned review by Ludovic Terren and Rosa Borge Bravo (2021) found the *opposite* of an echo chamber effect, where more politically involved individuals appear to seek out more counter-attitudinal information rather than less. For example, Elizabeth Dubois and Grant Blank (2018) examined the relationship between political interest and media diversity on the one hand, and the likelihood of being in an echo chamber on the other. To do this, they asked their participants how interested they were in politics and assessed how often they visited (online and offline) news sources from across the political spectrum for news about politics. As a measure of the degree to which individuals were prone to being in an echo chamber, they asked a series of questions such as "When looking for news or political information, how often, if ever, do you read something you disagree with?" With a sample of 2,000 individuals (representative of the United Kingdom), they found that higher levels of political interest and especially media diversity were related to a *lower* chance of being in an echo chamber: people with higher interest in politics and more diverse media diets were also more likely to report reading information they disagreed with and seeking out news sources different from those they normally read. Dubois and Blank (2018, p. 740) therefore conclude that "looking at the entire multi-media environment, we find little evidence of an echo chamber. This applies even to people who are not interested in politics."

However, the above study used self-report data collected through surveys, which doesn't necessarily translate to how people behave in the real world. One of the difficulties in studying echo chamber formation is how to combine survey data with people's behavior on social media (Rathje et al., 2022;

Robertson et al., 2023). Gregory Eady and colleagues (2019) addressed this problem by linking survey data to their respondents' public Twitter accounts. They investigated how much people encounter news content from sources from the opposite side of the political spectrum, by looking both at how many people follow counter-attitudinal accounts and how much they encounter content from these accounts. They found that for people who follow news organizations on Twitter, "there is generally more overlap than divergence in the ideological distributions of media accounts followed by the most liberal and most conservative [Twitter users]." In other words, they don't find strong evidence that social media users sort themselves into mutually exclusive information environments. However, the authors note that there does appear to be asymmetry across the political spectrum: 61 percent of the strongest conservatives in their sample followed no or very few news outlets equally or more left-leaning than the *New York Times*, indicating that more polarized individuals may also be more likely to end up in echo chambers. Eady and colleagues also caution against only looking at social media behavior and ignoring offline behavior (such as watching news on TV), as a large proportion of these strong conservatives did say they watched news on mainstream television channels (see also Geiß et al., 2021).

Another study by Seth Flaxman, Sharad Goel, and Justin Rao (2016) used the browser history data of about 50,000 people who regularly read online news to look at how news consumption relates to social media behavior. They found that social media (and search engine) use was associated with increased ideological polarization, but also with an *increase* in exposure to counter-attitudinal news content (i.e., news from the opposite side of the political spectrum). This means that it doesn't appear to be the case that people who rely strongly on social media for their news actively avoid information they don't like: rather, these people may be more likely to be voracious news consumers in general, even if they usually prefer to consume news that is in line with their beliefs over content that runs counter to them.

In mid-2023, a team of researchers led by Joshua Tucker from New York University and Talia Jomini Stroud from the University of Texas at Austin published four huge studies (using data from millions of US Facebook and Instagram users) into the relationship between social media, algorithmic recommendation, and political behaviors and attitudes (González-Bailón et al., 2023; Guess et al., 2023a, 2023b; Nyhan et al., 2023). These studies were the result of a large-scale collaboration between Tucker and Stroud's research team and Meta, which owns Facebook, Instagram, Threads, and WhatsApp. They found that, in the United States, ideological segregation on social media is both high and asymmetrical, where a substantial part of Facebook's news ecosystem is consumed exclusively by conservatives (González-Bailón et al., 2023).

However, the studies showed no clear evidence that Facebook and Instagram are fueling polarization. Removing reshared content from people's

Facebook feeds for three months decreased the consumption of political news (including from untrustworthy sources) and lowered news knowledge levels, but didn't affect political polarization or other political attitudes (Guess et al., 2023b). Showing people content in reverse chronological order (instead of using Facebook's and Instagram's own feed algorithms) reduced the time users spent on the platforms, decreased the amount of uncivil content and content from both cross-cutting and like-minded sources, but *increased* the amount of political and untrustworthy content and content from moderate sources. However, this intervention didn't affect people's self-reported levels of political and affective polarization either (Guess et al., 2023a). To test if the echo chamber effect might be driving polarization, Brendan Nyhan and colleagues (2023) experimentally reduced exposure to content from like-minded sources on people's Facebook feeds by about a third. Doing so measurably increased exposure to cross-cutting content and reduced exposure to uncivil language, but had no effect on people's belief in false claims, ideological extremity, or (again) measures of political and affective polarization.

That said, some researchers were also critical of these studies (Kupfer-schmidt, 2023). For example, Stephan Lewandowsky (University of Bristol) noted that a feed that displays posts in reverse chronological order may not be the best comparison to Facebook and Instagram's normal feed algorithm. Instead, the researchers could have looked at the effects of an algorithm that, for example, discourages polarizing or toxic language. David Garcia from the University of Konstanz argued that the time window used in these studies (three months) may not be enough to detect effects that take place over longer time periods. He makes a comparison with climate change: changing the social media feeds of some individuals may be a bit like cutting carbon emissions in a few towns or cities. Doing so doesn't alleviate the effects of climate change at the local level, even though we know carbon emissions drive climate change globally. Joe Bak-Coleman (Columbia School of Journalism) also called the collaboration "restrictive," noting that Meta (and not the researchers) was responsible for processing the raw data due to piracy concerns; this means that there continues to be a lack of democratic access to such important data, which complicates the independent scrutiny of findings.

Speaking more broadly, while echo chambers might be relatively common on social media, people don't receive all, or even most, of their news online. In a cross-national comparison of news audiences, Richard Fletcher and Rasmus Kleis Nielsen (2017) found a "surprising" amount of overlap between audiences in terms of the news they consume, and relatively little evidence for audience fragmentation. They also found no evidence that online audiences are more fragmented than offline ones, which speaks against the idea that online environments facilitate echo chamber formation more than traditional media. In another study, Fletcher, Robertson, and Nielsen (2021) showed that while (political) social media echo chambers do exist in many countries, about

5 percent of people actually find themselves in one. The likelihood of being in an echo chamber was highest among US liberals (about 10 percent), but much lower (2 or 3 percent) in different countries and for people of different ideological persuasions. This may imply that the echo chamber effect is not widespread enough to warrant serious concern. The aforementioned study by Bakshy and colleagues (2015, p. 1132), which investigated exposure to cross-cutting content on Facebook, also echoes the sentiments expressed by Eady and colleagues and Fletcher, Robertson, and Nielsen:

Although partisans tend to maintain relationships with like-minded contacts [...] on average more than 20% of an individual's Facebook friends who report an ideological affiliation are from the opposing party, leaving substantial room for exposure to opposing viewpoints. Furthermore, in contrast to concerns that people might "listen and speak only to the like-minded" while online, we found exposure to cross-cutting content along a hypothesized route: traditional media shared in social media.

Finally, social media only became an important source of news and other information very recently. In his book *Are Filter Bubbles Real?* (2019), Axel Bruns argues that concerns over echo chamber formation came about in a time of substantial political upheaval, while at the same time the way we create, disseminate, and consume news is changing rapidly. Historically, such technological innovations often come with "moral panics" about the potential dangers and harms of new technologies (which we also discussed in Chapters 2 and 3). Bruns argues that the emergence of new communications technologies *can* play an important role, for example in terms of driving public mobilization (as the radio did in 1930s Germany), but that the degree of harm they end up causing depends on the people who use them (see also O'Hara & Stevens, 2015). Ultimately, according to Bruns, just like we don't blame radio for the rise of fascism, we should be wary of falling for technological determinism when it comes to social media; "echo chambers" and "filter bubbles" are metaphors that he sees as ill defined, and our use of these terms can hamper our understanding of how communication technologies impact our daily lives (Bruns, 2021).

5.5 SO WHERE DO WE STAND?

The dynamics of echo chamber formation on social media are difficult to untangle. Some argue that the network structures of social media platforms expose people to content they like to a problematic degree, whereas others don't see much evidence of echo chambers existing to begin with, or at least don't believe that their existence is likely to have serious consequences for society. These sometimes contradictory viewpoints are in part a consequence of the methods we use to study echo chambers online and offline (Guess et al., 2018, p. 9; Terren & Borge-Bravo, 2021). Terren and Borge Bravo (2021) note that all studies they included in their review that find support for the echo chamber effect used social media trace data, whereas all the studies that reported evidence against echo chambers used self-report data (primarily collected through surveys). In other words, the two camps might be asking different questions: Do people form polarized clusters on social media around hot-button issues? The answer to this question often appears to be "yes." For example, echo chamber formation may take place at the issue level more than the user level. Pablo Barberá and colleagues (2015) examined information exchange between left-wing and right-wing Twitter users on six political and six nonpolitical issues. They found that information was primarily exchanged between like-minded individuals when it came to political topics (such as elections), but not for nonpolitical issues (e.g., current events such as the Super Bowl). They also noted that one high-profile event, the 2012 mass shooting at a primary school in Newtown, Connecticut, initially began as a platform-wide conversation but later evolved into a much more polarized state. This shows that, while people may not sort themselves into echo chambers where they're *only* exposed to content that agrees with their preexisting beliefs, partisan sorting can and does happen in specific circumstances, primarily in the context of political issues around which there already exists a degree of polarization.

But do people only consume ideologically like-minded media overall? Perhaps, but political content only makes up a small fraction of people's daily media diets (Allen et al., 2020; Nyhan et al., 2023). It's therefore critical not to conflate issue-based discussions on social media with media consumption more generally. More importantly, it remains very difficult to study individuals' behavior across platforms, especially at scale. Some platforms appear to be more extreme than others (Cinelli et al., 2020, 2021), and more extreme individuals might decide to leave more mainstream social media platforms and opt to join networks with less oversight in terms of content moderation. This makes looking beyond individual platforms and analyzing how likely people are to end up in echo chambers very complicated.[1]

In the end, a nuanced view of the scale and scope of the echo chamber problem might come down to how we define the term. C. Thi Nguyen (2020), a philosophy professor at the University of Utah, draws a distinction between echo chambers ("a social epistemic structure from which other relevant voices have been actively excluded and discredited") and *epistemic bubbles* ("a social epistemic structure in which other relevant voices have been left out, perhaps accidentally"). While social media platforms and the network structures they produce may not deterministically give rise to Nguyen's definition of echo

---

[1] A possible exception to this problem is the aforementioned collaboration between Meta and the research team led by Tucker and Stroud, which has resulted in several highly insightful publications (González-Bailón et al., 2023; Guess et al., 2023a, 2023b; Nyhan et al., 2023). Then again, these kinds of collaboration may engender mutual dependencies between certain research teams and tech platforms, which come with their own problems (Roozenbeek & Zollo, 2022). We discuss this further in Chapters 7 and 8.

chambers, their homophilic tendencies may ensure that epistemic bubbles are common. And while the worst early predictions about the consequences of echo chamber formation for society and the democratic process haven't come to pass, the fact that people are exposed to different information from different sources can nonetheless complicate how information is communicated, especially information that is of relevance to the public at large.

5.6 CONCLUSION

In this chapter, we have discussed echo chambers and filter bubbles. The main question we have tried to answer is whether echo chambers are likely to pose a risk to society by ensuring that people only see information they like and are shielded from information they dislike. Studies conducted on social media tend to show that online networks tend to be homophilic, that people usually prefer to be exposed to information that agrees with their preexisting beliefs, and that echo chambers can facilitate the spread of misinformation in some circumstances. These phenomena may complicate the efficacy of public-good communication efforts (such as fact-checks), although it's not clear if this also leads to polarization (with several recent studies showing no effect). At the same time, pessimistic predictions about the potential of echo chambers to produce isolated communities who have nothing in common and live in separate realities have not come to pass for most people (although some social media platforms exist in relative isolation and tend to attract more extreme users).

PART III

COUNTERING MISINFORMATION

6

Laws and Regulation

6.1 INTRODUCTION

Chapters 6–8 cover the range of proposed solutions and remedies to counter misinformation. Anastasia Kozyreva and colleagues (2020) identify four entry points for policy interventions to tackle misinformation (and other digital challenges): *laws and ethics* (such as regulations and ethical guidelines); *technology* (e.g., automated content detection); *education* (e.g., media and information literacy); and *psychology/behavioural sciences* (boosting, nudging, and "techno-cognition"). Here, we focus on the first category. We discuss how governments and supranational institutions have tried to tackle misinformation through laws and regulations. Our focus is on the European Union, United Kingdom, and United States, although we also take a brief look at anti-misinformation legislation in other countries and continents. It's important to note that neither of us is a legal scholar, and we have at best a tenuous grasp of what's legal and what isn't. Jon stole a Jawbreaker from a candy shop once when he was little, which is apparently frowned upon. Sander rode the tram to school in central Amsterdam for free as a teenager, which as it turns out is not free (he frequently rants about why it should be). We will therefore keep this chapter relatively brief and matter-of-fact,[1] and highly recommend checking out the sources we've relied on for this chapter (Edwards, 2022; Gallo & Cho, 2021; Nuñez, 2020; Prendergast, 2019; Wardle & Derakhshan, 2017).

6.2 COUNTERING MISINFORMATION AROUND THE WORLD

In their report *Information Disorder: Toward an Interdisciplinary Framework for Research and Policymaking* (2017), Claire Wardle and Hossein Derakhshan

---

[1] Also because Jon read Lev Tolstoy's *War and Peace* for his undergraduate degree and still has nightmares about how long it went on for. Do unto others, etc.

TABLE 6.1 Overview of suggested anti-misinformation interventions for tech companies and government actors

Tech companies could:	National governments could:
1. Create an international advisory council.	1. Commission research to map information disorder.
2. Provide researchers with the data related to initiatives aimed at improving public	2. Regulate ad networks.
3. discourse.	3. Require transparency around Facebook ads.
4. Provide transparent criteria for any algorithmic changes that down-rank content.	4. Support public service media organizations and local news outlets.
5. Work collaboratively.	5. Roll out advanced cybersecurity training.
6. Highlight contextual details and build visual indicators.	6. Enforce minimum levels of public service news on to the platforms.
7. Eliminate financial incentives.	
8. Crack down on computational amplification.	**Education ministries could:**
9. Adequately moderate non-English content.	1. Work internationally to create a standardized news literacy curriculum.
10. Pay attention to audio/visual forms of mis- and disinformation.	2. Work with libraries.
11. Provide metadata to trusted partners.	3. Update journalism school curricula.
12. Build fact-checking and verification tools.	
13. Build "authenticity engines."	
14. Work on solutions specifically aimed at minimizing the impact of filter bubbles:	
a. Let users customize feed and search algorithms.	
b. Diversify exposure to different people and views.	
c. Allow users to consume information privately.	
d. Change the terminology used by the social networks.	

Adapted from Wardle and Derakhshan (2017).

put together a series of recommendations for tech companies and national governments to counter misinformation. We've summarized these recommendations in Table 6.1. Importantly, Wardle and Derakhshan refrain from recommending governments from passing new legislation to make spreading or creating misinformation illegal. Instead, they focus on the regulation of ad networks and social media companies, providing support to public and local media, and promoting news literacy.

Not every government has followed Wardle's and Derakhshan's recommendations. Daniel Funke and Daniela Flamini (2018) put together a handy guide of the actions governments around the world have taken to counter misinformation. They identify the following categories of actions: laws that make creating, posting, or sharing misinformation illegal; Internet shutdowns; and conducting media literacy campaigns.

Most countries have laws on the books that make certain types of speech illegal, such as slander, libel, and fraud (Bannon, 2022). However, some governments have passed (or tried to pass) legislation specifically aimed at curbing misinformation, particularly online. Within Europe, Italy created an online portal in 2018 where people could report instances of misinformation to the police (Funke, 2018). France passed a law in the same year which allows French courts to rule if news stories reported during election campaigns are credible or should be taken down (Young, 2018). Greece's anti-disinformation law, passed in 2021, made it a crime to spread misinformation that is "capable of causing concern or fear to the public or undermining public confidence in the national economy, the country's defense capacity or public health" (Human Rights Watch, 2021; Stamouli, 2022). Similar laws were also passed in Hungary and Poland (Reporters Without Borders, 2020, 2021). Internet shutdowns are a common occurrence in Turkey, where the government has (temporarily) shut down platforms such as Twitter and TikTok, for example, after the earthquake that hit the country in February 2023 (Article 19, 2023).

Outside of Europe, China has implemented a series of laws criminalizing the spread of rumors that "undermine economic and social order" (Funke & Flamini, 2018; Repnikova, 2018), the most recent addition of which is a 2023 law prohibiting the spread of "deepfakes" and other forms of synthetic misinformation (China Law Translate, 2022; Hamilton, 2023). In 2022, a Chinese government official floated the idea of a ban on "fabricating and disseminating fake information online," in part because he believed that misinformation was responsible for fueling tensions between China and other countries: "there are often people online who, for some purpose, package a foreigner's vicious remarks against China as the view of everyone in that country towards China in order to incite the Chinese people's dissatisfaction and hostility towards said country and its people" (Kwan, 2022). Russia has laws in place that criminalize disseminating "false" information about the Russian armed forces, which can carry up to fifteen years in prison (Jack, 2022). In 2023, the Indian government was also considering prohibiting tech platforms from hosting information considered to be "fake" or "false" (Reuters, 2023).

Many of these laws have been criticized by academics, journalists, and human rights organizations because they pose a risk to the freedom of expression (Human Rights Watch, 2021; Media Defence, 2021; Repnikova, 2018; Reporters Without Borders, 2020, 2021; Stamouli, 2022). A common criticism is the lack of a clear definition of misinformation: if a law prohibits the spread of "false" information, who determines what's true and false, or harmful and harmless, and how can we be sure that these "arbiters of truth" are as objective as possible? Also, democratic countries that pass strict anti-misinformation laws run the risk of authoritarian regimes pointing to these laws as justification for cracking down on dissidents and independent journalists. The complications of these kinds of legislation are such that many countries have stayed away from making misinformation illegal outright.[2]

Instead, some countries have therefore opted to make social media platforms responsible for removing misinformation and other forms of harmful content. The most well-known example of such a law is the German *Netzwerkdurchsetzungsgesetz* or NetzDG, which translates to Network Enforcement Act.[3] This law, which was passed in 2018 and amended in 2021 (Library of Congress, 2021), mandates that social media platforms with more than 2 million users remove misinformation and hate speech within twenty-four hours after posting, or risk paying a fine of up to 50 million euros. Organizations such as Human Rights Watch (2018) expressed concern about this new law because of skewed incentives: social media platforms risk being fined if they don't remove content that the law says should be removed, but face no consequences if they remove content that is not illegal under the German government's definition. This means that they have a strong incentive to remove content that resides in this "gray zone," rather than leave it online, which poses a huge risk for freedom of speech. However, analyses of the impact of the NetzDG have painted a somewhat different picture (Echikson & Knodt, 2018; Zurth, 2021): pessimistic predictions about the wanton removal of non-misinformation have, broadly speaking, not come to pass. Instead, social media companies' own content moderation policies appear to have had a much stronger influence on what kinds of content are allows on their platforms. At the same time, however, the NetzDG doesn't seem to have had a huge impact on the proliferation of misinformation and hate speech on German social media; in other words, neither the pessimism nor the optimism about the law was entirely justified. As of 2023, Brazil was considering a similar law, which would penalize tech companies for failing to report instances of misinformation on their platforms (Paul, 2023).

6.3 THE DIGITAL SERVICES ACT (EU)

In response to the gamut of challenges brought about by the almost universal adoption of the Internet and social media as forms of communication, the European Commission has spent years developing a comprehensive framework for the regulation of digital services, aptly titled the Digital Services Act

---

[2] In fact, one of us (Sander) attended a meeting back in 2017 on the invitation of David Kaye, then the United Nations Special Rapporteur for the Protection of the Freedom of Speech, who believed that, when it comes to fake news, "regulation and censorship are the absolute wrong paths to deal with it" (Wilton Park, 2017).

[3] Good luck pronouncing the German name if you happen to be reading this chapter in front of an audience. Maybe it works as a cure for insomnia; you never know.

(DSA). This Act, along with the Digital Markets Act (DMA), which is similar in scope, were submitted by the Commission to the European Parliament and the Council of the European Union in December 2020, were approved in July 2022, and entered into force in November 2022. The goal of the DSA is to harmonize the disparate legal frameworks of European Union countries and subject tech platforms to the same regulations. Broadly speaking, the DSA contains the following provisions (European Commission, 2023a, 2023b):

- allowances for social media users to flag illegal content;
- allowances for platforms to cooperate with "trusted flaggers" to remove illegal content;
- rules to trace sellers on online marketplaces and combat scammers;
- new safeguards for social media users, including the possibility to challenge platforms' decision-making (e.g., with respect to moderation decisions);
- transparency measures for social media platforms, including on recommender algorithms;
- obligations for very large platforms and search engines to prevent abuse;
- an obligation for platforms to mitigate against risks such as mis- and disinformation, election manipulation, cyber violence against women, and/or harms to minors;
- bans on targeted advertising for some categories (e.g., children, ethnicity, political views, sexual orientation);
- a ban on "dark patterns" on social media platforms' interface (dark patterns are misleading tricks that can manipulate users into making decisions they don't want to make);
- new rules for social media data access for researchers;
- a crisis response mechanism in cases of serious threats to public health and safety.

These rules apply everywhere in the European single market, including to entities that offer services in the EU but aren't based there. Importantly, the DSA doesn't itself define what counts as "illegal" content. This is regulated by other EU legislation (e.g., when it comes to terrorist content or illegal hate speech) or at the level of individual member states.

The DSA distinguishes between illegal content and content that is harmful but not illegal ("lawful but awful"). To tackle this kind of content, large platforms must perform an annual risk assessment and take risk mitigation measures in response to, for example, disinformation, hoaxes, and manipulation during pandemics. While the DSA doesn't contain explicit rules for mitigating misinformation, it forms a so-called "co-regulatory framework" for online harms, together with the Code of Practice on Disinformation (Culloty et al., 2021; European Commission, 2022) and the European Democracy Action Plan (European Commission, 2020). The Code of Practice on Disinformation is a nonbinding agreement between tech platforms, advertisers, fact-checkers, researchers, and the European Commission which sets out guidelines for countering mis- and disinformation. Its provisions include demonetizing misinformation producers, developing tools to help users better identify and flag misinformation, improving researchers' access to data, and extending fact-checking coverage. An analysis by Eileen Culloty and colleagues (2021) of the effectiveness of the Code of Practice in countering misinformation during the COVID-19 pandemic found that, while the Code provides a substantial step forward, there were also important structural weaknesses: content labels and fact-checks were often not applied to relevant content, the results of actions taken by platforms were often not reported, and there were substantial differences between EU member states in terms of reporting and data access. This is in part due to the fact that the Code is nonbinding, which complicates its enforcement.

6.4 THE ONLINE SAFETY BILL (UK)

The Online Safety Bill is a large piece of legislation first drafted under UK prime minister Theresa May in 2018. The bill was primarily aimed at protecting children, in part motivated by the suicide of a fourteen-year-old girl who had been fed a steady stream of self-harm and suicide-related videos on her Instagram feed (Scott & Dickson, 2023). The bill mandates that social media platforms do the following (UK Government, 2022):

- remove illegal content quickly or prevent it from appearing in the first place;
- prevent children from accessing harmful and age-inappropriate content;
- enforce age limits and age-checking measures;
- ensure the risks and dangers posed to children on the largest social media platforms are more transparent, including by publishing risk assessments;
- provide parents and children with clear and accessible ways to report problems online when they arise;
- empower adult Internet users with tools so that they can tailor the type of content they see and can avoid potentially harmful content if they do not want to see it on their feeds.

After the outbreak of the full-scale invasion of Ukraine by Russia in February 2022, the UK government amended the proposed bill to also focus on tackling foreign disinformation, by adding "disinformation" to the list of priority offenses in the bill (Milmo, 2022). The bill was slated to become law in late 2023 (UK Parliament, 2021, 2023), but has been fraught with difficulties. An investigation by Politico into the negotiations over its provisions within the UK government found that the bill lacked momentum and strong support from key ministers, and there was concern that the final version would end up satisfying no one (Scott & Dickson, 2023).

6.5 THE UNITED STATES

The First Amendment to the United States constitution states that "Congress shall make no law [...] abridging the freedom of speech, or of the press." The US Supreme Court has taken this to mean that the government cannot impose limits on speech, except in cases of obscenity, defamation, fraud, "fighting words," incitement, threats, speech integral to criminal conduct, or child pornography (Killion, 2019). The Supreme Court has also long been wary of any new laws that restrict speech, which limits the government's ability to pass new legislation to counter misinformation similar to the UK and the EU (Bannon, 2019, 2022; Gallo & Cho, 2021; Prendergast, 2019). The bill that probably comes closest is the Honest Ads Act, a bipartisan piece of legislation proposed in 2023 that aims to "prevent foreign interference in future elections and improve the transparency of online political advertisements" (Gallagher, 2023). This bill was proposed in response to investigations into Russian interference in US elections, and is aimed primarily at reining in political advertising by foreign actors, both online and offline. If passed, it would mean increased transparency with respect to funding structures of political communications, and create uniform disclosure standards for online ads and ads shown on TV and radio. As of this writing, the bill has bipartisan support, but it's unclear whether it will end up becoming law.

Complicating the picture further, legal scholars have noted that "fact-checking the news is an exercise that the government could not possibly do with credibility" (Gielow Jacobs, 2022). In May 2023, the US Supreme Court sided with Google and other social media companies in two separate but very similar cases: *Twitter v. Taamneh et al.* (Supreme Court of the United States, 2023) and *Gonzalez v. Google*. Both cases challenged Section 230, a US statute that protects tech companies from liability for content produced by other people that is posted on social media platforms (Bartels, 2023). *Taamneh* was brought by family members of Nawras Alassaf, who was killed in a 2017 terror attack at the Reina nightclub in Istanbul. The *Gonzalez* case had come about after the parents of Nohemi Gonzalez, a twenty-three-year old student who died in the 2015 Paris terror attacks, sued Google, arguing that YouTube (which is owned by Google) recommended extremist content and promoted ISIS propaganda to its users. In both cases, the Supreme Court concluded that the plaintiffs had failed to state a claim under the Anti-Terrorism Act, which allows victims of terror attacks to sue people and organizations who "aided and abetted" the attacks (Quinn, 2023). This basically means that the Supreme Court was not convinced that social media companies are liable for the content that is posted on their platforms: in their words, the plaintiffs "failed to allege that [social media companies] provided substantial aid to the [attacks] or otherwise consciously participated in it – much less that [they] so pervasively and systemically assisted ISIS as to render them liable for every ISIS attack" (Supreme Court of the United States, 2023).

However, this doesn't mean that the US has never had impactful media content regulations in place. From 1949 until 1987, the US Federal Communications Commission (FCC) enforced the so-called "fairness doctrine," which stated that broadcast license holders were required to cover issues of public importance, and to do so in a fair manner. In practice, this meant that broadcasters had to present opposing views on controversial and important matters for society. In 1987, the FCC itself found that the fairness doctrine (as it was used at the time at least) violated the First Amendment rights of broadcasters, and stopped enforcing it, although some parts remained intact until 2000 and the doctrine was only formally repealed in 2011 (Ruane, 2010). Some have argued that the repeal of the fairness doctrine led to the rise of right-wing talk radio and twenty-four-hour news channels, which some believe has played a role in fueling political polarization in the United States (Matzko, 2021). However, it's important to note that the fairness doctrine only applied to broadcasting licenses, not cable TV, and it's unlikely that it would have impacted channels such as Fox News, which was launched in 1996 (Caldera, 2020).

Instead of direct regulation, some US government entities have preferred promoting media literacy and creating materials to help people identify misinformation themselves. For example, the Department of State has invested in a series of campaigns aimed at helping people identify the tactics used in (foreign) disinformation (US Department of State, 2023). The Cybersecurity and Infrastructure Security Agency (CISA) published an infographic (2019) called *The War on Pineapple: Understanding Foreign Interference in 5 Steps*, which explains how to recognize "information operations" through the lens of a creative example of a polarizing topic: whether pineapple belongs on pizza. The reasoning here is that, although many people disagree over whether pineapple is a legitimate pizza topping, it's not *politically* polarizing per se. The infographic then explains how disinformation agents might try to exacerbate existing tensions and fuel polarization around this topic, which is the goal of many real-world disinformation campaigns.

6.6 CONCLUSION

In this chapter, we have discussed how mis- and disinformation have been tackled by governments and supranational entities around the world. Some countries have adopted new legislation making the spread or creation of misinformation illegal; this has often been met with criticism by human rights organizations: for instance, because governments cannot act as neutral arbiters of truth. The UK and EU have adopted expansive regulatory frameworks that regulate not only misinformation, but rather the online information space in its entirety. The Online Safety Bill and the Digital Services Act impose new limitations and duties on tech companies and social media platforms to ensure transparency and increased scrutiny. However, these frameworks have also been widely criticized for being simultaneously too far-reaching and relatively toothless, and it remains to be seen how effective both pieces of legislation will turn out to be. The United States is generally wary of any new legislation that imposes limits on speech, and doesn't currently have legislative initiatives that are as broad in scope as those in the UK and EU. Instead, some entities in the US have tried out investing in communications campaigns about mis- and disinformation; these are aimed at individuals (and not companies or misinformation producers), and their effectiveness is evaluated in a very different way. In the final two chapters, we discuss the evidence behind these and other kinds of individual-level misinformation interventions, and how they have been implemented in the real world.

7

Interventions to Combat Misinformation

7.1 INTRODUCTION

In the previous chapter, we discussed the legislative side of countering misinformation. But governments (and other regulatory entities) don't just have the law at their disposal: they (and nongovernment entities) can also leverage insights from psychology and behavioral science to reduce the spread of and susceptibility to misinformation. In this chapter we review the evidence behind the anti-misinformation interventions that have been designed and tested since misinformation research exploded in popularity around 2016. For this chapter, we draw on a review paper Jon wrote together with two colleagues, Eileen Culloty and Jane Suiter from Dublin City University (Roozenbeek, Culloty, et al., 2023). However, that paper is more expansive and detailed than this chapter can be for brevity reasons, and contains several recommendations for policymakers and tech companies that we're unable to cover here. Also, several other reviews have been published in recent years that employ somewhat different categorizations, discuss different publications, and arrive at different conclusions from us. These are worth having a look at, especially the very thorough review by Pica Johansson and colleagues (Bergsma & Carney, 2008; Czerniak et al., 2023; Y. Green et al., 2023; Gwiaździński et al., 2023; Hartwig et al., 2023; Janmohamed et al., 2021; Jeong et al., 2012; Johansson et al., 2022; Kozyreva et al., 2022; O'Mahony et al., 2023; Saltz et al., 2021; Traberg et al., 2022; Vahedi et al., 2018; van der Linden, 2022; Whitehead et al., 2023; Ziemer & Rothmund, 2022).

Anastasia Kozyreva and colleagues (2022) also put together a toolbox of interventions to counter misinformation. Their website (https://intervention stoolbox.mpib-berlin.mpg.de/) contains a lot of useful and practical information about the efficacy and applicability of many of the interventions we discuss in this chapter.[1] Finally, our research program has focused heavily on developing

---

[1] A research project sponsored by the US Social Science Research Council, led by Lisa Fazio, David Rand, and Stephan Lewandowsky, aims to compare the efficacy of these interventions in a single study (Social Science Research Council, 2022).

and testing a series of anti-misinformation interventions; we'll briefly mention this work here where relevant, but discuss it in much more detail in the next chapter.

7.2 TYPES OF MISINFORMATION INTERVENTIONS

There are two categories of intervention that seek to counter misinformation: *individual-level* and *system-level* interventions (Chater & Loewenstein, 2022; Kozyreva et al., 2020; Roozenbeek, Culloty, et al., 2023). System-level interventions tackle the *supply side* of misinformation, and include not only legislation (which we discussed in the previous chapter) but also changes to recommender algorithms (Guess et al., 2023a), addressing tech companies' business models, and political measures such as reducing polarization. Individual-level interventions target either people's behavior (usually what kinds of information they share with others on social networks) or susceptibility to misinformation (e.g., by reducing the likelihood of falling for misinformation). We've broken up individual-level interventions into four categories, using a modified categorization scheme originally developed by Anastasia Kozyreva and colleagues (2020) and previously used in the above-mentioned review paper (Roozenbeek, Culloty, et al., 2023): *boosting* skills or competences (media/digital literacy, critical thinking, and prebunking); *nudging* people by making changes to social media platforms' choice architecture; *debunking* misinformation through fact-checking; and (automated) *content labeling*. Figure 7.1, taken from Roozenbeek et al. (2023), shows an overview of the various system-level and individual-level interventions that are available to counter misinformation.

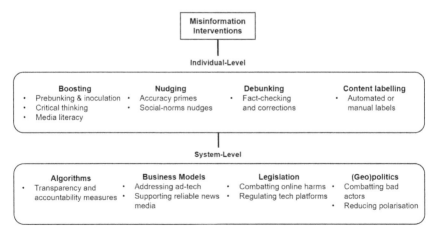

FIGURE 7.1 System-level and individual-level misinformation interventions. *Source:* Taken from Roozenbeek, Culloty, & Suiter (2023).

7.3 BOOSTING

Boosting interventions are competence-focused, in the sense that they seek to "improve people's competence to make their own choices" (Hertwig & Grüne-Yanoff, 2017, p. 974).[2] Boosts are always voluntary and don't require making changes to people's choice environments. This makes them different from nudges, which are behavior-focused and involve making changes to how people interact with the information environment they encounter (more on this later). The benefit of boosting interventions is that they're noninvasive and are unlikely to pose substantial ethical challenges. For example, taking a media literacy class is unlikely to infringe on one's right to free expression. The downside of boosts is that they require people to decide to participate: if some-one doesn't *want* to learn, they won't, and the boost won't be very beneficial to them. We'll discuss three types of boosting intervention: media and information literacy, critical thinking, and prebunking.

7.3.1 Media and Information Literacy

Media and Information Literacy (MIL) is an umbrella term that encom-passes media literacy, information literacy, news literacy, and digital literacy (Carlsson, 2019; UNESCO, 2021). Media literacy focuses especially on young people, and covers not only trainings on how to spot mis- and disinformation, but also information on how to detect sponsored advertising, bias awareness, and empowering people to participate in media content production (Potter, 2020). Information literacy emphasizes competences such as finding and eval-uating reliable information sources. News literacy focuses on content produc-tion and revolves around teaching people about how news and other kinds of content are produced (Tully et al., 2020). Finally, digital literacy interventions foster the skills required to navigate digital environments (Reddy et al., 2022).

Within the context of countering misinformation, MIL interventions are often designed for use in classrooms and other educational settings. To give a few examples, researchers at the University of Uppsala run the News Evaluator Project (Nyhetsvärderaren, https://nyhetsvarderaren.se/in-english), which is a series of instructional materials to help boost competences such as source criticism and civic online reasoning. These materials were extensively evalu-ated by the research team that developed them (led by our colleagues Thomas Nygren and Carl-Anton Axelsson), and are used in Swedish MIL curricula around the country (Axelsson et al., 2021; Nygren, 2019; Nygren et al., 2019; Nygren & Guath, 2019, 2021). Another high-profile example is the Civic Online Reasoning program (https://cor.stanford.edu/) led by Joel Breakstone

---

[2]   A team of researchers led by Ralph Hertwig and Stefan Herzog put together a cool website about the science of boosting: www.scienceofboosting.org/.

and Sam Wineburg at Stanford University. This program includes a wide range of free educational materials and even full-fledged curricula for teaching skills such as critical ignoring, lateral reading, click restraint, and source critique. This research team has also conducted a wide range of evaluations of the effectiveness of various curricula, and shown that they are broadly effective at fostering key competences for navigating digital environments (Breakstone et al., 2021; McGrew et al., 2017, 2019; Wineburg et al., 2022).

A downside of MIL interventions that take place in classrooms is their scalability: most adults don't go to school and may be unlikely to voluntarily take a MIL class when offered. This means that the majority of the population won't immediately benefit from these kinds of intervention (Lee, 2018). Researchers have therefore looked for ways to deploy MIL interventions in online environments. For example, Folco Panizza and colleagues (2022) designed a social media pop-up that explains how to use lateral reading techniques (i.e., evaluating the credibility of a source by looking for additional information through search engines or other sources). They found that displaying the pop-up significantly increased the use of lateral reading strategies. Andrew Guess and colleagues (2020) tested whether reading a set of media literacy tips (a short, informative infographic with tips such as "check the credibility of the source") could help people better distinguish true from false information in a large study conducted in the United States and India. They found that the tips were highly effective at improving people's ability to spot false news content in both countries. However, in India, the intervention was only effective for a sample of highly educated individuals, and not for a sample of people from a mostly rural area.

Although MIL interventions are often effective at achieving their goals (boosting relevant competences), the research into their efficacy continues to suffer from several limitations. Most importantly, there is a distinct lack of research from non-Western countries, and what has been published doesn't always show encouraging results. For instance, both Sumitra Badrinathan (2021) and Ayesha Ali and Ihsan Ayyub Qazi (2021) found that educational interventions were mostly ineffective for rural participants in India and Pakistan, respectively. This shows that we lack a decent understanding of how to make interventions work in settings where especially Western researchers don't tend to go (Ghai, 2021, 2022). There is, however, also some cause for optimism: in a field experiment with about 9,000 participants in Kenya, Susan Athey and colleagues (2023) found that a five-day text message educational course was effective at reducing intentions to share misinformation. The treatment that was designed to counter emotion-based manipulation techniques was particularly effective (more so than the treatment that targeted reasoning-based techniques or a combination of both).

There are also conceptual challenges. MIL interventions research uses a wide range of measures and assessment methods, which makes it difficult to compare different studies and interventions to one another (Potter & Thai, 2016). In addition, it's unclear if all types of MIL interventions are effective. A study by Mo Jones-Jang and colleagues (2019) showed that while information literacy was effective at boosting people's ability to identify misinformation, media, news, and digital literacy interventions were not; this suggests that more research is needed to probe what exactly makes MIL interventions effective. Finally, the efficacy of especially long-running MIL interventions (such as school curricula) is very difficult to assess. Longitudinal studies are hard and expensive to conduct, which makes optimizing interventions very complicated (Bulger & Davison, 2018).

7.3.2 Critical Thinking

Interventions aimed at boosting critical thinking typically intend to build skills related to people's ability to assess arguments, question underlying assumptions, and evaluate the quality of information (Duron et al., 2006). Critical thinking is related to media and information literacy, but not exactly the same: critical thinking may not be a domain-specific skill, but may instead be a transferable skill that can be applied in a variety of issue domains, not only misinformation (Axelsson et al., 2021; Moore, 2014).

In general, it appears that educational interventions are effective at teaching critical thinking. A meta-analysis about critical thinking in US college settings by Cristopher Huber and Nathan Kuncel (2016) concluded that "critical thinking skills and dispositions improve substantially over a normal college experience." However, the authors also note the following (conclusion section):

Although the set of specific skills measured by critical thinking tests is important, spending more time on them involves trade-offs with other important skills. The evidence suggests that basic competencies such as reading and mathematics are more amenable to improvement beyond the gains currently observed, and the need is arguably more desperate.

In other words, curricula and other interventions that seek to boost critical thinking skills in specific domains are less effective than the overall effect of going to college. College students become better at critical thinking overall as they progress through their degree, whereas individual interventions don't appear to work very well. Still, within the domain of misinformation, Lauren Lutzke and colleagues (2019) found that critical thinking guidelines did boost people's ability to evaluate the credibility of misinformation (and non-misinformation) about climate change on Facebook. However, compared to MIL interventions and prebunking (see below), the research on critical thinking is limited: a systematic review by Paul Machete and Marita Turpin (2020) only identified three studies that directly dealt with critical thinking as a way to identify misinformation.

Other researchers have noted that many studies on critical thinking suffer from methodological shortcomings (El Soufi & See, 2019; Todd & O'Brien, 2016), which renders much of the evidence collected so far inconclusive.

Conceptually, scholars such as danah boyd (2018) have argued that the very notion of "critical thinking" can be weaponized by malicious actors seeking to confuse and obfuscate rather than clarify. They mention the example of RT (formerly Russia Today), a Kremlin-funded news outlet whose motto is "Question More." RT asking its readers to think critically about the science behind climate change, boyd argues, is not a genuine effort to appraise evidence in a better or more accurate way, but rather a way to leverage the idea of critical thinking to sow doubt about a well-established field of science. Adopting a critical stance by default, according to boyd and others (Beene & Greer, 2021), is not helpful. However, others have argued that it's important to distinguish between constructive skepticism and dysfunctional cynicism (Quiring et al., 2021); how to achieve this in a reliable way through interventions, however, isn't entirely clear.

7.3.3 Prebunking

The term "prebunking" (preemptive debunking) is now widely used, but we have no idea where it came from. We thought it was John Cook (another misinformation researcher who started using the term around 2016, around the same time as Sander), but when we asked him about it, he didn't know who came up with it either. We then looked online to find out when "prebunking" was first used, but to little avail. Nonetheless, prebunking refers to any kind of intervention that is deployed *before* people are exposed to misinformation. Or, according to Urban Dictionary (a top scholarly resource): "to debunk lies you know are coming in advance." While you could argue that this would mean that media literacy curricula should fall under the "prebunking" banner, the term usually refers to short-acting interventions that can be deployed on social media or are easily accessible online (e.g., browser games: see below). Various approaches to prebunking exist. For instance, Nadia Brashier and colleagues (2021) showed their study participants a simple banner that read "this article was rated false by independent fact-checkers" before they saw a false headline. Li Qian Tay and colleagues (2021) provided participants with a more detailed refutation of the misinformation that they saw shortly after (pointing out why the information was false or misleading).[3]

The most common framework for prebunking misinformation is inoculation theory, which was originally conceptualized in the 1960s by William

---

[3] For those interested in more practical resources, together with Jigsaw and BBC Media Action, we (but mostly Trisha Harjani, then a research assistant at our lab in Cambridge) put together a practical guide to designing and testing prebunking interventions (Harjani et al., 2022).

McGuire and Demetrios Papageorgis (McGuire, 1964, 1970; McGuire & Papageorgis, 1961b, 1962; Papageorgis & McGuire, 1961),[4] and later refined by scholars such as Michael Pfau, Bobi Ivanov, Kimberly Parker, John Banas, and Josh Compton (Banas & Miller, 2013; Compton, 2013, 2020, 2021; Compton & Pfau, 2009; Ivanov et al., 2011, 2012, 2018, 2022; Parker et al., 2012, 2016; Pfau, 1995; Pfau & Burgoon, 1988; Richards & Banas, 2018). Inoculation theory is grounded in a biological metaphor: much like how a medical vaccine (usually) consists of a weakened dose of the real pathogen, which prompts the body to produce antibodies, the process of psychological "vaccination" (or inoculation) involves preemptively exposing people to a "weakened dose" of an unwanted persuasion attempt, which should then increase resistance against subsequent persuasion attempts. The persuasive message is "weakened" by adding two components: a warning of an impending attack on one's beliefs or attitudes (e.g., "warning: some people might be out to manipulate you"), and a preemptive refutation of the upcoming manipulation attempt: for example, by explaining why the information is false (Compton, 2013). By doing this, people are both warned that their beliefs might be under attack and provided with the cognitive tools to resist future attempts to manipulate them. A meta-analysis by John Banas and Stephen Rains (2010) found that inoculation interventions are generally effective at conferring resistance against unwanted persuasion.

Inoculation theory became of significant interest for misinformation researchers around 2017. Both John Cook, Ulrich Ecker, and Stephan Lewandowsky (2017) and Sander and his colleagues at Yale (van der Linden, Leiserowitz, et al., 2017) tested whether inoculation could be used to reduce susceptibility to misinformation about climate change, both with some success: after inoculation, participants in both studies had a more accurate perception of the scientific consensus, and the inoculation treatment managed to reduce the adverse impacts of exposure to misinformation (van der Linden, Maibach, et al., 2017).[5]

There are two important theoretical distinctions when it comes to inoculation interventions: *passive* versus *active* inoculation (McGuire & Papageorgis, 1961a; Traberg et al., 2022), and *issue-based* versus *technique-based* (or logic-based) inoculation (Cook et al., 2017; Roozenbeek, Traberg, et al., 2022). Passive inoculation interventions provide people with the counterarguments needed to resist unwanted persuasion, for example by reading a piece of text or watching a video. Active inoculations, on the other hand, involve actively generating your own counterarguments: such interventions ask their participants to think

---

4   Pronounced "papa gorgeous," you can't change our minds.
5   It's useful to note that a replication of John Cook's study (Schmid-Petri & Bürger, 2021) didn't find the same effects as the original, in the sense that there was no effect of the inoculation on the perceived scientific consensus on climate change. This may have been due to the fact that the sample used in the replication (from Germany) generally already had lower baseline belief in misinformation compared to participants in the original study. A similar effect occurred in a replication of Sander's study from 2017 (Williams & Bond, 2020).

about why a piece of information might be false or misleading, and come up with their own strategies for countering it: for example, by playing a game.

Issue-based inoculation interventions tackle a specific argument or false claim that you don't want people to fall for: for example, specific misleading information about climate change (Maertens et al., 2020; van der Linden, Leiserowitz, et al., 2017; Williams & Bond, 2020). Technique-based inoculation interventions tackle the underlying rhetorical strategies and manipulation techniques that are often used to mislead or misinform, such as logical fallacies (Roozenbeek, van der Linden, et al., 2022), fake experts (Cook et al., 2017), trolling (Lees et al., 2023), or astroturfing (Zerback et al., 2021). The advantage of technique-based interventions over issue-based ones is that improving people's ability to spot a misleading rhetorical strategy potentially applies to a wide range of content, whereas issue-based interventions can only be expected to be effective for the specific argument or claim that people were inoculated against. However, if you can predict with reasonable certainty what misleading claims people are likely to be exposed to in the near future (e.g., about election fraud around an important election), issue-based interventions may be most effective.

Passive inoculations were shown to successfully boost resistance against misinformation in a variety of issue domains, including extremism (Braddock, 2019), COVID-19 (Basol et al., 2021), astroturfing comments (Zerback et al., 2021), and vaccine misinformation (Jolley & Douglas, 2017). More recently, researchers have begun to explore the use of short inoculation videos, which can be useful because video is a popular format that can easily be rolled out on social media: for example, as advertisements. Inoculation videos have been successfully tested in the realms of Islamist and Islamophobic propaganda (Lewandowsky & Yesilada, 2021), extremist propaganda (Hughes et al., 2021), and vaccine misinformation (Piltch-Loeb et al., 2022). We (Jon and Sander) have also helped create a series of inoculation videos and rolled them out as ads on YouTube (Roozenbeek, van der Linden, et al., 2022), but we will discuss this study in more detail in the next chapter.

Active inoculation interventions tend to come in the form of online games (Shi, 2023). The aforementioned John Cook, in collaboration with creative agency Goodbeast, created Cranky Uncle (www.crankyuncle.com/), a hilarious game where players learn about fourteen different techniques of science denial (in the context of climate change), such as the promotion of fake experts, cherry-picking, and various logical fallacies (Cook, 2020). The game is free to play and can be played in a browser or downloaded as an app. A qualitative evaluation of the Cranky Uncle game showed promising results for the game's use as an educational tool both inside and outside of classroom settings (Cook et al., 2022). Another very interesting (and effective) active intervention is the Spot the Troll quiz, in which people learn how to identify online trolls and other types of disingenuous messaging. Jeff Lees and colleagues (2023) showed that taking the quiz significantly increased people's ability to distinguish troll comments from genuine content. Finally, we have also worked on a series of inoculation games ourselves, including Bad News (www.getbadnews.com/), Harmony Square (www.harmonysquare.game/), Go Viral! (www.goviralgame.com/), and Cat Park (www.catpark.game/). We'll discuss how we tested these interventions in the next chapter.

In general, prebunking interventions are mostly effective at reducing susceptibility to misinformation. However, they also have several important downsides (some of which we will discuss in Chapter 8). Most importantly, like MIL interventions, most prebunking interventions are rather lengthy and rely on voluntary uptake, and people who don't want to learn about how to spot misinformation will not benefit from them. This problem can be circumvented somewhat by making the interventions as entertaining as possible: for example, by using humor (Compton, 2018; Cook et al., 2022; Vraga et al., 2019). That said, what one person finds funny doesn't necessarily appeal to others,[6] making it necessary to continuously work on developing more and more interventions that appeal to different preferences. It's also important to note that people have to trust the source of the intervention; some people might be distrustful of an inoculation video about how smoking is secretly good for you produced by a tobacco company, and you might argue that this would be pretty reasonable. Similarly, if the production of prebunking interventions is not done in a transparent and open manner, people might be distrustful about their ultimate purpose, and refuse to engage with them.

Another limitation is that even successful prebunking interventions don't always exclusively impact people's evaluations of false or misleading information, but can also impact people's evaluation of factual information (Hameleers, 2023). This "real news" effect is commonly observed across a range of studies and for many different types of misinformation intervention (K. Clayton et al., 2020; Guess et al., 2020; Hoes et al., 2023; Modirrousta-Galian & Higham, 2023), although this discussion requires some nuance: prebunking interventions don't necessarily make people more skeptical of *all* information, but rather make them more skeptical of information that they already feel ambiguous about even without an intervention; their evaluations of information that is obviously true are not affected (Modirrousta-Galian & Higham, 2023). We discuss this phenomenon in detail in the next chapter.

7.4 NUDGES

In their famous book *Nudge: Improving Decisions about Health, Wealth, and Happiness* (2008, p. 6), Richard Thaler and Cass Sunstein (whose work on echo chambers we discussed in Chapter 5) define a "nudge" as "any aspect of the choice architecture that alters people's behavior in a predictable way without

---

[6] Looking at you, *Big Bang Theory*.

forbidding any options or significantly changing their economic incentive." Nudges come in many forms. One well-known example is moving the sugary or fatty products in the supermarket aisle from eye-level to foot-level to reduce how much unhealthy food people buy. In the context of misinformation, the unifying factor of nudges is that they seek to address some kind of unwanted information behavior, usually the sharing of misinformation with others. The potential advantages of nudges are numerous: they're cheap, nonintrusive, easy to implement, and highly scalable. Some social media companies have started implementing nudges in their choice architectures. Twitter, for instance, has asked people if they're sure they want to share or retweet a link if they haven't clicked on it.

The underlying assumption of nudge-based interventions is that a substantial proportion of social media users not only share unwanted content but are also "nudgeable" (de Ridder et al., 2021): people cannot be nudged into doing something they don't want to do. Nudgeable social media users therefore don't share misinformation knowingly and willingly (i.e., because they believe the misinformation to be true and want to tell others about it), but instead do so because they are in "irrational" modes of thinking. If these conditions are met, subtle changes to social media users' choice environments should positively affect their news-sharing decisions. Gordon Pennycook and David Rand (2019, 2021), whose work we also discussed in Chapter 4, have proposed that people tend to share misinformation (by which they mean false news headlines or "fake news": see Chapter 1) because of a failure to be mindful of accuracy. This, they argue, can happen because social media environments can be distracting and shift our attention away from the importance of sharing only accurate content with others. Their proposed solution is therefore to nudge people's attention *toward* accuracy: subtly reminding them of the concept of accuracy should prevent them from sharing misinformation when they encounter it in their social media feed. It's worth noting that this only works if people don't believe the misinformation that they see to be accurate to begin with; interventions that shift attention to accuracy only impact the sharing of misinformation that is accidental, and not deliberate.

Pennycook and Rand have proposed a series of interventions which they have collectively dubbed "accuracy prompts" or "accuracy nudges" (Epstein et al., 2021; Pennycook & Rand, 2022). There are different types of accuracy prompt intervention, which vary in terms of their intensity, effect size, length, and underlying mechanisms, but have in common that they all intend to improve the quality of people's news sharing decisions. The simplest and most well-known type of accuracy prompt consists of asking people to evaluate the accuracy of a single, nonpolitical news headline (Pennycook et al., 2020, 2021). People are shown a random news headline and asked "to the best of your knowledge, is the above headline accurate? Yes/No." This "evaluation" treatment should then activate the concept of accuracy in people's minds, which subsequently improves the quality of their sharing decisions: they become either less likely to share false news headlines, more likely to share true news headlines, or both. This approach was shown to work in the context of both COVID-19 misinformation (Pennycook et al., 2020) and political misinformation (Pennycook et al., 2021). In a major publication in *Nature* (2021), Gordon Pennycook and colleagues also conducted a field study where they deployed this type of intervention on Twitter. They built a Twitter bot that sent people (a sample of mostly conservative US Twitter users) a direct message on Twitter, asking them to evaluate the accuracy of a single headline. Even though not every recipient read the message, the authors were still able to show that this "nudge" boosted the quality of the sources that people shared: although the effects were very small, Twitter users who received the nudge appeared to share slightly fewer news articles from sources with low quality ratings from fact-checkers (such as Breitbart) and more news from high-quality sources such as the *New York Times* and CNN. In an internal meta-analysis of accuracy prompt interventions, Pennycook and Rand (2022) concluded that overall, accuracy prompts are a "replicable and generalizable" approach for reducing the spread of misinformation.

However, this type of accuracy nudge intervention has also been met with some criticism. Several replications, including one we conducted, showed either no effect of the intervention on people's sharing decisions or a very small one (Gavin et al., 2022; Pretus et al., 2021; Rasmussen et al., 2022; Roozenbeek, Freeman, et al., 2021). Furthermore, four out of fourteen studies included in the accuracy prompt meta-analysis (Pennycook & Rand, 2022) showed no significant main effect, and a further three showed small effects that were just about significant. Thus, while an overall effect of this type of accuracy nudge on news-sharing intentions does appear to exist, this effect may be so small that you need a very large sample to detect it. This may be partially due to the fact that this type of intervention is a behavioral prime, where rather than giving people explicit instructions about the intended outcome of the intervention (e.g., "don't share misinformation with others!"), the intervention subtly and implicitly reminds people of the importance of accuracy. Such behavioral primes are known to be very difficult to replicate (Chivers, 2019; Schimmack, 2020; Schimmack et al., 2017).

Nonetheless, this criticism is specific to the single-headline "accuracy nudge" intervention, and other types of nudge (or prompt) intervention are more robust. For instance, Lisa Fazio (2020) found that asking people to pause for a while to consider why a headline is true or false substantially reduced people's willingness to share false headlines, and Pennycook and Rand (2022) report robust effect sizes for other "accuracy prompt" interventions such as PSA videos and media literacy tips. In addition, social norms around the sharing of news and other content also appear to be a promising avenue for intervention: both Andı and Akesson (2021) and Gimpel and colleagues

(2021) found that emphasizing injunctive norms (what behavior most people approve or disapprove of: for example, "most people think sharing fake news is bad") could reduce the proportion of people who are willing to share false news with others. Ziv Epstein and colleagues (2021) put together an "accuracy prompt toolkit" that contains many different kinds of nudge intervention. Finally, in a field experiment conducted on Twitter, Matthew Katsaros and colleagues (2021) designed an intervention that prompted Twitter users about to post harmful or hateful content with an opportunity to pause and reconsider what they wrote. Promisingly, this intervention led to a 6 percent reduction in the posting of offensive tweets, compared to a control group. This highlights the real-world applicability of nudge interventions.

Although nudges are a highly promising approach to countering misinformation, they're also beset by several challenges. Most importantly, it's incredibly difficult to translate promising findings from lab studies to real-world settings. Stefano DellaVigna and Elizabeth Linos (2022) compared the effectiveness of nudge interventions (unrelated to misinformation) in lab studies and that of the same interventions when implemented in the field. They found that interventions were about four to six times less effective in the field than in the lab (although the effect remained detectable). This means that we can expect a substantial reduction in effect size when implementing nudge interventions in settings where people don't have to pay attention, which highlights the importance of starting out with robust effect sizes in lab studies. Furthermore, it appears that nudges become less effective the more people are exposed to them. A study by Shusaku Sasaki and colleagues (2021) found that the nudge effect wore off after only a few exposures, indicating that nudges may not retain their initial effectiveness (although we need more research to verify if this is the case on social media as well).

7.5 DEBUNKING AND FACT-CHECKING

Debunking involves correcting misinformation after exposure (Bode & Vraga, 2018).[7] It's one of the most popular approaches to tackling misinformation: websites such as Snopes, FullFact and StopFake have large numbers of followers and reach millions of people, and many tech companies have extensive fact-checking policies in place. Meta (formerly Facebook) runs a worldwide fact-checking program where it pays third-party fact-checkers to evaluate and label content that is posted on Facebook, WhatsApp, and Instagram.[8]

---

[7]   Debunking and fact-checking are similar terms but not entirely synonymous: debunking always pertains to misinformation, whereas you could fact-check a story and rate it "true" (Roozenbeek, Culloty, et al., 2023).
[8]   For full disclosure: Sander has been an adviser to Meta's fact-checking program. He can't use the Zuckerbucks he receives as compensation to buy anything other than more Zuckerbucks, but he's told that they go up in value over time.

Luckily, there appears to be scientific consensus about the effectiveness of debunking. A series of meta-analyses and review papers (Chan et al., 2017; Walter et al., 2020; Walter & Murphy, 2018; Walter & Tukachinsky, 2020) has shown that, overall, correcting misperceptions reduces belief in misperceptions. This sounds almost tautological, but it's an important finding: overall, people are willing to change their belief in a false claim when presented with corrective information. Research teams like the one run by Andreas Vlachos (Guo et al., 2022; Schlichtkrull et al., 2023; Thorne & Vlachos, 2018) have made great strides in improving automated fact-checking, which can potentially scale up fact-checking efforts on social media to a considerable degree. In 2020 a team of researchers led by Stephan Lewandowsky, John Cook, and Ulrich Ecker put together a practical guide to debunking, the *Debunking Handbook*, which explains the science of debunking and how to leverage it for effectively correcting misinformation online (Lewandowsky et al., 2020).

In the 2010s, concerns were raised about debunking accidentally provoking an *increased* belief in misperceptions (Nyhan & Reifler, 2010; C. Peter & Koch, 2015), a phenomenon which became known as the "backfire effect." For example, a study led by Mohsen Mosleh (2021) found that Twitter users who were corrected for posting false political news increased the subsequent sharing of toxic and low-quality content. However, recent review studies have shown that these backfire effects are extremely rare and not reliably observed (Ecker, Lewandowsky, et al., 2020; Swire-Thompson et al., 2020, 2022; Wood & Porter, 2019). The risks of debunking "side effects" are therefore considered to be very low.[9]

That said, like all misinformation interventions, debunking faces several challenges. First, debunking is not universally effective for everyone across all issue domains: correcting health misinformation appears to be easier than correcting misinformation about politics and marketing (Chan et al., 2017; Porter & Wood, 2021; Walter et al., 2020; Walter & Murphy, 2018). A recent meta-analysis on the effectiveness of debunking science-relevant (including health-related) misinformation found no overall significant effects (Chan & Albarracín, 2023), particularly for misinformation about politically polarizing topics. The content of the debunking message itself matters as well. For example, less detailed fact-checks appear to be less effective than more detailed ones (Ecker, O'Reilly, et al., 2020; Paynter et al., 2019). Another problem is source credibility: how trustworthy people perceive the source of a fact-check to be strongly affects how likely someone is to accept a correction. In other words, if you don't like the source of the fact-check, you likely won't believe it (Bode & Vraga, 2018, 2021; Ecker & Antonio, 2021; Guillory & Geraci, 2013; Vraga & Bode, 2017). A study led by Drew Margolin (2017) also showed that Twitter users were much more likely to accept a fact-check if it came from an account

---

[9] Still, like prebunking (as we'll see in the next chapter), every anti-misinformation intervention has benefits as well as potential side effects to consider.

that they followed than if it came from a stranger. Problematically, Michael Hameleers and Toni van der Meer (2019) found that people are much more likely to engage with corrections that are congruent with their prior (political) attitudes, and usually ignore those that contradict their prior beliefs.

More generally, the study on debunking on Facebook by Fabiana Zollo and colleagues (2017), which we discussed in Chapter 5, showed that fact-checks don't reach a lot of people who tend to consume conspiratorial content, possibly due to echo chamber formation. This means that it may be exceedingly difficult to provide effective corrections to social media users with the highest belief in misinformation; pessimistically speaking, many fact-checks may be preaching to the converted. Moreover, even if a correction successfully reduces a misbelief, it doesn't completely eliminate it: the "continued influence effect" (Ecker & Antonio, 2021; Lewandowsky et al., 2012; Walter & Tukachinsky, 2020) states that people continue to (partially) rely on misbeliefs and retrieve them from memory even after it has been successfully corrected. It's believed that this happens because information that was previously encoded in people's memory can continue to influence one's judgments, even if more recent information contradicts it (H. M. Johnson & Seifert, 1994).

Finally, as we discussed in Chapters 1 and 3, the most impactful misinformation is often not explicitly false, and judging whether something counts as misinformation can be highly subjective (Coleman, 2018). Because of this, fact-checking can be highly contentious and risks becoming politicized (Graves, 2016). This problem is compounded by the fact that some fact-checkers are dependent on large donors. Meta's third-party fact-checking program, for example, has been criticized for its lack of transparency (Sander denies any responsibility), and some have emphasized the risk of placing responsibility for what kinds of content are and aren't fact-checked in the hands of large corporations (BMJ, 2021; Nyhan, 2017).

7.6 (AUTOMATED) CONTENT LABELING

Because of the sheer volume of content uploaded to social media platforms, implementing misinformation interventions at scale is a daunting challenge. Some platforms therefore rely on automated methods to label and moderate content (Alaphilippe et al., 2019). Many of these methods rely on machine learning, and generally either classify content into categories (such as "misleading" or "false") or evaluate it against a database of known problematic sources or claims (Thorne & Vlachos, 2018). Content labels can come in the form of general or specific warnings (K. Clayton et al., 2020; Mena, 2019), fact-checks (Brashier et al., 2021), or news credibility labels (Aslett et al., 2022). Well-known examples of labels are NewsGuard, which rates the credibility of news sources, and Facebook's content labels, which provide context to what people are seeing on the platform (such as "satire page," "public official," and "fan page"). Twitter now also has a feature called Community Notes, where users can collaboratively add context to potentially misleading tweets.

Vincent Conzola and Michael Wogalter (2001) note that for content labels to be effective, they must attract enough attention for the information to be noticed, be clear enough that people can understand the message that is conveyed, and motivate people enough to take the required action (e.g., not sharing something with others when they otherwise would have). And indeed, Tatiana Celadin and colleagues (2023) found that displaying the trustworthiness of a news source reduced people's intentions to share false news posts. In a study on the effects of warning labels that were applied to Donald Trump's tweets about the 2020 US presidential elections, Orestis Papakyriakopoulos and Ellen Goodman (2022) found that, while adding labels didn't change Twitter users' engagement with or sharing of Trump's tweets overall, adding strong rebuttals and a degree of contextual overlap between the label and the tweets did reduce engagement. They conclude that the right kinds of labels may be a "plausible way to mitigate misinformation spread and toxic user engagement."

However, not all content labels appear to be effective. In a large study also conducted on Twitter, Kevin Aslett and colleagues (2022) investigated if news credibility labels can impact the quality of people's news diets and reduce belief in misinformation. They found that this was not the case: overall, the labels provoked very limited effects on news diet quality shortly after being introduced, and didn't reduce misperceptions. Similarly, Anne Oeldorf-Hirsch and colleagues (2020) found that fact-checking labels had little to no effect on the perceived accuracy of news memes and articles. It's also worth noting that automated detection methods are imperfect and can be unreliable; without humans to review judgments made by algorithms, there's always a risk of error-prone moderation (Banchik, 2021).

7.7 SOME REFLECTIONS ON MISINFORMATION INTERVENTIONS

With some exceptions, individual-level misinformation interventions appear to be effective at what they set out to achieve, be it reducing misperceptions, increasing resilience to manipulation, or nudging people into changing their (self-reported) behavior. However, are these kinds of individual-level solutions really the way to go? In an influential paper, Nick Chater and George Loewenstein (2022) argue that an excessive focus on individual-level solutions to societal problems (including but not limited to tackling misinformation) has "led behavioral public policy astray." They note that while some individual-level solutions are effective in the statistical sense, they at best combat the symptoms of larger underlying problems (Altay, 2022; Roozenbeek & Zollo, 2022). An overreliance on simple solutions and "quick fixes" may therefore draw necessary attention away from systemic problems, such as tech companies' recommender algorithms showing people dodgy content because it's good for ad revenue.

Then again, it's also true that individual-level misinformation interventions are unlikely to cause harm: fact-checks, prebunks, and nudges don't violate people's rights, even if some people may find them annoying. System-level solutions, such as legislation that puts limits on what kinds of content people can post online, may be much more effective in terms of reducing exposure or sharing of misinformation, but also carry significant risks such as posing a threat to freedom of expression (see Chapter 6). For example, analyses find that misinformation about election fraud dropped significantly after Twitter's decision to ban Donald Trump (Dwoskin & Timberg, 2021), but this also prompted Trump to start his own social media platform (Truth Social), resulting in audiences becoming even more fragmented and potentially more insulated from factual information. Cass Sunstein (2023) also disagrees strongly with the notion that individual-level solutions (such as nudges) can "crowd out" more aggressive approaches, calling it "preposterous." He argues that there is no evidence that the implementation of individual-level solutions makes system-level reforms less likely to occur.

To illustrate this, let's revisit Figure 1.5 from Chapter 1, but this time let's also look at what interventions might be considered for each type of content (verifiable falsehoods, misinformation that is misleading but not outright false, true but ambiguous information, and uncontroversial facts). In Chapter 1 we noted some of the difficulties with defining "misinformation": verifiable falsehoods and uncontroversial facts don't cause too much trouble in this respect, but it can be tremendously difficult to distinguish between misinformation that isn't outright false and non-misinformation of ambiguous veracity (e.g., because relevant context is left out, and so on).

Looking at Figure 7.2, we see that the difficulties we described in Chapter 1 rear their heads again when deciding on the appropriate intervention(s) to counter misinformation. Again, verifiable falsehoods and uncontroversial facts are relatively unproblematic: falsehoods can be removed or downranked by social media platforms without too much controversy, and other solutions such as nudging, debunking, content labeling, media literacy, and prebunking are all potentially effective as well. Uncontroversial (or reliable) news content can be labeled as such, digital literacy programs can educate people about how to identify reliable sources, and platforms can boost the visibility of reliable and trustworthy content. Our problems start when we try to tackle misinformation that isn't entirely false: such content is difficult to remove or downrank (because there might be substantial disagreement over whether it should be labeled as "misinformation," thus potentially evoking controversy). Accuracy prompts (see above) are known to work less well for misinformation that is seen as more persuasive (Arechar et al., 2022), and debunking, literacy, labeling, and prebunking interventions can work in principle but also require

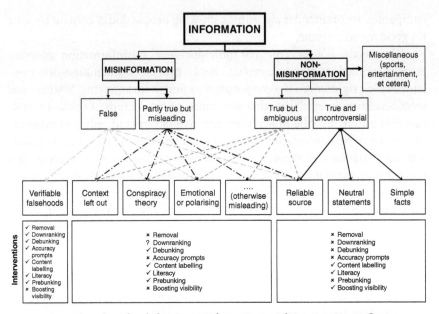

FIGURE 7.2 Flowchart for defining misinformation, with interventions. Crosses, ticks, and question marks indicate whether an intervention type is not suitable, suitable, or questionably useful for that type of (mis)information.

careful consideration: after all, you don't want to accidentally label something as misinformation that turns out to be true.

With all this in mind, the body of evidence that has been amassed over the last few years on the efficacy of misinformation interventions is growing rapidly, but continues to suffer from several shortcomings. Most importantly, as is a recurring theme throughout this book, there's a huge research gap for non-Western countries: we simply lack a lot of knowledge on what works and what doesn't in countries outside of the US and Western Europe. There's also not enough evidence on what works in the field; lab studies abound, but as we discussed above, it's not necessarily true that what works in a lab also works in real life (DellaVigna & Linos, 2022). This problem is compounded by the fact that researchers often lack access to social media data, and conducting experimental studies in social media settings is not only complicated but also extremely expensive (Roozenbeek & Zollo, 2022). There's a need to make access to data and funding more democratic and accessible, especially for researchers who don't work at rich, Western universities.

7.8 CONCLUSION

In this chapter, we've discussed the effectiveness of four categories of individual-level misinformation interventions: boosting (media and information literacy, critical thinking, and prebunking); nudging; debunking (and fact-checking);

and (automated) content labeling. These interventions have one of three goals: to improve relevant skills such as spotting manipulation techniques, source criticism, or lateral reading (in the case of boosting interventions and some content labels); to change people's behavior, most commonly improving the quality of their sharing decisions (for nudges and most content labels); or to reduce misperceptions and misbeliefs (in the case of debunking). We've argued that at least some interventions from each category are effective at what they set out to achieve, and more and more evidence continues to be gathered that builds our knowledge of what works and what doesn't. However, there are still open questions with respect to the cross-cultural and real-world effectiveness of many interventions, including over time, and there are important issues to consider when it comes to whether focusing too much on "fixing" individual beliefs or behavior doesn't distract from implementing more systemic solutions. In the next and final chapter, we will discuss our own research program on misinformation interventions. We will talk about what worked and what went well, but also about the nuances and limitations to our work.

8

Reflecting on Our Own Program of Research

8.1 INTRODUCTION

In the previous two chapters, we discussed various types of intervention to counter misinformation, ranging from introducing new legislation to educational programs and gentle nudges. We briefly touched on our own work, much of which has focused on intervention design and testing, in Chapter 7. In this chapter, we will look at this research in more detail. We'll first review the interventions we helped create and the studies we've conducted to test their effectiveness, most of which are rooted in inoculation theory. It's important to us that this chapter (and the book in general) remains balanced, so we will also discuss the constructive criticism that fellow scientists have expressed about our work over the last few years,[1] and the limitations of our approach to countering misinformation.

8.2 A PSYCHOLOGICAL "VACCINE" AGAINST MISINFORMATION?

To give a bit of background: we met in 2017, when Sander had just arrived in Cambridge as a new (and slightly mad) assistant professor of psychology and Jon was a (fully sane) Ph.D. student at the Department of Slavonic Studies. At the time, Jon was working on a side project on fake news together with a friend, Ruurd Oosterwoud, with whom he had studied Russian at Leiden University. Ruurd and Jon had just received some seed funding from the Stimuleringsfonds voor de Journalistiek, a Dutch government-backed fund that sponsors various journalistic projects. The idea was to create a game about misinformation from the perspective of the people who create it. This eventually led to the creation of a card game about propaganda and a demo browser game (https://getbadnews.com/nl/).

---

[1] As well as the, at times, eloquent criticism from Twitter users. It's important to take your critics seriously, especially if they accuse you of being a Bill Gates Big Pharma reptilian overlord. After all, what if they're right?

While Ruurd and Jon were working on this, the Dutch public broadcaster published a news article (NOS, 2017) about a new study led by Sander about "inoculating" people against climate change misinformation (van der Linden, Leiserowitz, et al., 2017).[2] This piqued Jon's interest, and he sent Sander an email asking to have a chat.[3] During this eclectic conversation, the idea was born that the game Jon was working on with Ruurd might work as an "inoculation" intervention, or a gamified "psychological vaccine," against misinformation. Over the next few weeks, we did a bit of reading and discovered that William McGuire, the progenitor of inoculation theory, had theorized that so-called "active" inoculation (where people are asked to generate their own counterarguments, rather than being provided with them) might yield substantial benefits in terms of the robustness and longevity of inoculation interventions (McGuire & Papageorgis, 1961a). This idea hadn't really been put into practice much at the time, but we figured that games might be a suitable avenue for active inoculation. In addition, John Cook (of Cranky Uncle fame; see Chapter 7) and his colleagues (2017) had just published a study in which they showed that inoculation theory could be used to successfully build resilience against argumentation *techniques*, as opposed to individual arguments. We found this very promising: what if you could design a game that inoculates people against the *ways* in which people are commonly misled and manipulated?

Together with Ruurd's new company (DROG) and Wim Hilberdink from Mediawijsheid Scholen, a Dutch media literacy organization, we first piloted this idea by conducting a small-scale randomized controlled trial with our propaganda card game at a Dutch high school. This went relatively well (considering the difficulties of doing field studies), and led to our first joint publication (Roozenbeek & van der Linden, 2018). While this paper was under review, we discussed how to proceed. All of us were enthusiastic about the idea of creating an English-language version of the game, incorporating insights from psychological science to potentially increase its effectiveness as an inoculation intervention. Incredibly, Jon's PhD supervisor, Rory Finnin, gave Jon permission to take time off from his dissertation to work on writing the content and story. Martijn Gussekloo, Bas Janson and Bas Breugelmans from design agency Gusmanson (www.gusmanson.nl/) were also part of the team. They were responsible for the game's graphic design and programming, and made valuable contributions to the overall gameplay and content. If you like how the games look, it's in large part thanks to them.

This collaborative effort eventually led to the *Bad News* game (www .getbadnews.com/). In the game, which takes about fifteen minutes, you play

---

[2] Inoculation theory is explained in Chapter 7, but to briefly recap: the theory posits that you can build resistance against unwanted persuasion attempts by preemptively exposing to a "weakened dose" of misinformation (kind of like a vaccine).

[3] By way of introduction, Jon is alleged to have said, "Hi, nice passport. I have the same one." Whether or not this is true we'll likely never know.

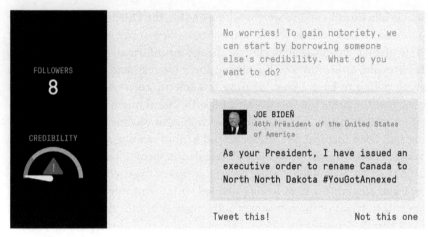

FIGURE 8.1 Screenshot from the *Bad News* game (www.getbadnews.com/), with the followers and credibility meters on the left. Players have the option to impersonate US President Joe Biden using a fake account.
Credit: TILT (www.tiltstudio.co/).

as a fake news magnate who tries to gain a following and build credibility in a simulated social media environment (reminiscent of Twitter).[4] Across six levels, you learn about six manipulation techniques that can be used in mis- and disinformation: impersonating fake accounts, emotional manipulation, polarizing audiences, spreading conspiracies, discrediting people through ad hominem attacks, and trolling people to evoke an emotional response.[5] Figure 8.1 shows what the game looks like in a browser.

Fred Lewsey, who works for Cambridge University's press office, has been an enormous help over the years increasing the visibility of our work (we call him "viral Fred"). He wrote a fantastic press release for our first publication and managed to time it with the launch of the game, which got us some press attention. In fact, so many people navigated to the *Bad News* website that it crashed Gusmanson's servers. In the years since then, the game has attracted millions of players (and bots, it turns out), and it became a resource used in classrooms and other educational settings in numerous countries. We noticed that there was demand for more games, and in the following years we (together with DROG and Gusmanson) also created *Harmony Square* and *Cat Park* (about political disinformation, funded by the US Department of Homeland Security and the

---

4   Lindsay Grace and Liang Songyi (2023) wrote a cool conceptual analysis of the *Bad News* and *Harmony Square* games (and other misinformation games), analyzing them through the lens of inoculation theory and transportation theory. Well worth a read.
5   There are many more ways of manipulating people than just these six techniques, but you have to start somewhere. We selected these techniques by reviewing the literature and from a report commissioned by NATO called *Digital Hydra* (Bertolin et al., 2017), which detailed the various strategies commonly used by mis- and disinformation producers. For a detailed discussion, see van der Linden and Roozenbeek (2020).

FIGURE 8.2 Landing pages for the *Bad News* (www.getbadnews.com/), *Harmony Square* (www.harmonysquare.game/), *Cat Park* (www.catpark.game/) and *Go Viral!* (www.goviralgame.com/) games.
Credit: TILT (www.tiltstudio.co/).

Global Engagement Center) and *Go Viral!* (about COVID-19 misinformation, funded by the UK Cabinet Office as part of a joint international campaign with the World Health Organization and United Nations; see GCSI, 2021). *Cat Park* won the 2023 Games for Change Award for "best civics game." Some games have been developed and tested but not yet publicly launched as of this writing: *Join This Group* (about misinformation on direct messaging apps, funded by WhatsApp), *Radicalise* (about recruitment strategies used by extremist organizations), *Bad Vaxx* (about vaccine misinformation, funded by the American Psychological Association and the US CDC), and *VaxBN* (about communicating with vaccine-hesitant patients, funded by the European Commission). Figure 8.2 shows screenshots of the landing pages of some of these games.

When *Bad News* was launched, we implemented a short survey within the game as a first test of the game's effectiveness as a way to improve people's ability to spot misinformation. The study design was simple: we showed people a series of Twitter posts at the start of the game. Two of these posts were normal tweets containing no misinformation techniques. The others were manipulative, in the sense that they made use of one of the manipulation techniques people learned about in the game. We asked *Bad News* players who agreed to take the survey to evaluate the reliability of each tweet on a 1–7 scale: 1 meant "very unreliable," and 7 meant "very reliable." After giving each tweet a rating, players progressed through the game as normal. At the end, we showed them the same tweets again, and again asked them to evaluate each tweet on the same 1–7 scale. Our idea was that if the game worked as intended, people should find manipulative tweets less reliable after playing than before, but not the "real" tweets (which didn't contain any misinformation), for which we expected ratings not to change, or at least not much. We were lucky: over the period of a month or two, about 15,000 people took the in-game survey. The results are shown in Figure 8.3.

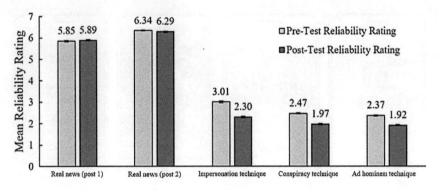

FIGURE 8.3 Reliability ratings of non-misinformation tweets (Real news post 1 and post 2) and misinformation-containing tweets (impersonation, conspiracy, and ad hominem techniques) before (pre-test) and after (post-test) playing the *Bad News* game. Error bars (barely visible due to the large sample size) represent 95 percent confidence intervals. *Source:* Adapted from Roozenbeek and van der Linden (2019).

Figure 8.3 shows that people found the tweets that contained some form of misinformation significantly less reliable after playing than before, whereas there was (almost) no change for the tweets that contained no misinformation. This was as we had hypothesized, and we published our results in the journal *Humanities and Social Sciences Communications* (Roozenbeek & van der Linden, 2019). However, this study design had some considerable limitations: there was no control group (the same people rated the tweets before and after playing), and we only asked people to evaluate a total of six different tweets, which made it difficult to generalize the findings.

To address these shortcomings, Melisa Basol, then a Ph.D. student in Cambridge (funded by the Gates Foundation[6]), led a randomized controlled study where she first had participants evaluate the reliability of a total of twenty-one tweets, three without misinformation and eighteen containing some form of misinformation (three tweets for each of the six techniques people lean about in the game). Participants were then assigned to either play the *Bad News* game or *Tetris* (which served as our control intervention). After this, participants again evaluated the same twenty-one tweets. Melisa found that people who played *Bad News* rated misinformation-containing tweets as much less reliable after playing than before, compared to the control group. In addition, *Bad News* players became significantly more confident in their ability to spot misinformation (which is useful because, if you're not very confident in your own abilities, you might be more easily manipulated). These results were again in line with our hypotheses, and provided further corroboration that the *Bad News* game made

---

[6] And no, neither Melisa nor the Gates foundation is putting microchips in your vaccines.

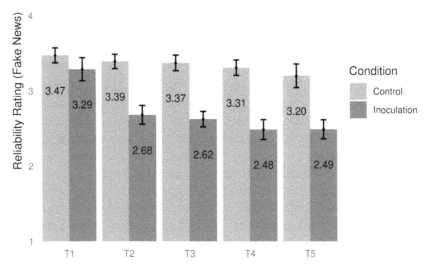

FIGURE 8.4 Reliability ratings of misinformation-containing tweets (averaged) for the inoculation (*Bad News*) and control (*Tetris*) conditions, before the intervention (T1), immediately after (T2), 1 week after (T3), 5 weeks after (T4), and 13 weeks after (T5). Error bars show 95 percent confidence intervals.
Source: Reprinted from Maertens, R., Roozenbeek, J., Basol, M., & van der Linden, S. (2021). Long-term effectiveness of inoculation against misinformation: Three longitudinal experiments. *Journal of Experimental Psychology: General, 27*(1), 1–16. With permission from American Psychological Association.

people substantially more skeptical of tweets containing misinformation (Basol et al., 2020).

Rakoen Maertens (now at the University of Oxford, whose work we also mentioned in Chapter 4), who was then a Ph.D. student in Cambridge as well, wrote his doctoral dissertation on the long-term effectiveness of inoculation interventions (Maertens, 2022). He ran a series of studies with more or less the same design as Melisa's (also with a *Bad News* and a *Tetris* group), but conducted regular follow-ups for two months after people played the game, where the same participants were again asked to evaluate a series of tweets (Maertens et al., 2021; Maertens, Roozenbeek, et al., 2023). The idea was to test if the inoculation effect we found immediately after gameplay remained detectable over time, and for how long. Rakoen found that the inoculation effect (the reduction in the reliability of misinformation-containing tweets) remained significant not only immediately after playing *Bad News*, but also one week, five weeks, and even thirteen weeks post-gameplay. However, the effect was gone after thirteen weeks for a group who had played the game but was not retested at all until thirteen weeks after. See Figure 8.4. In one of his studies, Rakoen also looked at the non-misinformation-containing tweets ("real news"). He found that people also became slightly more skeptical of real information in the first two studies he conducted. However, in a third study, he found that when he administered an equal number of misinformation and "real news" tweets that people are asked to evaluate, then there was no decrease in the reliability of "real news." More on this later.

Because the *Bad News* game kept attracting new players, we could keep collecting data via the in-game survey tool. We used this opportunity to run further studies and address reasonable critiques: we tested if there was still an effect if you asked people to evaluate *different* tweets before and after playing (rather than the same ones), finding that, while this did reduce the inoculation effect, it remained detectable (Roozenbeek, Maertens, et al., 2021). We also did a study where we showed people tweets with misinformation that had actually gone viral online instead of tweets that we made up ourselves, finding that the inoculation effect was very similar (Roozenbeek, Traberg, et al., 2022). One important nuance that emerged from this study is that the inoculation effect was much smaller for misinformation that didn't make explicit use of any of the manipulation techniques from the game; this means that we can't expect the game to work on any and all manipulation techniques, only the ones that people are inoculated against while playing. The rest is bonus or so-called "cross-protection" (kind of like a vaccine that protects against somewhat related strains but loses efficacy against others; see Parker et al., 2016). Because the *Bad News* game was translated into several languages, we also managed to collect survey data from Greece, Germany, Poland, and Sweden, finding the same pattern of results as we did for the English version (Roozenbeek, van der Linden, et al., 2020).

The other games we helped develop also allowed us to explore a bunch of open research questions about inoculation theory and misinformation interventions in general. For example, for the *Bad Vaxx* game, about vaccine misinformation, we (together with Melisa Basol, Ruth Elisabeth Appel from Stanford, and Becky Rayburn-Reeves and Jonathan Corbin, from Duke University) not only found that people who played the game were significantly better than a control group at discerning manipulative claims and neutral statements about vaccines, but also that game players became much better at correctly identifying which specific manipulation techniques were used in misleading social media posts about vaccinations. We also replicated our findings from prior studies for several other games using preregistered randomized designs: *Go Viral!* (Basol et al., 2021), *Radicalise* (Saleh et al., 2021, 2023), *Harmony Square* (Roozenbeek & van der Linden, 2020), and *Cat Park* (Neylan et al., 2023).[7] Two of our colleagues, Thomas Nygren and Carl-Anton Axelsson (Uppsala University), also ran tests with the *Bad News* game in Swedish high schools, to see if there are

---

[7] Preregistrations and making your data publicly available are trending topics in psychological science. This way, people can critique, check, reanalyze, and improve others' work whenever possible. For example, Geoff Cumming did a reanalysis of Melisa's 2020 study for his blog The New Statistics (Cumming, 2021).

benefits to playing the game in pairs or in a competitive classroom setting, as opposed to playing it alone; they found that, although the game boosted veracity discernment across all three conditions, students who played the game as part of a classroom competition found the game more interesting and fun than students who played it alone or in pairs (Axelsson et al., 2023).

This work was really fun and interesting to do, but games do have some noteworthy limitations as anti-misinformation interventions. First of all, they require that people opt into playing. This is a pretty big hurdle to overcome: most people have never played *Tetris*, for example (despite our best efforts by including it as a control intervention in many of our studies), which is probably one of the most famous video games ever made. But perhaps more importantly, they're difficult to scale on social media: only so many people would ever consider playing an educational game, and some people might not find *Bad News* or other games all that entertaining.[8] Humor also translates poorly, and there's no guarantee that what worked in English and other languages spoken in Western Europe will work elsewhere (more on that below). Also, creating and testing games is expensive and difficult, and they require constant maintenance.

We had been talking to Jigsaw (a research unit within Google) about adapting *Bad News* for a wider audience for some time, but to no avail. In 2020, our colleague Stephan Lewandowsky (University of Bristol) was also talking to Jigsaw about how to make inoculation interventions more scalable. We decided to join forces and collaboratively think through some ideas with Beth Goldberg, now Head of Research at Jigsaw (who has been a tremendous force in commissioning rigorous research to evaluate prebunking approaches at-scale across different universities and platforms). We decided to create short inoculation videos, each of which explaining a particular common manipulation technique in under ninety seconds. The idea was that these kinds of videos can be easily rolled out on social media, for example as YouTube ads (Google owns YouTube) or as PSA campaigns on Facebook or Twitter, potentially reaching millions of people. To do this, we enlisted the help of Luke Newbold and Sean Sears at Studio You London (https://studioyou.london/), a company that designs cool animated videos (among other things). Figure 8.5 shows screenshots from all the inoculation videos Luke and Sean have created so far.

We first ran a series of large randomized controlled trials with five of the videos from Figure 8.5, to test if watching the video (compared to watching a control video about something unrelated, like freezer burn) improved people's ability to discern misinformation from real news (Roozenbeek, van der Linden, et al., 2022). This turned out to be the case for all of them, and with

---

[8]   Also, we sometimes get tired listening to conference talks for fifteen minutes, so how can we expect *Bad News* players to pay attention for that long?

FIGURE 8.5 Overview of misinformation videos. The emotional language, false dilemmas, incoherence, scapegoating, and ad hominem videos were made together with Jigsaw. The conspiracies, fake experts, and polarization videos were commissioned by the UK Cabinet Office. The moving the goalposts, straw man fallacy, and whataboutism videos were funded jointly by the Irish Ministry of Foreign Affairs and the US Global Engagement Center, and developed together with Eileen Culloty, Jane Suiter, Kurt Braddock, and Mikey Biddlestone.

substantial effect sizes.[9] On top of that, we found that the videos were effective across the political spectrum, and even for people who are more susceptible to believing misinformation. But as we discussed in Chapter 7, lab results don't necessarily translate to the real world (DellaVigna & Linos, 2022). To test if the videos were also effective in a social media setting, Google enabled us to run a large YouTube ad campaign with two of the videos (emotional language and false dichotomies), where we showed about 1 million Americans who liked to watch political news one of the videos as a regular YouTube ad (usually this ad space is reserved for brand recognition polls, not scientific research). Some of these people were shown a single survey question (about eighteen hours after seeing the ad), in which they were asked to identify which (if any) manipulation technique was used in a headline. We administered six headlines in total (three per video). See Figure 8.6.

There was also a control group, which didn't see any inoculation videos as an ad but did get a survey question. This design allowed us to compare the proportion of correct responses in the treatment group and the control group for each survey question. In the end, we managed to collect about 22,000 responses (11,000 per group). The results are shown in Figure 8.7.

---

[9] About effect sizes: the average Cohen's d (the standardized difference between the inoculation and the control group for how good people are at correctly identifying a manipulation technique) was about $d = 0.50$, which is classified as a medium effect size.

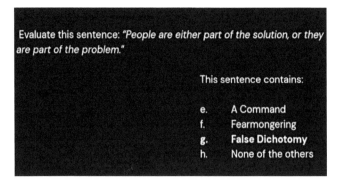

FIGURE 8.6 Example of a survey question from our YouTube field study (Roozenbeek, van der Linden et al., 2022).

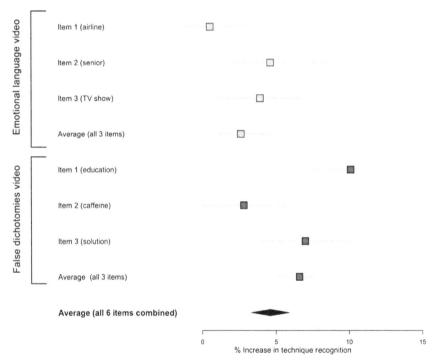

FIGURE 8.7 Results from our YouTube field study. The figure shows the average percent increase in correctly identified manipulation techniques for the treatment (video inoculation) group compared to the control group, for each item (headline) and averaged per video and overall. The figure shows that Item 1 (airline) overlaps with 0, indicating that there is no difference between the treatment and control group. All other items (with the exception of the caffeine item for the false dichotomies video) are significantly higher than 0, indicating that the treatment group gave the right answer significantly more often than the control group. Error bars show 95 percent confidence intervals.
Source: Taken from Roozenbeek, van der Linden et al. (2022).

This study demonstrated that showing inoculation videos as YouTube ads boosted people's ability to correctly identify manipulation techniques, even in a setting where they're free to not pay any attention to the videos. We found this result encouraging: apparently, the results from our lab studies could be replicated in a completely different setting, which bodes well for the potential of inoculation videos as a scalable intervention to reduce susceptibility to misinformation. Since this study was published in August 2022, Jigsaw has used a similar approach to counter disinformation about Ukrainian refugees in Poland, Slovakia, and the Czech Republic, reaching large numbers of social media users in each country with some encouraging results (Jigsaw, 2023). YouTube also created its own ad campaign with short prebunking videos inspired by this work, called Hit Pause. We've since also created a number of new videos (see Figure 8.5), all of which can be found on our website about inoculation theory and its application: www.inoculation.science/.

8.3 SIDE EFFECTS?

So far, so good; the inoculation games and videos seemed to work well, and (in part owing to luck and various kinds of privilege) our work was getting more attention from fellow scientists, tech companies, and the public than we had anticipated. However, like in medicine, no intervention is fully risk-free. Based on the feedback we have collected over the years, we noticed several things that could be improved that are important to consider for our work and misinformation intervention research more generally going forward. We'll discuss the games first, and the videos second.

8.3.1 The Games

First of all, it proved to be incredibly challenging to make the games work outside of Western contexts. Melisa Basol led a project funded by WhatsApp where we tested a Hindi-language version of the Join This Group game on a local sample in rural parts of India, in collaboration with the Digital Empowerment Foundation (DEF). We had tested the game on a UK sample before, and it worked fine (about the same as the other games). However, when we ran the study in India, we found no inoculation (or any) effects whatsoever. Trisha Harjani (then a research assistant at our lab) led the publication of this study (Harjani et al., 2023). By looking at the comments that study participants had given us, Trisha found that, while people sort of understood the purpose of the game they were playing, they didn't find it very useful or entertaining. There was also the problem that our participants weren't used to taking the kinds of survey we were administering, which meant that some people didn't know what was expected of them. Trisha concluded that "the typical data quality, representativeness, and methodological best practices for running such online experiments in India, and [non-Western] countries in general, is poorly understood and can impede the experimental process." Another issue was that we had to make substantial changes to the game for the Hindi localization, as the local organization we were working with was (rightly) concerned that our relatively "urban," nontraditional, and Western-style approach wouldn't resonate with citizens in rural India, where the situation was also more politically sensitive. Although we had a local partner, we (meaning Sander and Jon) had still seriously underestimated the complexity of doing studies in countries we didn't understand very well, and mistakenly assumed that what we believed works in Western settings should also work elsewhere.

But even in the US, a study we did led by Isobel Harrop (with Jens Madsen from the London School of Economics) showed mediocre results: in one out of three studies included in the publication (Harrop et al., 2023), the *Bad News* game did very little (although it did do something) to boost people's ability to spot misinformation. This could be due to problems with the sample quality (Prolific, our survey panel provider, was flooded by teenage girls for a while after a TikTok post went viral) or technical problems with the implementation of the survey, but this isn't entirely clear. Nonetheless, there was also some good news. Ananya Iyengar and colleagues (2022) conducted a replication of an earlier study of ours on a sample of urban (not rural) residents in India, and found positive effects on people ability to discern misinformation from real information. And in another study, led by Nabil Saleh (B4Development and Nudge Lebanon), we tested the *Radicalise* game (about manipulation techniques used by recruiters working for extremist organizations) on a sample of young people from areas of north Iraq previously under ISIS control (Saleh et al., 2023). We managed to replicate most (but not all) of the main effects from a previous study with the *Radicalise* game in the UK (Saleh et al., 2021), albeit at a much smaller effect size. Overall, we took this to mean that the delivery method of misinformation interventions matters a lot: a great deal of knowledge and expertise is needed to tailor interventions to different audiences.

More importantly, some scholars have pointed out significant nuances with respect to the effect of our inoculation games on people's evaluation of "real news" (i.e., news or social media content that doesn't contain any misinformation; see Chapter 1 for a discussion). Ariana Modirrousta-Galian and Phil Higham, from the University of Southampton, reanalyzed the data from five studies we'd published up until then using the *Bad News* and *Go Viral!* games (Modirrousta-Galian & Higham, 2023). Using an analytical approach called signal detection theory, they found that although some of our studies revealed significant positive effects on people's ability to discern between misinformation and real news, others didn't, so that the games basically "do not improve discrimination between true and fake news." Their analysis showed that the randomized controlled trials we'd conducted (Basol et al., 2020, 2021; Maertens et al., 2021) demonstrated that, rather than boosting recognition of misinformation alone, *Bad News* and *Go Viral!* players became more skeptical of true information ("real news") as well. In other words, their ability to distinguish true information from misinformation didn't increase (much) as a result of the game. Ariana and Phil argue in their paper that this result could be concerning because the games may inadvertently increase people's distrust in legitimate information: "reduced belief in true news can potentially have devastating consequences (e.g., rejecting the scientific truth that vaccines are important for personal and global health)" (p. 24). Furthermore, a team of students led by Stephen Lindsay conducted a series of four independent replications of an earlier *Bad News* study (Basol et al., 2020). Although they replicated the results from the original study, they also tested if playing the game made people more skeptical of real news (Graham et al., 2023). Their findings were largely in line with Ariana's and Phil's: in all four studies, the *Bad News* game made people more skeptical of misinformation as well as of "real" news, although in one of them the game did boost discriminative ability.

When we read these papers, we broadly agreed with much of this criticism, but also noted some important nuances, which we'll explain here. For instance, the argument that playing the *Bad News* game could cause people to suddenly stop believing in vaccines or climate change struck us as somewhat hyperbolic (also because there's no evidence that this is the case). More generally, the idea expressed by Michael Hameleers (2023) that prebunking interventions, even if they're entirely benign and well-meaning, may have "a negative impact on people's trust in factually accurate information and authentic news," relies (in our view) on set of rather pessimistic assumptions about human psychology and behavior: Is merely playing a simple game or reading a set of uncontroversial tips on how to spot misinformation really all it takes to reduce overall trust in accurate information enough to cause problems for society? This seems unlikely. Another explanation for this effect may be that making the concept of misinformation more salient in people's minds (temporarily) increases vigilance and therefore overall skepticism in treatment groups; this would be interesting but not necessarily problematic. In other words, interventions act as a starting point for critical thinking, but learning is more complicated than a one-off interaction with an intervention. This would also explain why the negative impact of anti-misinformation interventions on real news is not specific to games or inoculation per se, but appears to be a common side effect of many types of media literacy intervention (K. Clayton et al., 2020; M. Green et al., 2022; Guess et al., 2020; Hameleers, 2023; van der Meer et al., 2023).

Also, we noted that quite a few studies *did* show that the *Bad News* game and other games improved discriminative ability between real news and misinformation, as illustrated in Figure 8.3 above (e.g., Appel et al., 2023; Basol et al., 2021 Study 1; Iyengar et al., 2022; Ma et al., 2023; Maertens et al., 2021 Study 3; Roozenbeek & van der Linden, 2019). The studies that didn't (Basol et al., 2020, 2021 Study 2; Graham et al., 2023 Studies 1–3 but not study 4; Maertens et al.,

2021 Studies 1 and 2) all used a similar design: rating a large number of real and misinformation-containing social media posts both before (pre-test) and after the intervention (post-test). On the other hand, studies that used a pre-post design without a control group (e.g., Basol et al., 2021 Study 1; Roozenbeek & van der Linden, 2019) and studies without a pre-test and only a post-test (Appel et al., 2023) tend to show good effects of the games on discriminative ability. Whether you use balanced item sets (with equal numbers of misinformation and "real news" tweets) also seems to matter for whether you find improved discrimination. The way the studies are designed may therefore impact whether improved discriminative ability is observed. Nonetheless, an external meta-analysis (Lu et al., 2023) of inoculation studies found that overall, our interventions produce significant effects on truth discernment (d = 0.20).

Furthermore, it's not entirely correct to say that the inoculation games (or any other interventions, for that matter) make people more skeptical of *all* true information: their evaluations of obviously true information are unaffected (Modirrousta-Galian & Higham, 2023). Instead, the effect was largest for tweets containing true but ambiguous information (see Figure 1.5): that is, tweets that may be true but that people find somewhat implausible. If this is the case, and the games make people more skeptical of ambiguous information in general (even if it may be true), does this really mean that they have adverse consequences? What if this skepticism motivates people to search out more information about a (true) headline or article?

It's also true that the use of negative emotions (including fearmongering) has increased by over 100 percent in (US) mainstream media in the last decades relative to neutral content (Rozado et al., 2022); so perhaps people are merely correct in detecting that some "real news" also uses sensationalist techniques. After all, no scalable intervention can teach people facts about the world, only evaluation strategies (see also our discussion on "real news" in Chapter 1). When a person's media environment makes use of these fingerprints of misinformation, people may be more likely to notice it regardless of what is labelled as true news or misinformation. In short, healthy skepticism of the information we consume, we think at least, doesn't have to be bad; this only becomes a problem when skepticism turns into unhealthy cynicism, where people come to believe that nothing is true and reliable sources don't exist. If this is ever a consequence of any well-intended anti-misinformation intervention, it's probably rare: one study found that media literacy interventions may impact evaluations of credible headlines but not actually reduce trust in democracy or official institutions (Hoes et al., 2023). As we've argued in Chapter 3, sustained belief or attitude change is an unlikely consequence of consuming *any* single piece of information, let alone interventions that are designed to be beneficial (see also the discussion on backfire effects by Swire-Thompson et al., 2020; Wood & Porter, 2019).

Finally, it is important to assign the appropriate outcome measure to the purpose of an intervention (Guay et al., 2023): is it to boost people's ability to identify misinformation, to boost trust in true information, or perhaps both?

If you look at the history of the literature on conspiracy theories, for example, you find that most studies do not include measures of discernment between conspiratorial and non-conspiratorial claims (O'Mahony et al., 2023). Efficacy is established when the intervention does what it claims it does: reduce people's endorsement of conspiracy theories. Of course, it's legitimate to ask whether the intervention also makes people more suspicious of their neighbors, the mainstream media, or hundreds of other types of information sources: after all, a hypothetical intervention that tells people to not trust any information at all and be skeptical of everything they see (*especially* ivory tower psychologists such as ourselves) may effectively reduce belief in misinformation, but can hardly be called "effective" because the potential side effects are obvious. In other words, it's good to be careful about what an intervention actually teaches people.

That said, reasonable people can have very different opinions about the "right" level of skepticism toward news or information. After all of these discussions, we partially but not fully agreed with the criticism, but that doesn't mean the games were perfect or that we couldn't do anything to improve them. In fact, one advantage of the games is that we can change and improve them based on the feedback we receive from both the public and our colleagues. We therefore decided to find ways to improve the games' performance and reduce skepticism of real news and true information. One idea, which was proposed to us by Johannes Leder and Lukas Valentin Schellinger from the University of Bamberg, was to give players feedback on their ability to distinguish true news from misinformation in the game itself. The idea was that this would help consolidate the lessons learned in the game, which would (in theory) not only improve discriminative ability but also boost the longevity of the inoculation effect. Johannes and Lukas led two preregistered lab studies in which they indeed found that this was the case: including a short feedback exercise made *Bad News* players much better at correctly identifying both true news and misinformation, compared to playing the game without feedback (Leder et al., 2023). Also, the feedback led to measurably increased performance one week after playing the game.

After these lab studies, we set out to test how well the feedback tool worked in the *Harmony Square* and *Bad News* games themselves. We implemented simple feedback exercises in both games: at the end of the final level, players are shown a couple of headlines, some of which contain simple facts and some using a manipulation technique featured in the game. They are asked to indicate if they find the headline misleading or not, and then get feedback on their performance: for example, if they identify a true headline as misleading, they lose points and are told something like "Nope! That's just a headline; be careful not to be overly skeptical." If they get it right, they're given positive feedback and gain additional points. See Figure 8.8 for an example of what this feedback looks like in the *Bad News* game.

FIGURE 8.8   Examples of the feedback exercise in the *Bad News* game, with a neutral (top left) and misinformation (conspiracy technique, top right) headline, and a technique identification task (bottom left) and feedback after a correct answer (bottom right).
Credit: TILT (https://tiltstudio.co/).

We then also implemented a pre-post survey in both the *Harmony Square* and *Bad News* games to assess players' ability to distinguish true news from misinformation, and compare these effects for when the feedback tool was active in the game versus when it was turned off. The results were in line with the findings from the lab studies by Johannes and Lukas: discriminative ability improved substantially if you include the feedback tool,[10] and especially people's ability to identify true information. Encouragingly, these results were in line with a study testing an inoculation game we had no involvement in which incorporated similar feedback exercises, where the authors also found good effects on discriminative ability (Ma et al., 2023). These findings make sense from a psychological perspective as well: learning something works best if you apply the information you learned in some kind of task through active rehearsal (Bird et al., 2015). For example, reading about how to solve a differential equation works less well than also solving a few equations yourself as practice. So in the end, our games may have suffered from a design flaw in the form of a suboptimal learning environment, something which was fortunately easy to fix. Based on these findings, we now recommend that all misinformation

---

[10]   For example, for the *Harmony Square* game, the effect size for discriminative ability was about four times higher when the feedback tool was active than without feedback, a substantial improvement. We found pretty much the same for *Bad News*.

games implement a similar feedback exercise, to consolidate the lessons people learn in the game and apply them in a practical setting.

One possible downside is that the feedback exercise may make the game less entertaining, and more players may be inclined to drop out without finishing the game because they find the feedback task boring or annoying. We tried to mitigate this by integrating the feedback task with the rest of the game. Throughout *Bad News*, players are guided by a humorous but slightly mean moderator who tells them off if they make mistakes and gives them sarcastic compliments when they do well. This same moderator is in charge of the feedback task, asking players "If you're so smart, why don't you put those new 'skills' of yours to the test?" This, hopefully, feels natural enough to players that they don't mind going through the feedback exercise. That said, the game (like most individual-level misinformation interventions) relies entirely on people voluntarily deciding to engage with it, and there is an almost inevitable trade-off between maximizing playability and effectiveness.

8.3.2 The Videos

One important question that we were not able to address in our YouTube field study (Roozenbeek, van der Linden, et al., 2022) is if watching inoculation videos impacts how people behave online. It would be useful if the videos could also serve as a type of "nudge" (see Chapter 7) and, for example, improve the quality of the content that people share with others. So, for instance, the "emotional language" inoculation video (which is about evoking strong negative emotions to draw attention away from accuracy) might remind people that sharing emotionally manipulative content on social media could be harmful, and prevent them from sharing it. To see if this is the case, we collaborated with Jana Lasser (University of Graz), David Garcia (University of Konstanz), Stephan Lewandowsky (University of Bristol), and (again) Jigsaw to run a large Twitter ad campaign. We showed one group of Twitter users the emotional language inoculation video as a Twitter ad, and another group (the control group) an unrelated video. Jana then scraped the Twitter timelines of the users in both groups, and ran a series of sentiment classifiers on what people tweeted themselves, and what they shared and retweeted. This allowed us to compare the volume of tweets containing angry, sad, fearful, happy, and affectionate content between the inoculation and control groups. We hypothesized that people who saw the inoculation video ad would tweet and retweet less negative-emotional (sad, fearful, angry) content than the control group. The results are shown in Figure 8.9.

As you can see, there is absolutely no difference between the two groups. Across two separate studies, we found that there was no impact whatsoever of the inoculation video on what kinds of emotional content people shared with each other. However, there *may* have been a slight reduction in the number

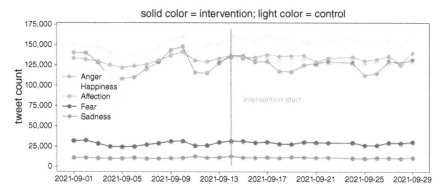

FIGURE 8.9 Results from our Twitter field study. The figure shows the tweet counts of tweets containing language related to anger, happiness, affection, fear, and sadness, for the intervention (inoculation video) and control groups, across September 2021. The vertical line marks the Twitter ad campaign start date. Figure created by Jana Lasser. *Source:* Taken from Roozenbeek, Lasser et al. (2023).

of retweets *overall,* in the sense that people who were shown an inoculation video appear to have reduced how much stuff they retweeted in general, for about a day or two (Roozenbeek, Lasser, et al., 2023). This would be in line with results from the Spot the Troll quiz study by Jeff Lees and colleagues (2023) mentioned in Chapter 7, which also found that people started tweeting and retweeting less content in general after taking the quiz, but more research is needed to verify this.

That said, our study was marred by several problems, not the least of which being Twitter's "fuzzy matching" policy: if you upload a list of Twitter usernames to the Twitter ad space and ask it to target them with an ad, Twitter only targets a random 30 percent of these users, and matches the rest based on a matching algorithm. This means that your ads only reach a maximum of 30 percent of the users you uploaded (in reality much less, because not everyone engages with an ad if they see it), which adds a huge amount of noise to the data and makes it complicated to do nuanced statistical analyses. Nonetheless, our study failed to show any meaningful impact of our interventions on people's behavior. Thus, while tackling misinformation *susceptibility* on social media seems attainable, reducing the sharing of unwanted content may be a substantially tougher challenge.

That said, some promising evidence of behavioral effects was found by Robert McPhedran and colleagues (2023), who assessed the effects of inoculation interventions on liking and sharing behavior in a simulated (not real!) social media environment. Not only did their inoculation intervention significantly reduce how much people engaged with misinformation posts, but it did so more effectively than content labels ("false" tags), and it also improved the quality of people's news sharing decisions. However, how these findings translate to actual social media environments is unclear; not only our study but also another one by Alexander Bor and colleagues (which tested if fact-checking videos reduce belief in and sharing of misinformation on Twitter) came up with negligible effects (Bor et al., 2021).

We came across another major limitation to our body of work very recently, when the first draft of this book was almost finished. Georgia Capewell, an undergraduate student in psychology at Cambridge, wanted to write her final dissertation on inoculation interventions. In search of a research question, Rakoen Maertens (Georgia's dissertation supervisor together with Jon and Sander) mentioned some interesting results from another study that he had just conducted (Maertens, Roozenbeek, et al., 2023): he found that if people watched an inoculation video and evaluated a series of social media posts directly after (an item rating task we use to assess if the intervention improves discrimination between manipulative and neutral social media content), then the longevity of the intervention was very good: ten and even thirty days after watching the video, inoculated participants were still significantly better than control group participants at distinguishing misinformation from non-misinformation. However, he also included a group that saw the inoculation video but *didn't* rate any social media posts immediately after viewing, and instead *only* did so ten days later. For this group, the inoculation effect was completely gone after ten days. Rakoen suspected that the social media post evaluation task itself played a role in the longevity of the intervention: similar to the feedback task we implemented in the games, maybe actively rehearsing the lessons from the video just after watching it substantially enhanced its effectiveness?

To test this, Georgia designed a study with two treatment groups (Capewell, 2023; Capewell et al., 2023). One group that watched an inoculation video (along with two unrelated videos), then immediately rated a series of social media posts, and then rated the same social media posts again forty-eight hours later. The second group watched the same videos but *only* rated the social media posts after forty-eight hours (and not immediately after). She also included two control groups, which were similar to the two treatment groups except they watched a set of unrelated videos. What she found was very interesting: while the group that rated the social media posts immediately after watching the video continued to perform much better on the same task than both control groups forty-eight hours after, the group that only rated the social media posts after forty-eight hours performed *exactly* the same as the control group, with not even a hint of an inoculation effect left.[11] This shows that, without any rehearsal, the effect conferred by the video disappears

---

[11]   For the statistically inclined: the *p*-value for the difference between this treatment group and the control group was about $p = 0.85$. *P*-values range between 0 and 1, with values *above* 0.05 usually being taken to mean that there is no significant difference between groups. In other words, the effect was *completely* gone.

completely within two days, whereas with rehearsal it can remain detectable for almost a month.[12] This is a serious potential problem. Apparently, what makes the intervention effective is the intervention itself *plus* active rehearsal. Watching a video is not enough: people need to apply the lessons from the video in some kind of exercise for it to become embedded in their long-term memory. Of course, educational psychologists have known about the importance of rehearsal in learning for years (Bird et al., 2015), and so the results from Georgia's study really should have been no surprise to us, but they were.

More generally, however, Georgia's findings have consequences not just for inoculation videos but for many kinds of misinformation interventions, which are almost exclusively assessed using item rating tasks administered immediately post-intervention. How can we be sure that interventions such as media literacy tips, PSA videos or infographics are effective over time if we haven't tested if the item rating tasks are what strengthens the intervention's longevity? And most importantly, rehearsal tasks are relatively easy to implement in games (see above) and other more intensive media literacy interventions (such as educational programs), but they don't scale well: it's difficult enough to entice people to watch an inoculation video as a YouTube or Twitter ad, but how many people are going to *also* voluntarily rehearse what they learned in a video straight after? We think this number is likely very small, which has serious implications for the scalability of misinformation interventions on social media.

Lastly, over the years we've collaborated with many parties, including Google, Meta, the UK and US governments, the WHO, and the United Nations. Much of our work with these funders has involved testing and implementing prebunking and inoculation at scale. Although we've been fortunate to benefit from these collaborations, one might argue it's good PR for governments and especially corporations to work with university researchers in order to be *seen* to be doing something about an important societal problem (especially, it should be acknowledged, if the university is well known; in PR world this adds to the perceived credibility of the research). But considering the rather modest impact of psychological interventions (including our own), how much do individual-level solutions actually help to counter misinformation at scale, particularly compared to system-level interventions (see Chapter 7)? In other words, doesn't this work steer attention away from potentially much more impactful solutions, such as taking down content and exploring potential changes to recommender algorithms (Albarracín et al., 2018; Alfano et al., 2021; Faddoul et al., 2020; Hosseinmardi et al., 2021;

[12] In the YouTube study that we mentioned earlier (Roozenbeek, van der Linden, et al., 2022), we assessed people's ability to identify misinformation an average of eighteen hours after seeing the video without any immediate rehearsal, and found significant effects; optimistically, this means that, without rehearsal, the inoculation effect most likely disappears somewhere between eighteen and forty-eight hours after viewing.

Nyhan et al., 2023)? Or, even worse, couldn't ethically questionable actors (e.g., authoritarian governments) be incentivized to draw on our work to "inoculate" people against "misinformation" that isn't really misinformation at all?

These kinds of critiques are important and worth reflecting on. To be sure, it's hard to deny that especially Google and Meta have made substantial policy changes in part thanks to our work: for example, by running inoculation video campaigns in countries around the world. It's possible if not likely that these companies decided to invest in video-based inoculation campaigns in part because they do not impact their business model and because they're politically palatable; simply pointing out how to spot common manipulation techniques is unlikely to evoke massive political backlash, even in a political climate where the term "disinformation" itself has become politicized.

Then again, fighting misinformation isn't an "either-or" type of problem. we need both system-level change and to empower individuals to spot misinformation and hold tech companies and governments accountable so that more systematic change becomes part of the policy agenda. It's also probably not completely fair to say that inoculation has *replaced* system-level solutions (as Google and Meta are signatories to the EU Disinformation Code of Practice, which contains all sorts of provisions on reducing mis- and disinformation at the system level). Also, as we discussed in Chapters 6 and 7, effective system-level solutions are hard to come by (Nyhan et al., 2023), especially ones that don't pose a potential risk for freedom of expression online. Particularly when it comes to the kinds of content that our interventions have tried to address (which is usually *misleading* rather than outright false), relatively light-touch measures such as inoculation and media/digital literacy might be our best shot, at least for now.

More broadly, this discussion is situated within a debate about the role of social psychology in society: when looking at a particular societal phenomenon, psychologists tend to focus on individual attitudes, beliefs, and behaviors, and the interventions they develop also tend to reflect this preference. But these interventions exist alongside work from other fields such as political science, computer science, and economics. In the end, effectively tackling misinformation inevitably involves a multilayered defense system that includes perspectives from numerous viewpoints and disciplines. To end with an (imperfect) analogy: working at a food bank doesn't address the systemic causes of poverty and inequality, but that doesn't mean it's not valuable.

8.4 CONCLUSION

In this chapter, we've discussed the ups and downs of our own program of research on misinformation, which has involved creating "fake news" games and videos to reduce susceptibility to various common types of manipulation. Looking back on over six years of work, we're happy to see that our interventions have reached quite a few people. However, as with any treatment, there are also side effects and limitations that practitioners and policymakers should weigh carefully: limited cross-cultural generalizability, in some cases an unintentional effect of game-based interventions on people's evaluation of "real news" (likely the consequence of an imperfectly designed learning environment, which we've addressed by implementing feedback exercises in the games), a negligible impact of inoculation interventions on people's sharing behavior, and perhaps most importantly (potentially rapid) decay over time and the presence of testing effects: actively rehearsing the lessons from the interventions (e.g., about how to spot a particular manipulation technique) appears to be important for their longevity and effectiveness. These limitations have implications for anyone who wants to design (and test) an intervention to counter misinformation, and we hope that this chapter has been helpful in this respect.

REFERENCES

Acerbi, A. (2019). Cognitive Attraction and Online Misinformation. *Humanities and Social Sciences Communications*, 5(1), 15. https://doi.org/10.1057/s41599-019-0224-y

Alaphilippe, A., Gizikis, A., Hanot, C., & Bontcheva, K. (2019). *Automated Tackling of Disinformation*. https://doi.org/10.2861/368879

Albarracín, D., Romer, D., Jones, C. R., Hall Jamieson, K., & Jamieson, P. (2018). Misleading Claims About Tobacco Products in YouTube Videos: Experimental Effects of Misinformation on Unhealthy Attitudes. *Journal of Medical Internet Research*, 20(6), e229. https://doi.org/10.2196/jmir.9959

Alfano, M., Fard, A. E., Carter, J. A., Clutton, P., & Klein, C. (2021). Technologically Scaffolded Atypical Cognition: The Case of YouTube's Recommender System. *Synthese*, 199, 835–858. https://doi.org/10.1007/s11229-020-02724-x

Ali, A., & Qazi, I. A. (2021). Countering Misinformation on Social Media Through Educational Interventions: Evidence from a Randomized Experiment in Pakistan. *ArXiv Preprint*. https://doi.org/10.48550/arXiv.2107.02775

Allcott, H., & Gentzkow, M. (2017). Social Media and Fake News in the 2016 Election. *Journal of Economic Perspectives*, 31(2), 211–236. https://doi.org/10.1257/jep.31.2.211

Allen, J., Howland, B., Mobius, M., Rothschild, D., & Watts, D. J. (2020). Evaluating the Fake News Problem at the Scale of the Information Ecosystem. *Science Advances*, 6(14). https://doi.org/10.1126/sciadv.aay3539

Altay, S. (2022). How Effective Are Interventions against Misinformation? *PsyArxiv Preprints*. https://doi.org/10.31234/osf.io/sm3vk

Altay, S., Berriche, M., & Acerbi, A. (2022). Misinformation on Misinformation: Conceptual and Methodological Challenges. *PsyArxiv Preprints*. https://doi.org/10.31234/osf.io/edqc8

Altay, S., Berriche, M., Heuer, H., Farkas, J., & Rathje, S. (2023). A Survey of Expert Views on Misinformation: Definitions, Determinants, Solutions, and Future of the Field. *Harvard Kennedy School Misinformation Review*. https://doi.org/10.37016/mr-2020-119

Altay, S., de Araujo, E., & Mercier, H. (2022). "If This Account Is True, It Is Most Enormously Wonderful": Interestingness-If-True and the Sharing of True and False News. *Digital Journalism*, 10(3), 373–394. https://doi.org/10.1080/21670811.2021.1941163

Altay, S., Hacquin, A.-S., & Mercier, H. (2022). Why Do So Few People Share Fake News? It Hurts their Reputation. *New Media & Society*, 24(6), 1303–1324. https://doi.org/10.1177/1461444820969893

Altay, S., & Mercier, H. (2021). Happy Thoughts: The Role of Communion in Accepting and Sharing Epistemically Suspect Beliefs. *British Journal of Social Psychology*, 62(4), 1672–1692. https://doi.org/10.1111/bjso.12650

Amnesty International. (2015). *Ukraine: Homophobic Violence Mars Gay Pride Rally in Kyiv.* www.amnesty.org/en/latest/news/2015/06/homophobic-violence-mars-gay-pride-rally-in-kyiv/

Andı, S., & Akesson, J. (2021). Nudging Away False News: Evidence from a Social Norms Experiment. *Digital Journalism*, 9(1), 106–125. https://doi.org/10.1080/21670811.2020.1847674

Anti-Defamation League. (2019). *ADL Global 100: Eastern Europe.* https://global100.adl.org/map/eeurope

Appel, R. E., Roozenbeek, J., Rayburn-Reeves, R., Basol, M., Corbin, J., Compton, J., & van der Linden, S. (2023). Psychological Inoculation Improves Resilience to and Reduces Willingness to Share Vaccine Misinformation. *Under Review.*

Aral, S. (2022, April 6). Fake News about Our Fake News Study Spread Faster than Its Truth… Just as We Predicted. *Medium.* https://sinanaral.medium.com/fake-news-about-our-fake-news-study-spread-faster-than-its-truth-just-as-we-predicted-77db6d9ca8c8

Arechar, A., Allen, J., Berinsky, A. J., Cole, R., Epstein, Z., Garimella, K., Gully, A., Lu, J. G., Ross, R. M., Stagnaro, M. N., Zhang, Y., Pennycook, G., & Rand, D. (2022). Understanding and Reducing Online Misinformation Across 16 Countries on Six Continents. *PsyArxiv Preprints.* https://doi.org/10.31234/osf.io/a9frz

Article 19. (2023, March 3). *Turkey: Internet Throttling Violates Human Rights.* www.article19.org/resources/turkey-internet-throttling-violates-human-rights/

Arun, C. (2019). On WhatsApp, Rumours, and Lynchings. *Economic & Political Weekly*, 54(6).

Aslett, K., Guess, A. M., Bonneau, R., Nagler, J., & Tucker, J. A. (2022). News Credibility Labels Have Limited Average Effects on News Diet Quality and Fail to Reduce Misperceptions. *Science Advances*, 8(18). https://doi.org/10.1126/sciadv.abl3844

Athey, S., Cersosimo, M., Koutout, K., & Li, Z. (2023). Emotion-versus Reasoning-Based Drivers of Misinformation Sharing: A Field Experiment Using Text Message Courses in Kenya. *SSRN Electronic Journal.* https://doi.org/10.2139/ssrn.4489759

Axelsson, C.-A. W., Guath, M., & Nygren, T. (2021). Learning How to Separate Fake from Real News: Scalable Digital Tutorials Promoting Students' Civic Online Reasoning. *Future Internet*, 13(3), 60. https://doi.org/10.3390/fi13030060

Axelsson, C.-A. W., Nygren, T., Roozenbeek, J., & van der Linden, S. (2023). How Can a Serious Game against Misinformation Be Used in Classrooms? Impact and Effects of Collaboration and Competition. *Under Review.*

Badawy, A., Addawood, A., Lerman, K., & Ferrara, E. (2019). Characterizing the 2016 Russian IRA Influence Campaign. *Social Network Analysis and Mining*, 9(1), 31. https://doi.org/10.1007/s13278-019-0578-6

Badrinathan, S. (2021). Educative Interventions to Combat Misinformation: Evidence from a Field Experiment in India. *American Political Science Review*, 115(4), 1325–1341. https://doi.org/10.1017/S0003055421000459

Bakshy, E., Messing, S., & Adamic, L. A. (2015). Exposure to Ideologically Diverse News and Pinion on Facebook. *Science, 348*(6239), 1130–1132. https://doi.org/10.1126/science.aaa1160

Banas, J. A., & Miller, G. (2013). Inducing Resistance to Conspiracy Theory Propaganda: Testing Inoculation and Metainoculation Strategies. *Human Communication Research, 39*(2), 184–207. https://doi.org/10.1111/hcre.12000

Banas, J. A., & Rains, S. A. (2010). A Meta-Analysis of Research on Inoculation Theory. *Communication Monographs, 77*(3), 281–311. https://doi.org/10.1080/03637751003758193

Banchik, A. V. (2021). Disappearing acts: Content Moderation and Emergent Practices to Preserve at-Risk Human Rights–related Content. *New Media & Society, 23*(6), 1527–1544. https://doi.org/10.1177/1461444820912724

Bannon, V. C. (2019). *Free Speech and the Regulation of Social Media Content.* https://crsreports.congress.gov/product/pdf/R/R45650

Bannon, V. C. (2022). *False Speech and the First Amendment: Constitutional Limits on Regulating Misinformation.*

Baptista, J. P., & Gradim, A. (2022). Who Believes in Fake News? Identification of Political (A)Symmetries. *Social Sciences, 11*(10), 460. https://doi.org/10.3390/socsci11100460

Barberá, P. (2015). Birds of the Same Feather Tweet Together: Bayesian Ideal Point Estimation Using Twitter Data. *Political Analysis, 23*(1), 76–91. https://doi.org/10.1093/pan/mpu011

Barberá, P., Jost, J. T., Nagler, J., Tucker, J. A., & Bonneau, R. (2015). Tweeting From Left to Right: Is Online Political Communication More Than an Echo Chamber? *Psychological Science, 26*(10), 1531–1542. https://doi.org/10.1177/0956797615594620

Baron, J. (2019). Actively Open-minded Thinking in Politics. *Cognition, 188*, 8–18. https://doi.org/10.1016/j.cognition.2018.10.004

Baron, J., Scott, S., Fincher, K., & Emlen Metz, S. (2015). Why Does the Cognitive Reflection Test (Sometimes) Predict Utilitarian Moral Judgment (and Other Things)? *Journal of Applied Research in Memory and Cognition, 4*(3), 265–284. https://doi.org/10.1016/j.jarmac.2014.09.003

Bartels, M. (2023, February 22). Why Google's Supreme Court Case Could Rattle the Internet. *Scientific American.* www.scientificamerican.com/article/why-googles-supreme-court-case-could-rattle-the-internet/

Basol, M., Roozenbeek, J., Berriche, M., Uenal, F., McClanahan, W., & van der Linden, S. (2021). Towards Psychological Herd Immunity: Cross-cultural Evidence for Two Prebunking Interventions against COVID-19 Misinformation. *Big Data and Society, 8*(1). https://doi.org/10.1177/20539517211013868

Basol, M., Roozenbeek, J., & van der Linden, S. (2020). Good News about Bad News: Gamified Inoculation Boosts Confidence and Cognitive Immunity against Fake News. *Journal of Cognition, 3*(1), 1–9. https://doi.org/10.5334/joc.91

Bastos, M., Mercea, D., & Baronchelli, A. (2018). The Geographic Embedding of online Echo Chambers: Evidence from the Brexit Campaign. *PLOS ONE, 13*(11), e0206841. https://doi.org/10.1371/journal.pone.0206841

BBC News. (2012). *China Paper Carries Onion Kim Jong-un "heart-throb" Spoof.* www.bbc.com/news/world-asia-20518929

BBC News. (2018, July 19). *How WhatsApp Helped Turn an Indian Village into a Lynch Mob*. www.bbc.com/news/world-asia-india-44856910

BBC News. (2021). *Covid: Biden Orders Investigation into Virus Origin as Lab Leak Theory Debated*. www.bbc.com/news/world-us-canada-57260009

Becket, S. (2023, July 28). UFO Hearing Key Takeaways: What a Whistleblower Told Congress about UAPs. *CBS News*. www.cbsnews.com/news/ufo-hearing-congress-uap-takeaways-whistleblower-conference-david-grusch-2023/

Beene, S., & Greer, K. (2021). A call to Action for Librarians: Countering Conspiracy Theories in the Age of QAnon. *The Journal of Academic Librarianship*, *47*(1), 102292. https://doi.org/10.1016/j.acalib.2020.102292

Beever, S. (2022, September 16). King Charles Related to "real Dracula" Vlad the Impaler Who Butchered Enemies with Stake. *The Mirror*. www.mirror.co.uk/news/weird-news/king-charles-related-real-dracula-28008188

Bergsma, L. J., & Carney, M. E. (2008). Effectiveness of Health-promoting Media Literacy Education: A Systematic Review. *Health Education Research*, *23*(3), 522–542. https://doi.org/10.1093/her/cym084

Berinsky, A. J. (2018). Telling the Truth about Believing the Lies? Evidence for the Limited Prevalence of Expressive Survey Responding. *The Journal of Politics*, *80*(1). https://doi.org/10.1086/694258

Berlinski, N., Doyle, M., Guess, A. M., Levy, G., Lyons, B., Montgomery, J. M., Nyhan, B., & Reifler, J. (2023). The Effects of Unsubstantiated Claims of Voter Fraud on Confidence in Elections. *Journal of Experimental Political Science*, *10*(1), 34–49. https://doi.org/10.1017/XPS.2021.18

Berriche, M., & Altay, S. (2020). Internet Users Engage more with Phatic Posts than with Health Misinformation on Facebook. *Humanities and Social Sciences Communications*, *6*(1), 1–9. https://doi.org/10.1057/s41599-020-0452-1

Bertolin, G., Agarwal, N., Bandeli, K., Biteniece, N., & Sedova, K. (2017). *Digital Hydra: Security Implications of False Information Online*. https://stratcomcoe.org/publications/digital-hydra-security-implications-of-false-information-online/205

Bezimeni, U. (2011). Determinants of Age in Europe: A Pooled Multilevel Nested Hierarchical Time-Series Cross-Sectional Model. *European Political Science*, *10*, 86–91. https://doi.org/10.1057/eps.2010.12

Bird, C. M., Keidel, J. L., Ing, L. P., Horner, A. J., & Burgess, N. (2015). Consolidation of Complex Events via Reinstatement in Posterior Cingulate Cortex. *The Journal of Neuroscience*, *35*(43), 14426–14434. https://doi.org/10.1523/JNEUROSCI.1774-15.2015

BMJ. (2021). *The BMJ will Appeal after Facebook Fails to Act Over "Fact Check" of Investigation*. www.bmj.com/company/newsroom/the-bmj-announces-appeal-after-facebook-fails-to-act-over-incompetent-fact-check-of-investigation/

Bode, L., & Vraga, E. K. (2018). I Do Not Believe You: How Providing a Source Corrects Health Misperceptions across Social Media Platforms. *Information, Communication & Society*, *21*(10), 1337–1353. https://doi.org/10.1080/1369118X.2017.1313883

Bode, L., & Vraga, E. K. (2021). Correction Experiences on Social Media During COVID-19. *Social Media + Society*, *7*(2). https://doi.org/10.1177/20563051211008829

Bond, R. M., & Garrett, R. K. (2023). Engagement with Fact-Checked Posts on Reddit. *PNAS Nexus*, *2*(3). https://doi.org/10.1093/pnasnexus/pgad018

Bonneuil, C., Choquet, P.-L., & Franta, B. (2021). Early Warnings and Emerging Accountability: Total's Responses to Global Warming, 1971–2021. *Global Environmental Change*, *71*, 102386. https://doi.org/10.1016/j.gloenvcha.2021.102386

Bor, A., Osmundsen, M., Rasmussen, S. H. R., Bechmann, A., & Petersen, M. B. (2021). "Fact-Checking" Videos Reduce Belief in, but Not the Sharing of Fake News on Twitter. *PsyArxiv Preprints*. https://doi.org/10.31234/osf.io/a7huq

Borger, J. (2004). There Were No Weapons of Mass Destruction in Iraq. *The Guardian*. www.theguardian.com/world/2004/oct/07/usa.iraq1

Borukhson, D., Lorenz-Spreen, P., & Ragni, M. (2022). When Does an Individual Accept Misinformation? An Extended Investigation Through Cognitive Modeling. *Computational Brain & Behavior*, *5*, 244–260. https://doi.org/10.1007/s42113-022-00136-3

Boryga, A. (2021, April 8). A 'healthy' Doctor Died Two Weeks after Getting a COVID-19 Vaccine; CDC Is Investigating Why. *Chicago Tribune*. www.chicagotribune.com/coronavirus/fl-ne-miami-doctor-vaccine-death-20210107-afzysvqqjbgwnetcy5v6ec62py-story.html

Boudry, M., & Hofhuis, S. (2018). Parasites of the Mind. Why Cultural Theorists Need the Meme's Eye View. *Cognitive Systems Research*, *52*, 155–167. https://doi.org/10.1016/j.cogsys.2018.06.010

Boulianne, S., & Humprecht, E. (2023). Perceived Exposure to Misinformation and Trust in Institutions in Four Countries Before and During a Pandemic. *International Journal of Communication*, *17*, 2024–2047.

Bovet, A., & Makse, H. A. (2019). Influence of Fake News in Twitter during the 2016 US Presidential Election. *Nature Communications*, *10*(1), 7. https://doi.org/10.1038/s41467-018-07761-2

boyd, danah. (2018, March 9). You Think You Want Media Literacy… Do You?. *Medium*. https://medium.com/datasociety-points/you-think-you-want-media-literacy-do-you-7cad6af18ec2

Braddock, K. (2019). Vaccinating against Hate: Using Attitudinal Inoculation to Confer Resistance to Persuasion by Extremist Propaganda. *Terrorism and Political Violence*. https://doi.org/10.1080/09546553.2019.1693370

Brady, W. J., Wills, J. A., Jost, J. T., Tucker, J. A., & Van Bavel, J. J. (2017). Emotion Shapes the Diffusion of Moralized Content in Social Networks. *Proceedings of the National Academy of Sciences*, *114*(28), 7313–7318. https://doi.org/10.1073/pnas.1618923114

Brandt, A. M. (2012). Inventing Conflicts of Interest: A History of Tobacco Industry Tactics. *American Journal of Public Health*, *102*(1), 63–71. https://doi.org/10.2105/AJPH.2011.300292

Brashier, N. M., Pennycook, G., Berinsky, A. J., & Rand, D. G. (2021). Timing Matters when Correcting Fake News. *Proceedings of the National Academy of Sciences*, *118*(5). https://doi.org/10.1073/pnas.2020043118

Breakstone, J., Smith, M., Connors, P., Ortega, T., Kerr, D., & Wineburg, S. (2021). Lateral Reading: College Students learn to Critically Evaluate Internet Sources in an online Course. *Harvard Kennedy School (HKS) Misinformation Review*. https://doi.org/10.37016/mr-2020-56

Brennen, J. S., Simon, F., Howard, P. N., & Nielsen, R. K. (2020). *Types, Sources, and Claims of COVID-19 Misinformation*.

Brick, C. (2019). A Modest Proposal for Restoration Ecology. *Restoration Ecology*, 27(3), 485–487. https://doi.org/10.1111/rec.12943

British Museum. (2022). *The Flood Tablet*. www.britishmuseum.org/collection/object/W_K-3375

Broderick, R. (2014). Here's How a Fake Feminist Hashtag Like #EndFathersDay Gets Started and Why It'll Keep Happening. BuzzFeed. www.buzzfeednews.com/article/ryanhatesthis/end-fathers-day-and-feminist-troll-accounts

Broniatowski, D. A., Jamison, A. M., Qi, S., AlKulaib, L., Chen, T., Benton, A., Quinn, S. C., & Dredze, M. (2018). Weaponized Health Communication: Twitter Bots and Russian Trolls Amplify the Vaccine Debate. *American Journal of Public Health*, 108(10), 1378–1384. https://doi.org/10.2105/AJPH.2018.304567

Bronner, S. E. (2007). *A Rumor about the Jews: Antisemitism, Conspiracy, and the Protocols of Zion*. Oxford University Press.

Bronstein, M. M., Pennycook, G., Bear, A., Rand, D. G., & Cannon, T. (2019). Belief in Fake News Is Associated with Delusionality, Dogmatism, Religious Fundamentalism, and Reduced Analytic Thinking. *Journal of Applied Research in Memory and Cognition*, 8(1), 108–117. https://doi.org/10.1016/j.jarmac.2018.09.005

Bruns, A. (2019). *Are Filter Bubbles Real?* Polity Press.

Bruns, A. (2021). Echo Chambers? Filter Bubbles? The Misleading Metaphors That Obscure the Real Problem. In *Hate Speech and Polarization in Participatory Society* (pp. 33–48). Routledge. https://doi.org/10.4324/9781003109891-4

Bryanov, K., & Vziatysheva, V. (2021). Determinants of Individuals' Belief in Fake News: A Scoping Review Determinants of Belief in Fake News. *PLOS ONE*, 16(6), e0253717. https://doi.org/10.1371/journal.pone.0253717

Bulger, M., & Davison, P. (2018). The Promises, Challenges and Futures of Media Literacy. *Journal of Media Literacy Education*, 10(1), 1–21.

Burkhardt, J. M. (2017). Combating Fake News in the Digital Age. *Library Technology Reports*, 53(8). https://doi.org/978-0-8389-5991-6

Caldera, C. (2020, November 28). Fact Check: Fairness Doctrine Only Applied to Broadcast Licenses, Not Cable TV Like Fox News. *USA Today*. https://usatoday.com/story/news/factcheck/2020/11/28/fact-check-fairness-doctrine-applied-broadcast-licenses-not-cable/6439197002/

Camut, N. (2023, May 30). COVID Might Have Come from a Lab Leak, Says China's Former Top Scientist. *Politico*. www.politico.eu/article/covid-mightve-come-from-a-lab-leak-chinas-former-top-scientist-says/

Capewell, G. (2023). *The Booster Shot Effect in the Long-Term Effectiveness of Video-Based Inoculation Interventions* [Undergraduate dissertation]. University of Cambridge.

Capewell, G., Maertens, R., van der Linden, S., & Roozenbeek, J. (2023). Misinformation Interventions Decay Rapidly without an Immediate Post-Test. Under Review.

Carbonaro, G. (2022). 40% of Americans Think 2020 Election Was Stolen, Just Days Before Midterms. *Newsweek*. www.newsweek.com/40-americans-think-2020-election-stolen-days-before-midterms-1756218

Carlsson, U. (2019). *Understanding Media and Information Literacy (MIL) in the Digital Age: A Question of Democracy*. UNESCO. https://jmg.gu.se/digitalAssets/1742/1742676_understanding-media-pdf-original.pdf

CBS News. (2011, October 28). *Vlad the Impaler: How Is Prince Charles, Queen Elizabeth Related to Him?* www.cbsnews.com/news/vlad-the-impaler-how-is-prince-charles-queen-elizabeth-related-to-him/

Celadin, T., Capraro, V., Pennycook, G., & Rand, D. G. (2023). Displaying News Source Trustworthiness Ratings Reduces Sharing Intentions for False News Posts. *Journal of Online Trust and Safety, 1*(5). https://doi.org/10.54501/jots.v1i5.100

Center for Countering Digital Hate. (2021). *The Disinformation Dozen: Why Platforms must Act on Twelve Leading online Anti-Vaxxers.*

Central Election Commission of Ukraine. (2014). *Extraordinary Parliamentary Election 2014.* https://web.archive.org/web/20171019075244/http://www.cvk.gov.ua/pls/vnd2014/wp039e?PT001F01=910

Chan, M. P. S., & Albarracín, D. (2023). A Meta-Analysis of Correction Effects in Science-Relevant Misinformation. *Nature Human Behaviour.* https://doi.org/10.1038/s41562-023-01623-8

Chan, M. P. S., Jones, C. R., Hall Jamieson, K., & Albarracín, D. (2017). Debunking: A Meta-Analysis of the Psychological Efficacy of Messages Countering Misinformation. *Psychological Science, 28*(11), 1531–1546. https://doi.org/10.1177/0956797617714579

Channel 4. (2017). *C4 Study Reveals only 4% Surveyed Can Identify True or Fake News.* www.channel4.com/info/press/news/c4-study-reveals-only-4-surveyed-can-identify-true-or-fake-news

Chater, N., & Loewenstein, G. (2022). The i-Frame and the s-Frame: How Focusing on Individual-Level Solutions Has Led Behavioral Public Policy Astray. *Behavioral and Brain Sciences,* 1–60. https://doi.org/10.1017/S0140525X22002023

China Law Translate. (2022, December 11). *Provisions on the Administration of Deep Synthesis Internet Information Services.* www.chinalawtranslate.com/en/deep-synthesis/

Chivers, T. (2019). What's Next for Psychology's Embattled Field of Social Priming. *Nature, 576,* 200–202. https://doi.org/10.1038/d41586-019-03755-2

Cinelli, M., De Fransisci Morales, G., Galeazzi, A., & Starnini, M. (2021). The Echo Chamber Effect on Social Media. *Proceedings of the National Academy of Sciences, 118*(9), e2023301118. https://doi.org/10.1073/pnas.2023301118

Cinelli, M., Quattrociocchi, W., Galeazzi, A., Valensise, C. M., Brugnoli, E., Schmidt, A. L., Zola, P., Zollo, F., & Scala, A. (2020). The COVID-19 Social Media Infodemic. *Scientific Reports, 10*(1), 16598. https://doi.org/10.1038/s41598-020-73510-5

Clayton, K., Blair, S., Busam, J. A., Forstner, S., Glance, J., Green, G., Kawata, A., Kovvuri, A., Martin, J., Morgan, E., Sandhu, M., Sang, R., Scholz-Bright, R., Welch, A. T., Wolff, A. G., Zhou, A., & Nyhan, B. (2020). Real Solutions for Fake News? Measuring the Effectiveness of General Warnings and Fact-Check Tags in Reducing Belief in False Stories on Social Media. *Political Behavior, 42*(4), 1073–1095. https://doi.org/10.1007/s11109-019-09533-0

Clayton, N. S., Dally, J. M., & Emery, N. J. (2007). Social Cognition by Food-Caching Corvids. The Western Scrub-Jay as a Natural Psychologist. *Philosophical Transactions of the Royal Society B: Biological Sciences, 362*(1480), 507–522. https://doi.org/10.1098/rstb.2006.1992

Coan, T. G., Boussalis, C., Cook, J., & Nanko, M. O. (2021). Computer-assisted Classification of Contrarian Claims about Climate Change. *Scientific Reports*, *11*(22320). https://doi.org/10.1038/s41598-021-01714-4

Cohn, N. (1966). *Warrant for Genocide: The Myth of the Jewish World-Conspiracy and the Protocols of the Elders of Zion*. Harper & Row.

Coleman, S. (2018). The Elusiveness of Political Truth: From the Conceit of Objectivity to Intersubjective Judgement. *European Journal of Communication*, *33*(2), 157–171. https://doi.org/10.1177/0267323118760319

Compton, J. (2013). Inoculation Theory. In J. P. Dillard & L. Shen (Eds.), *The SAGE Handbook of Persuasion: Developments in Theory and Practice* (2nd ed., pp. 220–236). SAGE Publications, Inc. https://doi.org/10.4135/9781452218410

Compton, J. (2018). Inoculation against/with Political Humor. In J. C. Baumgartner & A. B. Becker (Eds.), *Political Humor in a Changing Media Landscape: A New Generation of Research* (pp. 95–113). Lexington Books.

Compton, J. (2020). Prophylactic Versus Therapeutic Inoculation Treatments for Resistance to Influence. *Communication Theory*, *30*(3), 330–343. https://doi.org/10.1093/ct/qtz004

Compton, J. (2021). Threat and/in Inoculation Theory. *International Journal of Communication*, *15*, 4294–4306. https://doi.org/10.1932–8036/2021FEA0002

Compton, J., & Pfau, M. (2009). Spreading Inoculation: Inoculation, Resistance to Influence, and Word-of-Mouth Communication. *Communication Theory*, *19*(1), 9–28. https://doi.org/10.1111/j.1468-2885.2008.01330.x

Conzola, V. C., & Wogalter, M. S. (2001). A Communication–Human Information Processing (C–HIP) Approach to Warning Effectiveness in the Workplace. *Journal of Risk Research*, *4*(4), 309–322. https://doi.org/10.1080/13669870110062712

Cook, J. (2020). *Cranky Uncle Game: Building Resilience against Misinformation*. https://crankyuncle.com/game/

Cook, J., Ecker, U. K. H., Trecek-King, M., Schade, G., Jeffers-Tracy, K., Fessmann, J., Kim, S. C., Kinkead, D., Orr, M., Vraga, E. K., Roberts, K., & McDowell, J. (2022). The Cranky Uncle game – Combining Humor and Gamification to Build Student Resilience against Climate Misinformation. *Environmental Education Research*. https://doi.org/10.1080/13504622.2022.2085671

Cook, J., Lewandowsky, S., & Ecker, U. K. H. (2017). Neutralizing Misinformation Through Inoculation: Exposing Misleading Argumentation Techniques Reduces their Influence. *PLOS ONE*, *12*(5), 1–21. https://doi.org/10.1371/journal.pone.0175799

Copeland, D. A. (2006). *The Idea of a Free Press: The Enlightenment and Its Unruly Legacy*. Northwestern University Press.

Crockett, M. J. (2017). Moral Outrage in the Digital Age. *Nature Human Behaviour*, *1*(11), 769–771. https://doi.org/10.1038/s41562-017-0213-3

Culloty, E., Park, K., Feenane, T., Papaevangelou, C., Conroy, A., & Suiter, J. (2021). *CovidCheck: Assessing the Implementation of EU Code of Practice on Disinformation in Relation to COVID-19*. https://doras.dcu.ie/26472/

Cumming, G. (2021, September 2). Psychological Inoculation? Prebunking? Assessing the Bad News Game That Targets Fake News. The New Statistics. https://thenewstatistics.com/itns/2021/09/02/psychological-inoculation-prebunking-assessing-the-bad-news-game-that-targets-fake-news/

Cybersecurity and Infrastructure Security Agency. (2019, June). *THE WAR ON PINEAPPLE: Understanding Foreign Interference in 5 Steps.* www.dhs.gov/sites/default/files/publications/19_0717_cisa_the-war-on-pineapple-understanding-foreign-interference-in-5-steps.pdf

Czerniak, K., Pillai, R., Parmar, A., Ramnath, K., Krocker, J., & Myneni, S. (2023). A Scoping Review of Digital Health Interventions for Combating COVID-19 Misinformation and Disinformation. *Journal of the American Medical Informatics Association, 30*(4), 752–760. https://doi.org/10.1093/jamia/ocad005

Da San Martino, G., Barrón-Cedeño, A., Wachsmuth, H., Petrov, R., & Nakov, P. (2020). SemEval-2020 Task 11: Detection of Propaganda Techniques in News Articles. *Proceedings of the Fourteenth Workshop on Semantic* Evaluation, 1377–1414.

Dan, V., Paris, B., Donovan, J., Hameleers, M., Roozenbeek, J., van der Linden, S., & von Sikorski, C. (2021). Visual Mis-and Disinformation, Social Media, and Democracy. *Journalism & Mass Communication Quarterly, 98*(3), 641–664. https://doi.org/10.1177/10776990211035395

Davis, A. (2010). New Media and Fat Democracy: The Paradox of Online Participation. *New Media & Society, 12*(5), 745–761. https://doi.org/10.1177/1461444809341435

de Ridder, D., Kroese, F., & van Gestel, L. (2021). Nudgeability: Mapping Conditions of Susceptibility to Nudge Influence. *Perspectives on Psychological Science, 17*(2), 346–359. https://doi.org/10.1177/1745691621995183

de Waal, J. R. (2018). Brexit and Trump Voters Are more Likely to Believe in Conspiracy Theories. YouGov. https://yougov.co.uk/topics/international/articles-reports/2018/12/14/brexit-and-trump-voters-are-more-likely-believe-co

Debies-Carl, J. S. (2017). Pizzagate and Beyond: Using Social Research to Understand Conspiracy Legends. *Skeptical Inquirer, 41*(6).

Deer, B. (2004). Revealed: MMR Research Scandal. *The Times.* www.thetimes.co.uk/article/revealed-mmr-research-scandal-7ncfntn8mjq

Del Vicario, M., Bessi, A., Zollo, F., Petroni, F., Scala, A., Caldarelli, G., Stanley, H. E., & Quattrociocchi, W. (2016). The Spreading of Misinformation Online. *Proceedings of the National Academy of Sciences, 113*(3), 554–559. https://doi.org/10.1073/pnas.1517441113

Delirrad, M., & Mohammadi, A. B. (2020). New Methanol Poisoning Outbreaks in Iran Following COVID-19 Pandemic. *Alcohol and Alcoholism, 55*(4), 347–348. https://doi.org/10.1093/alcalc/agaa036

DellaVigna, S., & Linos, E. (2022). RCTs to Scale: Comprehensive Evidence from Two Nudge Units. *Econometrica, 90*(1), 81–116. https://doi.org/10.3982/ECTA18709

Diaz Ruiz, C., & Nilsson, T. (2023). Disinformation and Echo Chambers: How Disinformation Circulates on Social Media Through Identity-Driven Controversies. *Journal of Public Policy & Marketing, 42*(1), 18–35. https://doi.org/10.1177/07439156221103852

Dittmar, J. E. (2011). Information Technology and Economic Change: The Impact of The Printing Press. *The Quarterly Journal of Economics, 126*(3), 1133–1172. https://doi.org/10.1093/qje/qjr035

Dizikes, P. (2018). Study: On Twitter, False News Travels Faster than True Stories. MIT News. https://news.mit.edu/2018/study-twitter-false-news-travels-faster-true-stories-0308

Dubois, E., & Blank, G. (2018). The Echo Chamber Is Overstated: The Moderating Effect of Political Interest and Diverse Media. *Information, Communication & Society*, 21(5), 729–745. https://doi.org/10.1080/1369118X.2018.1428656

Duron, R., Limbach, B., & Waugh, W. (2006). Critical Thinking Framework for Any Discipline. *International Journal of Teaching and Learning in Higher Education*, 17(2), 160–166.

Dwoskin, E., & Timberg, C. (2021, January 16). *Misinformation Dropped Dramatically the Week after Twitter Banned Trump and Some Allies. The Washington Post*. www.washingtonpost.com/technology/2021/01/16/misinformation-trump-twitter/

Dyer, O. (2021a). Covid-19: China Pressured WHO Team to Dismiss Lab Leak Theory, Claims Chief Investigator. *BMJ, 374*. https://doi.org/10.1136/bmj.n2023

Dyer, O. (2021b). Covid-19: China Pressured WHO Team to Dismiss Lab Leak Theory, Claims Chief Investigator. *BMJ, 374*(n2023). https://doi.org/10.1136/bmj.n2023

Eady, G., Nagler, J., Guess, A. M., Zilinsky, J., & Tucker, J. A. (2019). How Many People Live in Political Bubbles on Social Media? Evidence From Linked Survey and Twitter Data. *SAGE Open*, 9(1). https://doi.org/10.1177/2158244019832705

Eady, G., Pashkalis, T., Zilinsky, J., Bonneau, R., Nagler, J., & Tucker, J. A. (2023). Exposure to the Russian Internet Research Agency Foreign Influence Campaign on Twitter in the 2016 US Election and Its Relationship to Attitudes and Voting Behavior. *Nature Communications*, 14(62). https://doi.org/10.1038/s41467-022-35576-9

Echikson, W., & Knodt, O. (2018). *Germany's NetzDG: A key Test for Combatting Online Hate*. http://wp.ceps.eu/wp-content/uploads/2018/11/RR%20N02018-09_Germany's%20NetzDG.pdf

Ecker, U. K. H., & Antonio, L. M. (2021). Can You Believe It? An Investigation into the Impact of Retraction Source Credibility on the Continued Influence Effect. *Memory & Cognition*, 49, 631–644. https://doi.org/10.3758/s13421-020-01129-y

Ecker, U. K. H., Lewandowsky, S., & Chadwick, M. (2020). Can Corrections Spread Misinformation to New Audiences? Testing for the Elusive Familiarity Backfire Effect. *Cognitive Research: Principles and Implications*, 5(1), 41. https://doi.org/10.1186/s41235-020-00241-6

Ecker, U. K. H., Lewandowsky, S., Cook, J., Schmid, P., Fazio, L. K., Brashier, N., Kendeou, P., Vraga, E. K., & Amazeen, M. A. (2022). The Psychological Drivers of Misinformation Belief and Its Resistance to Correction. *Nature Reviews Psychology*, 1(1), 13–29. https://doi.org/10.1038/s44159-021-00006-y

Ecker, U. K. H., O'Reilly, Z., Reid, J. S., & Chang, E. P. (2020). The Effectiveness of Short-format Refutational Fact-checks. *British Journal of Psychology*, 111(1), 36–54. https://doi.org/10.1111/bjop.12383

Edwards, L. (2022, January 25). *How to Regulate Misinformation*. https://royalsociety.org/blog/2022/01/how-to-regulate-misinformation/

El Soufi, N., & See, B. H. (2019). Does Explicit Teaching of Critical Thinking Improve Critical Thinking Skills of English Language Learners in Higher Education? A Critical Review of Causal Evidence. *Studies in Educational Evaluation*, 60, 140–162. https://doi.org/10.1016/j.stueduc.2018.12.006.

Emery, D. (2016). Did the 1938 Radio Broadcast of 'War of the Worlds' Cause a Nationwide Panic? *Snopes*. www.snopes.com/fact-check/war-of-the-worlds/

Epstein, Z., Berinsky, A. J., Cole, R., Gully, A., Pennycook, G., & Rand, D. G. (2021). Developing an Accuracy-prompt Toolkit to Reduce COVID-19 Misinformation Online. *Harvard Kennedy School (HKS) Misinformation Review.* https://doi .org/10.37016/mr-2020-71

European Center for Populism Studies. (2022). *Information Warfare.* www .populismstudies.org/Vocabulary/information-warfare/

European Commission. (2020). *European Democracy Action Plan.* https:// commission.europa.eu/strategy-and-policy/priorities-2019-2024/new-push-european-democracy/european-democracy-action-plan_en

European Commission. (2022). *The 2022 Code of Practice on Disinformation.* https:// digital-strategy.ec.europa.eu/en/policies/code-practice-disinformation

European Commission. (2023a, April 25). *Questions and Answers: Digital Services Act*.* https://ec.europa.eu/commission/presscorner/detail/en/QANDA_20_2348

European Commission. (2023b, May 5). *The Digital Services Act package.* https://digital-strategy.ec.europa.eu/en/policies/digital-services-act-package

Faddoul, M., Chaslot, G., & Farid, H. (2020). A Longitudinal Analysis of YouTube's Promotion of Conspiracy Videos. *ArXiv Preprint.*

Faragó, L., Kende, A., & Krekó, P. (2020). We Only Believe in News That We Doctored Ourselves: The Connection Between Partisanship and Political Fake News. *Social Psychology, 51*, 77–90. https://doi.org/10.1027/1864-9335/a000391

Faragó, L., Krekó, P., & Orosz, G. (2023). Hungarian, Lazy, and Biased: The Role of Analytic Thinking and Partisanship in Fake News Discernment on a Hungarian Representative Sample. *Scientific Reports, 13*(1), 178. https://doi.org/10.1038/s41598-022-26724-8

Fazio, L. K. (2020). Pausing to Consider Why a Headline Is True or False Can Help Reduce the Sharing of False News. *Harvard Misinformation Review, 1*(2). https://doi.org/10.37016/mr-2020-009

Fazio, L. K., Brashier, N. M., Payne, B. K., & Marsh, E. J. (2015). Knowledge Does Not Protect against Illusory Truth. *Journal of Experimental Psychology: General, 144*(5), 993–1002. https://doi.org/10.1037/xge0000098

Fazio, L. K., Pillai, R. M., & Patel, D. (2022). The Effects of Repetition on Belief in Naturalistic Settings. *Journal of Experimental Psychology: General, 151*(10), 2604–2613. https://doi.org/10.1037/xge0001211

Fazio, L. K., Rand, D. G., & Pennycook, G. (2019). Repetition Increases Perceived Truth Equally for Plausible and Implausible Statements. *Psychonomic Bulletin & Review, 26*(5), 1705–1710. https://doi.org/10.3758/s13423-019-01651-4

Fazio, L. K., & Sherry, C. L. (2020). The Effect of Repetition on Truth Judgments Across Development. *Psychological Science, 31*(9), 1150–1160. https://doi .org/10.1177/0956797620939534

Federal Communications Commission. (2020). *History of Commercial Radio.* www .fcc.gov/media/radio/history-of-commercial-radio

Ferrara, E. (2017). Disinformation and Social Bot Operations in the Run Up to the 2017 French Presidential Election. *CoRR, abs/1707.0.*

Flaxman, S., Goel, S., & Rao, J. M. (2016). Filter Bubbles, Echo Chambers, and online News Consumption. *Public Opinion Quarterly, 80*(Specialissue1), 298–320. https://doi.org/10.1093/poq/nfw006

Fletcher, R., & Nielsen, R. K. (2017). Are News Audiences Increasingly Fragmented? A Cross-National Comparative Analysis of Cross-Platform News Audience Fragmentation and Duplication. *Journal of Communication, 67*(4), 476–498. https://doi.org/10.1111/jcom.12315

Fletcher, R., Robertson, C. T., & Nielsen, R. K. (2021). How Many People Live in Politically Partisan Online News Echo Chambers in Different Countries? *Journal of Quantitative Description: Digital Media, 1.* https://doi.org/10.51685/jqd.2021.020

Foster, C. A., & Branch, G. (2018). Do People Really Think Earth Might Be Flat? *Scientific American.* https://blogs.scientificamerican.com/observations/do-people-really-think-earth-might-be-flat/

Fox, M. (2018). Fake News: Lies Spread Faster on Social Media than Truth Does. *NBC News.* www.nbcnews.com/health/health-news/fake-news-lies-spread-faster-social-media-truth-does-n854896

Franta, B. (2018). Early oil Industry Knowledge of CO_2 and Global Warming. *Nature Climate Change, 8*, 1024–1025. https://doi.org/10.1038/s41558-018-0349-9

Frederick, S. (2005). Cognitive Reflection and Decision Making. *Journal of Economic Perspectives, 19*(4), 25–42. https://doi.org/10.1257/089533005775196732

Freelon, D., & Wells, C. (2020). Disinformation as Political Communication. *Political Communication, 37*(2), 145–156. https://doi.org/10.1080/10584609.2020.1723755

Funke, D. (2018, January 19). Italians Can Now Report Fake News to the Police. Here's Why That's problematic. *Poynter.* www.poynter.org/fact-checking/2018/italians-can-now-report-fake-news-to-the-police-heres-why-thats-problematic/

Funke, D., & Flamini, D. (2018). A Guide to Anti-misinformation Actions around the World. *Poynter.* www.poynter.org/ifcn/anti-misinformation-actions/

Gabbatt, A. (2023, June 6). US Urged to Reveal UFO Evidence after Claim That It has Intact Alien Vehicles. *The Guardian.* www.theguardian.com/world/2023/jun/06/whistleblower-ufo-alien-tech-spacecraft

Gajanan, Ma. (2017). White House's Sean Spicer Stands by False Claim That Donald Trump's Inauguration Was the "Most-Watched" Ever. *Time Magazine.* https://time.com/4643927/sean-spicer-white-house-donald-trump-inauguration-press-briefing/

Galey, P. (2022). Ukraine Admits the "Ghost of Kyiv" Isn't Real, but the Myth Was Potent for a Reason. *NBC News.* www.nbcnews.com/news/world/ukraine-admits-ghost-kyiv-isnt-real-wartime-myth-russia-rcna26867

Gallagher, M. (2023, April 17). Gallagher, Kilmer Introduce Bipartisan, Bicameral Legislation to Bring Transparency and Accountability to Online Political Ads. Gallagher.House.Gov. https://gallagher.house.gov/media/press-releases/gallagher-kilmer-introduce-bipartisan-bicameral-legislation-bring-transparency

Gallo, J. A., & Cho, C. Y. (2021). Social Media: Misinformation and Content Moderation Issues for Congress. https://crsreports.congress.gov/product/pdf/R/R46662

Gallup. (2022, July). Tobacco and Smoking. https://news.gallup.com/poll/1717/tobacco-smoking.aspx

Garcia, D., & Rimé, B. (2019). Collective Emotions and Social Resilience in the Digital Traces After a Terrorist Attack. *Psychological Science, 30*(4), 617–628. https://doi.org/10.1177/0956797619831964

Garcia-Pelegrin, E., Schnell, A. K., Wilkins, C., & Clayton, N. S. (2021). Exploring the Perceptual Inabilities of Eurasian Jays (Garrulus glandarius) Using Magic Effects. *Proceedings of the National Academy of Sciences, 118*(24). https://doi.org/10.1073/pnas.2026106118

Garrett, R. K. (2019). Social Media's Contribution to Political Misperceptions in U.S. Presidential Elections. *PLOS ONE, 14*(3), e0213550. https://doi.org/10.1371/journal.pone.0213500

Garrett, R. K., & Bond, R. M. (2021). Conservatives' Susceptibility to Political Misperceptions. *Science Advances, 7*(23), eabf1234. https://doi.org/10.1126/sciadv.abf1234

Gavin, L., McChesney, J., Tong, A., Sherlock, J., Foster, L., & Tomsa, S. (2022). Fighting the Spread of COVID-19 Misinformation in Kyrgyzstan, India, and the United States: How Replicable Are Accuracy Nudge Interventions? *Technology, Mind, and Behavior, 3*(3). https://doi.org/10.1037/tmb0000086

GCSI. (2021, February 18). *GCS International Joins the Fight against Health Misinformation Worldwide.* https://gcs.civilservice.gov.uk/news/gcs-international-joins-the-fight-against-health-misinformation-worldwide/

Geiß, S., Magin, M., Jürgens, P., & Stark, B. (2021). Loopholes in the Echo Chambers: How the Echo Chamber Metaphor Oversimplifies the Effects of Information Gateways on Opinion Expression. *Digital Journalism, 9*(5), 660–686. https://doi.org/10.1080/21670811.2021.1873811

Gerasimov, V. (2016). The Value of Science Is in the Foresight: New Challenges Demand Rethinking the Forms and Methods of Carrying out Combat Operations. *Military Review* (January/February). www.armyupress.army.mil/portals/7/military-review/archives/english/militaryreview_20160228_art008.pdf

Ghai, S. (2021). It's Time to Reimagine Sample Diversity and Retire the WEIRD Dichotomy. *Nature Human Behaviour, 5*(8), 971–972. https://doi.org/10.1038/s41562-021-01175-9

Ghai, S. (2022). Expand Diversity Definitions Beyond their Western Perspective. *Nature, 602*(7896), 211–211. https://doi.org/10.1038/d41586-022-00330-0

Ghai, S., Magis-Weinberg, L., Stoilova, M., Livingstone, S., & Orben, A. (2022). Social Media and Adolescent Well-being in the Global South. *Current Opinion in Psychology, 46*(101318). https://doi.org/10.1016/j.copsyc.2022.101318

Gielow Jacobs, L. (2022). Freedom of Speech and Regulation of Fake News. *The American Journal of Comparative Law, 70*(Supplement_1), i278–i311. https://doi.org/10.1093/ajcl/avac010

Gimpel, H., Heger, S., Olenberger, C., & Utz, L. (2021). The Effectiveness of Social Norms in Fighting Fake News on Social Media. *Journal of Management Information Systems, 38*(1), 196–221. https://doi.org/10.1080/07421222.2021.1870389

Glantz, S. A., Slade, J., Bero, L. A., Hanauer, P., & Barnes, D. E. (1996). *The Cigarette Papers.* University of California Press.

Godlee, F. (2011). The Fraud Behind the MMR Scare. *BMJ, 342*(d22). https://doi.org/10.1136/bmj.d22

Goebbels, J. (1934). Speech to the 1934 Nuremberg Party Rally. In P. R. Baines & N. J. O'Shaughnessy (Eds.), *Propaganda. Volume 1: Historical Origins, Definitions and the Changing Nature of Propaganda* (pp. 151–158). SAGE Publications.

Goel, V., Raj, S., & Ravichandran, P. (2019, July 18). How WhatsApp Leads Mobs to Murder in India. *New York Times*. www.nytimes.com/interactive/2018/07/18/technology/whatsapp-india-killings.html

González-Bailón, S., Lazer, D., Barberá, P., Zhang, M., Allcott, H., Brown, T., Crespo-Tenorio, A., Freelon, D., Gentzkow, M., Guess, A. M., Iyengar, S., Kim, Y. M., Malhotra, N., Moehler, D., Nyhan, B., Pan, J., Rivera, C. V., Settle, J., Thorson, E., … Tucker, J. A. (2023). Asymmetric Ideological Segregation in Exposure to Political News on Facebook. *Science, 381*(6656), 392–398. https://doi.org/10.1126/science.ade7138

Goodman, M. (2008). *The Sun and the Moon: The Remarkable True Account of Hoaxers, Showmen, Dueling Journalists, and Lunar Man-Bats in Nineteenth-Century New York*. Basic Books.

Grace, L., & Liang, S. (2023). Examining Misinformation and Disinformation Games Through Inoculation Theory and Transportation Theory. *Proceedings of the 56th Hawaii International Conference on System Sciences*.

Graham, M., Skov, B., Gilson, Z., Heise, C., Fallow, K. M., & Lindsay, D. S. (2023). Mixed News about the Bad News Game. *Journal of Cognition, 6*(1), 58. https://doi.org/10.5334/joc.324

Grant, T. D. (2015). Annexation of Crimea. *The American Journal of International Law, 109*(1), 68–95.

Graves, L. (2016). *Deciding What's True: The Rise of Political Fact-Checking in American Journalism*. Columbia University Press.

Green, M., McShane, C. J., & Swinbourne, A. (2022). Active Versus Passive: Evaluating the Effectiveness of Inoculation Techniques in Relation to Misinformation about Climate Change. *Australian Journal of Psychology, 74*(1). https://doi.org/10.1080/00049530.2022.2113340

Green, Y., Gully, A., Roth, Y., Roy, A., Tucker, J. A., & Wanless, A. (2023). Evidence-Based Misinformation Interventions: Challenges and Opportunities for Measurement and Collaboration. https://carnegieendowment.org/2023/01/09/evidence-based-misinformation-interventions-challenges-and-opportunities-for-measurement-and-collaboration-pub-88661

Greenemeier, L. (2018). False News Travels 6 Times Faster on Twitter than Truthful News. PBS Newshour. www.pbs.org/newshour/science/false-news-travels-6-times-faster-on-twitter-than-truthful-news

Greifeneder, R., Jaffé, M., Newman, E. J., & Schwartz, N. (2020). *The Psychology of Fake News: Accepting, Sharing, and Correcting Misinformation*. Psychology Press. https://doi.org/10.4324/9780429295379

Grimes, D. R. (2016). On the Viability of Conspiratorial Beliefs. *PLOS ONE, 11*(1), e0147905. https://doi.org/10.1371/journal.pone.0147905

Grinberg, N., Joseph, K., Friedland, L., Swire-Thompson, B., & Lazer, D. (2019). Fake News on Twitter during the 2016 U.S. Presidential Election. *Science, 363*(6425), 374–378. https://doi.org/10.1126/science.aau2706

Guay, B., Berinsky, A., Pennycook, G., & Rand, D. G. (2023). How to Think about Whether Misinformation Interventions Work. *Nature Human Behaviour, 7*(8), 1231–1233. https://doi.org/10.1038/s41562-023-01667-w

Guess, A. M., Lerner, M., Lyons, B., Montgomery, J. M., Nyhan, B., Reifler, J., & Sircar, N. (2020). A Digital Media Literacy Intervention Increases Discernment

Between Mainstream and False News in the United States and India. *Proceedings of the National Academy of Sciences, 117*(27), 15536–15545. https://doi.org/10.1073/pnas.1920498117

Guess, A. M., Lyons, B., Nyhan, B., & Reifler, J. (2018). *Avoiding the Echo Chamber about Echo Chambers: Why Selective Exposure to Like-Minded Political News Is Less Prevalent than You Think.* https://kf-site-production.s3.amazonaws.com/media_elements/files/000/000/133/original/Topos_KF_White-Paper_Nyhan_V1.pdf

Guess, A. M., Malhotra, N., Pan, J., Barberá, P., Allcott, H., Brown, T., Crespo-Tenorio, A., Dimmery, D., Freelon, D., Gentzkow, M., González-Bailón, S., Kennedy, E., Kim, Y. M., Lazer, D., Moehler, D., Nyhan, B., Rivera, C. V., Settle, J., Thomas, D. R., … Tucker, J. A. (2023a). How Do Social Media Feed Algorithms Affect Attitudes and Behavior in an Election Campaign? *Science, 381*(6656), 398–404. https://doi.org/10.1126/science.abp9364

Guess, A. M., Malhotra, N., Pan, J., Barberá, P., Allcott, H., Brown, T., Crespo-Tenorio, A., Dimmery, D., Freelon, D., Gentzkow, M., González-Bailón, S., Kennedy, E., Kim, Y. M., Lazer, D., Moehler, D., Nyhan, B., Rivera, C. V., Settle, J., Thomas, D. R., … Tucker, J. A. (2023b). Reshares on Social Media Amplify Political News but Do Not Detectably Affect Beliefs or Opinions. *Science, 381*(6656), 404–408. https://doi.org/10.1126/science.add8424

Guess, A. M., Nagler, J., & Tucker, J. (2019). Less Than You Think: Prevalence and Predictors of Fake News Dissemination on Facebook. *Science Advances, 5*(1). https://doi.org/10.1126/sciadv.aau4586

Guillory, J. J., & Geraci, L. (2013). Correcting Erroneous Inferences in Memory: The Role of Source Credibility on the Continued Influence Effect. *Journal of Applied Research in Memory and Cognition, 2*(4), 201–209. https://doi.org/10.1016/j.jarmac.2013.10.001

Guo, Z., Schlichtkrull, M., & Vlachos, A. (2022). A Survey on Automated Fact-Checking. *Transactions of the Association for Computational Linguistics,* 178–206. https://doi.org/10.1162/tacl_a_00454

Gwiaździński, P., Gundersen, A. B., Piksa, M., Krysińska, I., Kunst, J. R., Noworyta, K., Olejniuk, A., Morzy, M., Rygula, R., Wójtowicz, T., & Piasecki, J. (2023). Psychological Interventions Countering Misinformation in Social Media: A Scoping Review. *Frontiers in Psychiatry, 13.* https://doi.org/10.3389/fpsyt.2022.974782

Hall Jamieson, K., & Capella, J. N. (2008). *Echo Chamber: Rush Limbaugh and the Conservative Media Establishment.* Oxford University Press.

Hameleers, M. (2023). The (Un)Intended Consequences of Emphasizing the Threats of Mis-and Disinformation. *Media and Communication, 11*(2). https://doi.org/10.17645/mac.v11i2.6301

Hameleers, M., & van der Meer, T. G. L. A. (2019). Misinformation and Polarization in a High-Choice Media Environment: How Effective Are Political Fact-Checkers? *Communication Research, 47*(2), 227–250. https://doi.org/10.1177/0093650218819671

Hamilton, D. (2023, May 10). ChatGPT User in China Detained for Creating and Spreading Fake News, Police Say. AP News. https://apnews.com/article/chatgpt-china-deepfakes-criminal-detention-7985cf38ffa33b09d3ad4f8ea5299967

Harff, D., Bollen, C., & Schmuck, D. (2022). Responses to Social Media Influencers' Misinformation about COVID-19: A Pre-Registered Multiple-Exposure Experiment. *Media Psychology*, 25(9), 1–20. https://doi.org/10.1080/15213269.202 2.2080711

Harjani, T., Basol, M., Roozenbee, J., & van der Linden, S. (2023). Gamified Inoculation against Misinformation in India: A Randomised Control Trial. *Journal of Trial and Error*. https://doi.org/10.36850/e12

Harjani, T., Roozenbeek, J., Biddlestone, M., van der Linden, S., Stuart, A., Iwahara, M., Piri, B., Xu, R., Goldberg, B., & Graham, M. (2022). *A Practical Guide to Prebunking Misinformation*. Interventions. https://interventions.withgoogle .com/static/pdf/A_Practical_Guide_to_Prebunking_Misinformation.pdf

Harrop, I., Roozenbeek, J., Madsen, J. K., & van der Linden, S. (2023). Inoculation Can Reduce the Perceived Reliability of Polarizing Social Media Content. *International Journal of Communication*, 16, 1–24.

Hartwig, K., Doell, F., & Reuter, C. (2023). The Landscape of User-Centered Misinformation Interventions – A Systematic Literature Review. *ArXiv Preprints*. https://doi.org/10.48550/arXiv.2301.06517

Hassan, A., & Barber, S. J. (2021). The Effects of Repetition Frequency on the Illusory Truth Effect. *Cognitive Research: Principles and Implications*, 6(38). https://doi .org/10.1186/s41235-021-00301-5

He, Z. (1994). Diffusion of Movable Type in China and Europe: Why Were There Two Fates?. *International Communication Gazzette*, 53(3), 153–173. https://doi .org/10.1177/001654929405300301

Henderson, E. L., Simons, D. J., & Barr, D. J. (2021). The Trajectory of Truth: A Longitudinal Study of the Illusory Truth Effect. *Journal of Cognition*, 4(1). https:// doi.org/10.5334/joc.161

Hertwig, R., & Grüne-Yanoff, T. (2017). Nudging and Boosting: Steering or Empowering Good Decisions. *Perspectives on Psychological Science*, 12(6), 973–986. https://doi.org/10.1177/1745691617702496

Ho, S. S., Chuah, A. S. F., Kim, N., & Tandoc, E. C. (2022). Fake News, Real Risks: How online Discussion and Sources of Fact-Check Influence Public Risk Perceptions Toward Nuclear Energy. *Risk Analysis*, 42(11), 2569–2583. https://doi.org/10.1111/ risa.13980

Hoes, E., Aitken, B., Zhang, J., Gackowski, T., & Wojcieszak, M. (2023). Prominent Misinformation Interventions Reduce Misperceptions but Increase Skepticism. *PsyArxiv Preprints*. doi: 10.31234/osf.io/zmpdu

Holbert, R. L. (2013). Developing a Normative Approach to Political Satire: An Empirical Perspective. *International Journal of Communication*, 7, 305–323.

Holbrook, J. (2001). Republic.com by Cass R Sunstein. *Harvard Journal of Law & Technology*, 14(2), 753–766.

Hopkins, C. D., & Snyder, G. (2022, May 17). The Military's UFO Database Now has Info from about 400 Reported Incidents. *NPR*. www.npr.org/2022/05/17/1099410910/ ufo-hearing-congress-military-intelligence

Hornsey, M. J., Bierwiaczonek, K., Sassenberg, K., & Douglas, K. M. (2022). Individual, Intergroup and Nation-Level Influences on Belief in Conspiracy Theories. *Nature Reviews Psychology*, 2(2), 85–97. https://doi.org/10.1038/s44159-022-00133-0

Horowitz, D. L. (2000). *The Deadly Ethnic Riot*. University of California Press.

Horton, R. (2021). Offline: The Origin Story – Division Deepens. *The Lancet, 398*(10318), 2221. https://doi.org/10.1016/S0140-6736(21)02833-6

Hosseinmardi, H., Ghasemian, A., Clauset, A., Mobius, M., & Rothschild, D. (2021). Examining the Consumption of Radical Content on YouTube. *Proceedings of the National Academy of Sciences of the United States of America, 118*(32), e2101967118. https://doi.org/10.1073/pnas.2101967118

Hsia, R. P.-C. (1992). *Trent 1475: Stories of a Ritual Murder Trial.* Yale University Press.

Huber, C. R., & Kuncel, N. R. (2016). Does College Teach Critical Thinking? A Meta-Analysis. *Review of Educational Research, 86*(2), 431–468. https://doi.org/10.3102/0034654315605917

Hughes, B., Braddock, K., Miller-Idriss, C., Goldberg, B., Criezis, M., Dashtgard, P., & White, K. (2021). Inoculating against Persuasion by Scientific Racism Propaganda: The Moderating Roles of Propaganda Form and Subtlety. *PsyArxiv Preprints.* https://doi.org/10.31235/osf.io/ecqn4

Human Rights Watch. (2018). *Germany: Flawed Social Media Law.* www.hrw.org/news/2018/02/14/germany-flawed-social-media-law

Human Rights Watch. (2021, November 17). *Greece: Alleged 'Fake News' Made a Crime.* www.hrw.org/news/2021/11/17/greece-alleged-fake-news-made-crime

Hunt, E. (2017). Trump's Inauguration Crowd: Sean Spicer's Claims Versus the Evidence. *The Guardian.* www.theguardian.com/us-news/2017/jan/22/trump-inauguration-crowd-sean-spicers-claims-versus-the-evidence

Hutchings, S., & Szostek, J. (2015). Dominant Narratives in Russian Political and Media Discourse during the Ukraine Crisis. In A. Pikulicka-Wilcewska & R. Sakwa (Eds.), *Ukraine and Russia.* E-International Relations Publishing.

Institute for the Study of War. (2023). *Ukraine Conflict Updates.* www.understandingwar.org/backgrounder/ukraine-conflict-updates

Ivanov, B., Miller, C. H., Compton, J., Averbeck, J. M., Harrison, K. J., Sims, J., Parker, K. A., & Parker, J. L. (2012). Effects of Postinoculation Talk on Resistance to Influence. *Journal of Communication, 62*(4), 701–718.

Ivanov, B., Parker, K. A., & Compton, J. (2011). The Potential of Inoculation in Reducing Post-Purchase Dissonance: Reinforcement of Purchase Behavior. *Central Business Review, 30*, 10–16.

Ivanov, B., Parker, K. A., & Dillingham, L. L. (2018). Testing the Limits of Inoculation-Generated Resistance. *Western Journal of Communication, 82*(5), 648–665. https://doi.org/10.1080/10570314.2018.1454600

Ivanov, B., Rains, S. A., Dillingham, L. L., Parker, K. A., Geegan, S. A., & Barbati, J. L. (2022). The Role of Threat and Counterarguing in Therapeutic Inoculation. *Southern Communication Journal, 87*(1), 15–27. https://doi.org/10.1080/1041794X.2021.1983012

Iyengar, A., Gupta, P., & Priya, N. (2022). Inoculation against Conspiracy Theories: A Consumer Side Approach to India's Fake News Problem. *Applied Cognitive Psychology.* https://doi.org/10.1002/acp.3995

Jack, V. (2022, March 22). Russia Expands Laws Criminalizing "Fake News." *Politico.* www.politico.eu/article/russia-expand-laws-criminalize-fake-news/

Jama, A., Ali, M., Lindstrand, A., Butler, R., & Kulane, A. (2018). Perspectives on the Measles, Mumps and Rubella Vaccination among Somali Mothers in Stockholm. *International Journal of Environmental Research and Public Health, 15*(11), 2428. https://doi.org/10.3390/ijerph15112428

Jankowicz, N. (2020). *How to Lose the Information War: Russia, Fake News, and the Future of Conflict.* I.B.Tauris & Co.

Janmohamed, K., Walter, N., Nyhan, K., Khoshnood, K., Tucker, J. D., Sangngam, N., Altice, F. L., Ding, Q., Wong, A., Schwitzky, Z. M., Bauch, C. T., De Choudhury, M., Papakyriakopoulos, O., & Kumar, N. (2021). Interventions to Mitigate COVID-19 Misinformation: A Systematic Review and Meta-Analysis. *Journal of Health Communication, 26*(12), 846–857. https://doi.org/10.1080/10810730.2021.2021460

Jenke, L. (2023). Affective Polarization and Misinformation Belief. *Political Behavior.* https://doi.org/10.1007/s11109-022-09851-w

Jeong, S.-H., Cho, H., & Hwang, Y. (2012). Media Literacy Interventions: A Meta-Analytic Review. *Journal of Communication, 62*(3), 454–472. https://doi.org/10.1111/j.1460-2466.2012.01643.x

Jigsaw. (2023, February 13). Defanging Disinformation's Threat to Ukrainian Refugees. *Medium.* https://medium.com/jigsaw/defanging-disinformations-threat-to-ukrainian-refugees-b164dbbc1c60

Johansson, P., Enock, F., Hale, S., Vidgen, B., Bereskin, C., Margetts, H., & Bright, J. (2022). How Can We Combat online Misinformation? A Systematic Overview of Current Interventions and Their Efficacy. *ArXiv Preprint.* https://doi.org/10.48550/arXiv.2212.11864

Johnson, H. M., & Seifert, C. M. (1994). Sources of the Continued Influence Effect: When Misinformation in Memory Affects Later Inferences. *Journal of Experimental Psychology: Learning, Memory, and Cognition, 20*(6), 1420–1436. https://doi.org/10.1037/0278-7393.20.6.1420

Johnson, S. B., Park, H. S., Gross, C. P., & Yu, J. B. (2017). Use of Alternative Medicine for Cancer and Its Impact on Survival. *JNCI: Journal of the National Cancer Institute, 110*(1), 121–124. https://doi.org/10.1093/jnci/djx145

Jolley, D., & Douglas, K. M. (2017). Prevention Is Better Than Cure: Addressing Anti-Vaccine Conspiracy Theories. *Journal of Applied Social Psychology, 47*(8), 459–469. https://doi.org/10.1111/jasp.12453

Jolley, D., & Paterson, J. L. (2020). Pylons Ablaze: Examining the Role of 5G COVID-19 Conspiracy Beliefs and Support for Violence. *British Journal of Social Psychology, 59*(3), 628–640. https://doi.org/10.1111/bjso.12394

Jones, S. G. (2022). *Russia's Ill-Fated Invasion of Ukraine: Lessons in Modern Warfare.*

Jones-Jang, S. M., Mortensen, T., & Liu, J. (2019). Does Media Literacy Help Identification of Fake News? Information Literacy Helps, but Other Literacies Don't. *American Behavioral Scientist, 65*(2), 371–388. https://doi.org/10.1177/0002764219869406

Jost, J. T., van der Linden, S., Panagopoulos, C., & Hardin, C. D. (2018). Ideological Asymmetries in Conformity, Desire for Shared Reality, and the Spread of Misinformation. *Current Opinion in Psychology, 23*, 77–83. https://doi.org/10.1016/j.copsyc.2018.01.003

Kahan, D. M. (2013). Ideology, Motivated Reasoning, and Cognitive Reflection. *Judgment and Decision Making, 8*(4), 407–424. http://journal.sjdm.org/13/13313/jdm13313.pdf

Kahn, R., & Cerf, V. (2000). Al Gore and the Internet. *The Register.* www.theregister.com/2000/10/02/net_builders_kahn_cerf_recognise/

Kaminska, I. (2017, January 17). A Lesson in Fake News From the Info-Wars of Ancient Rome. *Financial Times.* www.ft.com/content/aaf2bb08-dca2-11e6-86ac-f253db7791c6

Kapantai, E., Christopoulou, A., Berberidis, C., & Peristeras, V. (2021). A Systematic Literature Review on Disinformation: Toward a Unified Taxonomical Framework. *New Media & Society, 23*(5), 1301–1326. https://doi.org/10.1177/1461444820959296

Kata, A. (2010). A Postmodern Pandora's Box: Anti-Vaccination Misinformation on the Internet. Vaccine. https://doi.org/10.1016/j.vaccine.2009.12.022

Kata, A. (2012). Anti-Vaccine Activists, Web 2.0, and the Postmodern Paradigm – An Overview of Tactics and Tropes Used Online by the Anti-Vaccination Movement. *Vaccine, 30*(25), 3778–3789. https://doi.org/10.1016/j.vaccine.2011.11.112

Katsaros, M., Yang, K., & Fratamico, L. (2021). Reconsidering Tweets: Intervening During Tweet Creation Decreases Offensive Content. *Proceedings of the Sixteenth International AAAI Conference on Web and Social Media (ICWSM 2022)*, 477–487. https://ojs.aaai.org/index.php/ICWSM/article/view/19308/19080

Kean, L., & Blumenthal, R. (2023, June 5). Intelligence Official Says U.S. Has Retrieved Craft of Non-human Origin. The Debrief. https://thedebrief.org/intelligence-officials-say-u-s-has-retrieved-non-human-craft/

Keller, F. B., Schoch, D., Stier, S., & Yang, J. (2020). Political Astroturfing on Twitter: How to Coordinate a Disinformation Campaign. *Political Communication, 37*(2), 256–280. https://doi.org/10.1080/10584609.2019.1661888

Killion, V. L. (2019, January 16). *The First Amendment: Categories of Speech.* Congressional Research Service. https://sgp.fas.org/crs/misc/IF11072.pdf

King, K. M., Kim, D. S., & McCabe, C. J. (2019). Random Responses Inflate Statistical Estimates in Heavily Skewed Addictions Data. *Drug and Alcohol Dependence, 183*, 102–110. https://doi.org/10.1016/j.drugalcdep.2017.10.033

Kirby, E. J. (2016, December 5). The City Getting Rich from Fake News. BBC News.

Kozyreva, A., Lewandowsky, S., & Hertwig, R. (2020). Citizens Versus the Internet: Confronting Digital Challenges With Cognitive Tools. *Psychological Science in the Public Interest, 21*(3), 103–156. https://doi.org/10.1177/1529100620946707

Kozyreva, A., Lorenz-Spreen, P., Herzog, S. M., Ecker, U. K. H., Lewandowsky, S., Hertwig, R., Basol, M., Berinsky, A. J., Betsch, C., Cook, J., Fazio, L. K., Geers, M., Guess, A. M., Maertens, R., Panizza, F., Pennycook, G., Rand, D. J., Rathje, S., Reifler, J., … Wineburg, S. (2022). Toolbox of Interventions against Online Misinformation and Manipulation. PsyArxiv Preprints. https://doi.org/10.31234/osf.io/x8ejt

Krause, N. M., Freiling, I., Beets, B., & Brossard, D. (2020). Fact-Checking as Risk Communication: The Multi-layered Risk of Misinformation in Times of COVID-19. *Journal of Risk Research, 23*(7–8), 1052–1059. https://doi.org/10.1080/13669877.2020.1756385

Krebs, J. R., & Dawkins, R. (1978). Animal Signals: Mind-Reading and Manipulation. In J. R. Krebs & N. B. Davies (Eds.), *Behavioural Ecology. An Evolutionary Approach.* (2nd ed., pp. 380–404). Blackwell Scientific Publications.

Kuklinski, J. H., Quirk, P. J., Jerit, J., Schwieder, D., & Rich, R. F. (2000). Misinformation and the Currency of Democratic Citizenship. *The Journal of Politics, 62*(3), 790–816. https://doi.org/10.1111/0022-3816.00033

Kumkale, T. G., & Albarracín, D. (2004). The Sleeper Effect in Persuasion: A Meta-Analytic Review. *Psychological Bulletin, 130*(1), 143–172. https://doi.org/10.1037/0033-2909.130.1.143

Kupferschmidt, K. (2023, July 27). Does Social Media Polarize Voters? Unprecedented Experiments on Facebook Users Reveal Surprises. *Science*. www.science.org/content/article/does-social-media-polarize-voters-unprecedented-experiments-facebook-users-reveal

Kwan, R. (2022, March 8). Chinese Government Adviser Calls for Law to Ban "Fake News." *The Guardian*. www.theguardian.com/world/2022/mar/08/chinese-government-adviser-calls-for-law-to-ban-fake-news

Kyrychenko, Y., Brik, T., & Roozenbeek, J. (2023). In-group Solidarity Drives Engagement on Social Media during Intergroup Conflict. *Under Review.*

Larson, H. J. (2020). *Stuck: How Vaccine Rumors Start-and Why They Don't Go Away*. Oxford University Press.

Lazer, D. M. J., Baum, M. A., Benkler, Y., Berinsky, A. J., Greenhill, K. M., Menczer, F., Metzger, M. J., Nyhan, B., Pennycook, G., Rothschild, D., Schudson, M., Sloman, S. A., Sunstein, C. R., Thorson, E. A., Watts, D. J., & Zittrain, J. L. (2018). The Science of Fake News: Addressing Fake News Requires a Multidisciplinary Effort. *Science*, 359(6380), 1094–1096. https://doi.org/10.1126/science.aao2998

Leder, J., Schellinger, L. V., Maertens, R., van der Linden, S., & Roozenbeek, J. (2023). Feedback Exercises Boost Discernment and Longevity for Gamified Misinformation Interventions. *PsyArXiv Preprints*. https://doi.org/10.31234/osf.io/7k2mt

Lee, N. M. (2018). Fake News, Phishing, and Fraud: A Call for Research on Digital Media Literacy Education Beyond the Classroom. *Communication Education*, 67(4), 460–466. https://doi.org/10.1080/03634523.2018.1503313

Lees, J., Banas, J. A., Linvill, D., Meirick, P. C., & Warren, P. (2023). The Spot the Troll Quiz Game Increases Accuracy in Discerning Between Real and Inauthentic Social Media Accounts. *PNAS Nexus*. https://doi.org/10.31219/osf.io/xu6mh

LEMMiNO. (2016, October 29). The Eight Spiders. *YouTube*. www.youtube.com/watch?v=OjlKIjLWq-Y

Leopold, J. (2017, March 6). Here Are The Official Photos Showing Trump's Inauguration Crowds Were Smaller Than Obama's. Buzzfeed. www.buzzfeednews.com/article/jasonleopold/the-national-park-service-has-released-official-photos-of-tr

Levada-Center. (2022). *The Attitude of Russians to Countries: November 2022*. www.levada.ru/en/2022/12/16/the-attitude-of-russians-to-countries-november-2022/

Levy, G., & Razin, R. (2019). Echo Chambers and Their Effects on Economic and Political Outcomes. *Annual Review of Economics*, 11(1), 303–328. https://doi.org/10.1146/annurev-economics-080218-030343

Lewandowsky, S., Cook, J., Ecker, U. K. H., Albarracín, D., Amazeen, M. A., Kendeou, P., Lombardi, D., Newman, E. J., Pennycook, G., Porter, E., Rand, D. G., Rapp, D. N., Reifler, J., Roozenbeek, J., Schmid, P., Seifert, C. M., Sinatra, G. M., Swire-Thompson, B., van der Linden, S., … Zaragoza, M. S. (2020). *The Debunking Handbook 2020*. https://doi.org/10.17910/b7.1182

Lewandowsky, S., Ecker, U. K. H., Seifert, C. M., Schwarz, N., & Cook, J. (2012). Misinformation and Its Correction: Continued Influence and Successful Debiasing. *Psychological Science in the Public Interest*, 13(3), 106–131. https://doi.org/10.1177/1529100612451018

Lewandowsky, S., Lloyd, E. A., & Brophy, S. (2018). When THUNCing Trumps Thinking: What Distant Alternative Worlds Can Tell Us about the Real World. *Argumenta, 3*(2), 217–231.

Lewandowsky, S., & Oberauer, K. (2016). Motivated Rejection of Science. *Current Directions in Psychological Science, 25*(4), 217–222. https://doi.org/ 10.1177/0963721416654436

Lewandowsky, S., Stritzke, W. G. K., Oberauer, K., & Morales, M. (2005). Memory for Fact, Fiction, and Misinformation: The Iraq War 2003. *Psychological Science, 16*(3), 190–195. https://doi.org/10.1111/j.0956-7976.2005.00802.x

Lewandowsky, S., & van der Linden, S. (2021). Countering Misinformation and Fake News Through Inoculation and Prebunking. *European Review of Social Psychology, 32*(2), 348–384. https://doi.org/10.1080/10463283.2021.1876983

Lewandowsky, S., & Yesilada, M. (2021). Inoculating against the Spread of Islamophobic and Radical-Islamist Disinformation. *Cognitive Research: Principles and Implications, 6*(57). https://doi.org/10.1186/s41235-021-00323-z

Library of Congress. (2021, June 8). *Germany: Network Enforcement Act Amended to Better Fight Online Hate Speech.* www.loc.gov/item/global-legal-monitor/2021-07-06/germany-network-enforcement-act-amended-to-better-fight-online-hate-speech/

Löblich, M., & Venema, N. (2021). Echo Chambers. In G. Balbi, N. Ribeiro, V. Schafer, & C. Schwarzenegger (Eds.), *Digital Roots: Historicizing Media and Communication Concepts of the Digital Age* (pp. 177–192). De Gruyter. https://doi .org/10.1515/9783110740202-010

Loomba, S. (2023). *Sparse and Partially Observed Large-Scale Networks: Analytic Statistics, Behaviour, and Structural Inference* [PhD Thesis]. Imperial College London.

Loomba, S., de Figueiredo, A., Piatek, S. J., de Graaf, K., & Larson, H. J. (2021). Measuring the Impact of COVID-19 Vaccine Misinformation on Vaccination Intent in the UK and USA. *Nature Human Behaviour.* https://doi.org/10.1038/ s41562-021-01056-1

Loomba, S., Götz, F. M., Maertens, R., Roozenbeek, J., de Figueiredo, A., & van der Linden, S. (2023). Ability to Detect Fake News Predicts Geographical Variation in COVID-19 Vaccine Uptake. *Under Review.* https://doi.org/10.1101/2023.05.10.23289764

Lopez, J., & Hillygus, D. S. (2018). Why So Serious?: Survey Trolls and Misinformation. *SSRN Electronic Journal.* https://doi.org/10.2139/ssrn.3131087

Lu, C., Hu, B., Li, Q., Bi, C., & Ju, X. D. (2023). Psychological Inoculation for Credibility Assessment, Sharing Intention, and Discernment of Misinformation: Systematic Review and Meta-Analysis. Journal of Medical Internet Research, 25, e49255.

Luskin, R. C., Sood, G., Park, Y. M., & Blank, J. (2018). Misinformation about Misinformation? Of Headlines and Survey Design. *Unpublished Manuscript.* www.gsood.com/research/papers/misinformation_misinformation.pdf

Lutzke, L., Drummond, C., Slovic, P., & Árvai, J. (2019). Priming Critical Thinking: Simple Interventions Limit the Influence of Fake News about Climate Change on Facebook. *Global Environmental Change, 58*, 101964. https://doi.org/10.1016/j .gloenvcha.2019.101964

Lyons, B., Montgomery, J. M., & Reifler, J. (2023). Partisanship and Older Americans' Engagement with Dubious Political News. *PsyArxiv Preprints.* doi: 10.31219/osf .io/etb89

Ma, J., Chen, Y., Zhu, H., & Gan, Y. (2023). Fighting COVID-19 Misinformation Through an Online Game Based on the Inoculation Theory: Analyzing the Mediating Effects of Perceived Threat and Persuasion Knowledge. *International Journal of Environmental Research and Public Health, 20*(2), 980. https://doi .org/10.3390/ijerph20020980

MacDonald, E. (2017, December 1). The Fake News that Sealed the Fate of Antony and Cleopatra. Brewminate. https://brewminate.com/the-fake-news-that-sealed-the-fate-of-antony-and-cleopatra/

Machete, P., & Turpin, M. (2020). The Use of Critical Thinking to Identify Fake News: A Systematic Literature Review (pp. 235–246). https://doi.org/ 10.1007/978-3-030-45002-1_20

Mackey, R. (2016). Disinformation, Not Fake News, Got Trump Elected, and It Is Not Stopping. *The Intercept.* https://theintercept.com/2016/12/06/ disinformation-not-fake-news-got-trump-elected/

Madsen, J. K., Bailey, R. M., & Pilditch, T. D. (2018). Large Networks of Rational Agents form Persistent Echo Chambers. *Scientific Reports, 8*, 12391. https://doi.org/ 10.1038/s41598-018-25558-7

Maertens, R. (2022). *The Long-Term Effectiveness of Inoculation against Misinformation: An Integrated Theory of Memory, Threat, and Motivation* [PhD dissertation]. University of Cambridge.

Maertens, R., Anseel, F., & van der Linden, S. (2020). Combatting Climate Change Misinformation: Longevity of Inoculation and Consensus Messaging Effects. *Journal of Environmental Psychology, 70*(101455). https://doi.org/10.1016/j .jenvp.2020.101455

Maertens, R., Götz, F. M., Golino, H. F., Roozenbeek, J., Schneider, C. R., Kyrychenko, Y., Kerr, J. R., Stieger, S., McClanahan, W. P., Drabot, K., He, J., & van der Linden, S. (2023). The Misinformation Susceptibility Test (MIST): A Psychometrically Validated Measure of News veracity Discernment. *Behavior Research Methods.* https://doi.org/10.3758/s13428-023-02124-2

Maertens, R., Roozenbeek, J., Basol, M., & van der Linden, S. (2021). Long-Term Effectiveness of Inoculation against Misinformation: Three Longitudinal Experiments. *Journal of Experimental Psychology: Applied, 27*(1), 1–16. https://doi .org/10.1037/xap0000315

Maertens, R., Roozenbeek, J., Simons, J., Lewandowsky, S., Maturo, V., Goldberg, B., Xu, R., & van der Linden, S. (2023). Psychological Booster Shots Targeting Memory Increase Long-Term Resistance against Misinformation. *PsyArxiv Preprints.* doi: 10.31234/osf.io/6r9as

Magnúsdóttir, R. (2018). *Enemy Number One: The United States of America in Soviet Ideology and Propaganda, 1945–1959.* Oxford University Press.

Margolin, D. B., Hannak, A., & Weber, I. (2017). Political Fact-Checking on Twitter: When Do Corrections Have an Effect? *Political Communication, 35*(2), 196–219. https://doi.org/10.1080/10584609.2017.1334018

Marineau, S. (2020). Fact Check US: What Is the Impact of Russian Interference in the US Presidential Election? The Conversation. https://theconversation.com/fact-check-us-what-is-the-impact-of-russian-interference-in-the-us-presidential-election-146711

Martin, D. (2018). #republic: Divided Democracy in the Age of Social Media, by Cass R. Sunstein. Princeton: Princeton University Press, 2017. 328 pp. ISBN: 978-0691175515. *Business Ethics Quarterly, 28*(3), 360–363. https://doi.org/10.1017/beq.2018.22

Matchanova, A., Woods, S. P., Neighbors, C., Medina, L. D., Podell, K., Beltran-Najera, I., Alex, C., Babicz, M. A., & Thompson, J. L. (2023). Are Accuracy Discernment and Sharing of COVID-19 Misinformation Associated with Older Age and Lower Neurocognitive Functioning? *Current Psychology*. https://doi.org/10.1007/s12144-023-04464-w

Mateo, E. (2018). The Ukraine Crisis: A Clash of Narratives? University Consortium. https://uc.web.ox.ac.uk/article/the-ukraine-crisis-a-clash-of-narratives

Matthias, M. (2022). The Great Moon Hoax of 1835 Was Sci-fi Passed Off as News. Encyclopaedia Brittanica. www.britannica.com/story/the-great-moon-hoax-of-1835-was-sci-fi-passed-off-as-news

Matzko, P. (2021). When Conservatives Forget the History of the Fairness Doctrine. www.cato.org/blog/when-conservatives-forget-history-fairness-doctrine

Mayyasi, A. (2016, May 17). The Surprising Reason Why Dr. John Harvey Kellogg Invented Corn Flakes. *Forbes.* www.forbes.com/sites/priceonomics/2016/05/17/the-surprising-reason-why-dr-john-harvey-kellogg-invented-corn-flakes/

Mazepus, H., Osmudsen, M., Bang-Petersen, M., Toshkov, D., & Dimitrova, A. (2023). Information Battleground: Conflict Perceptions Motivate the Belief in and Sharing of Misinformation about the Adversary. *PLOS ONE, 18*(3), e0282308. https://doi.org/10.1371/journal.pone.0282308

McCarthy, B. (2021, June 30). Misinformation and the Jan. 6 Insurrection: When 'Patriot Warriors' Were Fed Lies. PolitiFact. www.politifact.com/article/2021/jun/30/misinformation-and-jan-6-insurrection-when-patriot/

McGrew, S., Ortega, T., Breakstone, J., & Wineburg, S. (2017). The Challenge That's Bigger than Fake News: Civic Reasoning in a Social Media Environment. *American Educator, 41*(3), 4.

McGrew, S., Smith, M., Breakstone, J., Ortega, T., & Wineburg, S. (2019). Improving University Students' Web Savvy: An Intervention Study. *British Journal of Educational Psychology, 89*(3), 485–500. https://doi.org/10.1111/bjep.12279

McGuire, W. J. (1961). The Effectiveness of Supportive and Refutational Defenses in Immunizing and Restoring Beliefs against Persuasion. *Sociometry, 24*(2), 184. https://doi.org/10.2307/2786067

McGuire, W. J. (1964). Some Contemporary Approaches. *Advances in Experimental Social Psychology, 1*(C), 191–229. https://doi.org/10.1016/S0065-2601(08)60052-0

McGuire, W. J. (1970). A Vaccine for Brainwash. *Psychology Today, 3*(9), 36–64.

McGuire, W. J., & Papageorgis, D. (1961a). Resistance to Persuasion Conferred by Active and Passive Prior Refutation of the Same and Alternative Counterarguments. *Journal of Abnormal and Social Psychology, 63*, 326–332.

McGuire, W. J., & Papageorgis, D. (1961b). The Relative Efficacy of Various Types of Prior Belief-Defense in Producing Immunity against Persuasion. *Journal of Abnormal and Social Psychology*, 62(2), 327–337.

McGuire, W. J., & Papageorgis, D. (1962). Effectiveness of Forewarning in Developing Resistance to Persuasion. *Public Opinion Quarterly*, 26(1), 24–34. https://doi .org/10.1086/267068

McKew, M. K. (2018, February 4). How Twitter Bots and Trump Fans Made #ReleaseTheMemo Go Viral. *Politico.* www.politico.com/magazine/ story/2018/02/04/trump-twitter-russians-release-the-memo-216935/

McPhedran, R., Ratajczak, M., Mawby, M., King, E., Yang, Y., & Gold, N. (2023). Psychological Inoculation Protects against the Social Media Infodemic. *Scientific Reports*, 13(1), 5780. https://doi.org/10.1038/s41598-023-32962-1

Media Defence. (2021, December 14). *Are Fake News Laws the Best way to Tackle Disinformation?.* www.mediadefence.org/news/are-fake-news-laws-the-best-way-to-tackle-disinformation/

Melki, J., Tamim, H., Hadid, D., Makki, M., El Amine, J., & Hitti, E. (2021). Mitigating Infodemics: The Relationship between News Exposure and Trust and Belief in COVID-19 Fake News and Social Media Spreading. *PLOS ONE*, 16(6), e0252830. https://doi.org/10.1371/journal.pone.0252830

Mena, P. (2019). Cleaning Up Social Media: The Effect of Warning Labels on Likelihood of Sharing False News on Facebook. *Policy & Internet*, 12(2), 165–183. https://doi .org/10.1002/poi3.214

Mercier, H. (2017). Confirmation Bias – Myside Bias. In R. Pohl (Ed.), *Cognitive Illusions* (2nd ed., pp. 99–114). Routledge.

Mercier, H. (2020). *Not Born Yesterday: The Science of Who We Trust and What We Believe.* Princeton University Press.

Mercier, H., & Altay, S. (2022). Do Cultural Misbeliefs Cause Costly Behavior? In J. Musolino, J. Sommer, & P. Hemmer (Eds.), *The Cognitive Science of Beliefs* (pp. 193–208). Cambridge University Press. https://doi.org/10.1017/9781009001021

Mikkelson, D. (2001, April 22). Do People Swallow Eight Spiders Per Year? *Snopes.* www.snopes.com/fact-check/swallow-spiders/

Miller, N., & Campbell, D. T. (1959). Recency and Primacy in Persuasion as a Function of the Timing of Speeches and Measurements. *Journal of Abnormal and Social Psychology*, 59(1), 1–9. https://doi.org/10.1037/h0049330

Milmo, D. (2022, July 4). Legislation Aims to Shield UK Internet Users from State-Backed Disinformation. *The Guardian.* www.theguardian.com/uk-news/2022/jul/04/ legislation-aims-to-shield-uk-internet-users-from-state-backed-disinformation

Mirhoseini, M., Early, S., El Shamy, N., & Hassanein, K. (2023). Actively Open-Minded Thinking Is Key to Combating Fake News: A Multimethod Study. *Information & Management*, 60(3), 103761. https://doi.org/10.1016/j.im.2023.103761

Modirrousta-Galian, A., & Higham, P. A. (2023). Gamified Inoculation Interventions Do Not Improve Discrimination between True and Fake News: Reanalyzing Existing Research with Receiver Operating Characteristic Analysis. *Journal of Experimental Psychology: General.* https://doi.org/10.1037/xge0001395

Mokkonen, M., & Lindstedt, C. (2016). The Evolutionary Ecology of Deception. *Biological Reviews*, 91(4), 1020–1035. https://doi.org/10.1111/brv.12208

Moore, T. (2014). Wittgenstein, Williams and the Terminologies of Higher Education: A Case Study of the Term 'Critical.' *Journal of Academic Language & Learning, 8(1),* A95–A108.

Mosleh, M., Martel, C., Eckles, D., & Rand, D. G. (2021). Perverse Downstream Consequences of Debunking: Being Corrected by Another User for Posting False Political News Increases Subsequent Sharing of Low Quality, Partisan, and Toxic Content in a Twitter Field Experiment. *CHI '21: Proceedings of the 2021 CHI Conference on Human Factors in Computing Systems,* 1–13. https://doi.org/10.1145/3411764.3445642

Motta, M., & Stecula, D. (2021). Quantifying the Effect of Wakefield et al. (1998) on Skepticism about MMR Vaccine Safety in the U.S. *PLOS ONE, 16*(8), e0256395. https://doi.org/10.1371/journal.pone.0256395

National Park Service. (2017, March 3). National Mall & Memorial Parks Inauguration Information. www.nps.gov/aboutus/foia/foia-frd.htm

New York Times. (2004). FROM THE EDITORS; The Times and Iraq. *New York Times.* www.nytimes.com/2004/05/26/world/from-the-editors-the-times-and-iraq.html

Newman, M. S. (2019). So, Gutenberg Didn't Actually Invent Printing As We Know It. Literary Hub. https://lithub.com/so-gutenberg-didnt-actually-invent-the-printing-press/

Neylan, J., Biddlestone, M., Roozenbeek, J., & van der Linden, S. (2023). How to "inoculate" against multimodal misinformation: A conceptual replication of Roozenbeek and van der Linden (2020). *Scientific Reports, 13*(1), 18273. https://doi.org/10.1038/s41598-023-43885-2.

Nguyen, C. T. (2020). Echo Chambers and Epistemic Bubbles. *Episteme, 17*(2), 141–161. https://doi.org/10.1017/epi.2018.32

NOS. (2017, January 23). *Zo vaccineer je mensen tegen nepnieuws.* Nos.Nl. https://nos.nl/op3/artikel/2154559-zo-vaccineer-je-mensen-tegen-nepnieuws

Nuñez, F. (2020). Disinformation Legislation and Freedom of Expression. *UC Irvine Law Review, 10*(2). https://scholarship.law.uci.edu/ucilr/vol10/iss2/10

Nygren, T. (2019). *Fakta, fejk och fiktion: Källkritik, ämnesdidaktik och digital kompetens.* Natur & Kultur.

Nygren, T., Brounéus, F., & Svensson, G. (2019). Diversity and Credibility in Young People's News Feeds: A Foundation for Teaching and Learning Citizenship in a Digital Era. *Journal of Social Science Education, 18*(2), 87–109. www.jsse.org/index.php/jsse/article/view/917/1539

Nygren, T., & Guath, M. (2019). Swedish Teenagers' Difficulties and Abilities to Determine Digital News Credibility. *Nordicom Review, 40*(1), 23–42.

Nygren, T., & Guath, M. (2021). Students Evaluating and Corroborating Digital News. *Scandinavian Journal of Educational Research, 66*(1), 1–17. https://doi.org/10.1080/00313831.2021.1897876

Nyhan, B. (2017). Why the Fact-Checking at Facebook Needs to Be Checked. www.nytimes.com/2017/10/23/upshot/why-the-fact-checking-at-facebook-needs-to-be-checked.html

Nyhan, B., & Reifler, J. (2010). When Corrections Fail: The Persistence of Political Misperceptions. *Political Behavior, 32*(2), 303–330. https://doi.org/10.1007/s11109-010-9112-2

Nyhan, B., Settle, J., Thorson, E., Wojcieszak, M., Barberá, P., Chen, A. Y., Allcott, H., Brown, T., Crespo-Tenorio, A., Dimmery, D., Freelon, D., Gentzkow, M., González-Bailón, S., Guess, A. M., Kennedy, E., Kim, Y. M., Lazer, D., Malhotra, N., Moehler, D., ... Tucker, J. A. (2023). Like-Minded Sources on Facebook Are Prevalent but Not Polarizing. *Nature*. https://doi.org/10.1038/s41586-023-06297-w

Oeldorf-Hirsch, A., Schmierbach, M., Appelman, A., & Boyle, M. P. (2020). The Ineffectiveness of Fact-Checking Labels on News Memes and Articles. *Mass Communication and Society*, 23(5), 682–704. https://doi.org/10.1080/15205436.2020.1733613

Ognyanova, K., Lazer, D., Robertson, R. E., & Wilson, C. (2020). Misinformation in Action: Fake News Exposure Is Linked to Lower Trust in Media, Higher Trust in Government When Your Side Is in Power. *Harvard Kennedy School Misinformation Review*. https://doi.org/10.37016/mr-2020-024

O'Hara, K., & Stevens, D. (2015). Echo Chambers and Online Radicalism: Assessing the Internet's Complicity in Violent Extremism. *Policy & Internet*, 7(4), 401–422. https://doi.org/10.1002/poi3.88

O'Loughlin, J., Toal, G., & Kolosov, V. (2017). The Rise and Fall of "Novorossiya": Examining Support for a Separatist Geopolitical Imaginary in Southeast Ukraine. *Post-Soviet Affairs*, 33(2), 124–144. https://doi.org/10.1080/1060586X.2016.1146452

O'Mahony, C., Brassil, M., Murphy, G., & Linehan, C. (2023). The Efficacy of Interventions in Reducing Belief in Conspiracy Theories: A Systematic Review. *PLOS ONE*, 18(4), e0280902. https://doi.org/10.1371/journal.pone.0280902

Orben, A. (2020a). Teenagers, Screens and Social Media: A Narrative Review of Reviews and Key Studies. *Social Psychiatry and Psychiatric Epidemiology*, 55, 407–414. https://doi.org/10.1007/s00127-019-01825-4

Orben, A. (2020b). The Sisyphean Cycle of Technology Panics. *Perspectives on Psychological Science*, 15(5), 1143–1157. https://doi.org/10.1177/1745691620919372

Orben, A., Tomova, L., & Blakemore, S.-J. (2020). The Effects of Social Deprivation on Adolescent Development and Mental Health. *The Lancet Child Adolescent Health*, 4(8), 634–640. https://doi.org/10.1016/S2352-4642(20)30186-3

Oreskes, N., & Conway, E. M. (2010). *Merchants of Doubt: How a Handful of Scientists Obscured the Truth on Issues from Tobacco Smoke to Global Warming*. Bloomsbury Press.

Osmundsen, M., Bor, A., Bjerregaard Vahlstrup, P., Bechmann, A., & Petersen, M. B. (2021). Partisan Polarization Is the Primary Psychological Motivation behind Political Fake News Sharing on Twitter. *American Political Science Review*, 115(3), 999–1015. https://doi.org/10.1017/S0003055421000290

Panizza, F., Ronzani, P., Martini, C., Mattavelli, S., Morisseau, T., & Motterlini, M. (2022). Lateral Reading and Monetary Incentives to Spot Disinformation about Science. *Scientific Reports*, 12(1), 5678. https://doi.org/10.1038/s41598-022-09168-y

Papageorgis, D., & McGuire, W. J. (1961). The Generality of Immunity to Persuasion Produced by Pre-exposure to Weakened Counterarguments. *Journal of Abnormal and Social Psychology*, 62, 475–481.

Papakyriakopoulos, O., & Goodman, E. (2022). The Impact of Twitter Labels on Misinformation Spread and User Engagement: Lessons from Trump's Election Tweets. *Proceedings of the ACM Web Conference 2022*, 2541–2551. https://doi.org/10.1145/3485447.3512126

Pariser, E. (2011). *The Filter Bubble: What The Internet Is Hiding From You*. Penguin Books.

Park, H. S., & Yoon, E. P. (2009). Early movable metal types produced by lost-wax casting. *Metals and Materials International, 15*(1), 155–158. https://doi.org/10.1007/s12540-009-0155-z

Parker, K. A., Ivanov, B., & Compton, J. (2012). Inoculation's Efficacy with Young Adults' Risky Behaviors: Can Inoculation Confer Cross-Protection Over related but Untreated Issues? *Health Communication, 27*(3), 223–233. https://doi.org/10.1080/10410236.2011.575541

Parker, K. A., Rains, S. A., & Ivanov, B. (2016). Examining the "Blanket of Protection" Conferred by Inoculation: The Effects of Inoculation Messages on the Cross-protection of Related Attitudes. *Communication Monographs, 83*(1), 49–68. https://doi.org/10.1080/03637751.2015.1030681

Parks, M. (2021, March 25). Few Facts, Millions Of Clicks: Fearmongering Vaccine Stories Go Viral Online. *NPR*. www.npr.org/2021/03/25/980035707/lying-through-truth-misleading-facts-fuel-vaccine-misinformation?t=1621596471521&t=1622544913288

Paul, K. (2023, May 3). Brazil Receives Pushback from Tech Companies on 'Fake News' Bill. *The Guardian*. www.theguardian.com/world/2023/may/03/alphabet-google-fake-news-law

Paynter, J., Luskin-Saxby, S., Keen, D., Fordyce, K., Frost, G., Imms, C., Miller, S., Trembath, D., Tucker, M., & Ecker, U. (2019). Evaluation of a Template for Countering Misinformation: Real-World Autism Treatment Myth Debunking. *PLOS ONE, 14*(1), e0210746. https://doi.org/10.1371/journal.pone.0210746

Pennycook, G., Epstein, Z., Mosleh, M., Arechar, A., Eckles, D., & Rand, D. G. (2021). Shifting Attention to Accuracy Can Reduce Misinformation Online. *Nature, 592*, 590–595. https://doi.org/10.1038/s41586-021-03344-2

Pennycook, G., McPhetres, J., Zhang, Y., Lu, J. G., & Rand, D. G. (2020). Fighting COVID-19 Misinformation on Social Media: Experimental Evidence for a Scalable Accuracy-nudge Intervention. *Psychological Science, 31*(7), 770–780. https://doi.org/10.1177/0956797620939054

Pennycook, G., & Rand, D. G. (2019). Lazy, Not Biased: Susceptibility to Partisan Fake News Is Better Explained by Lack of Reasoning than by Motivated Reasoning. *Cognition, 188*, 39–50. https://doi.org/10.1016/j.cognition.2018.06.011

Pennycook, G., & Rand, D. G. (2020). Who Falls For Fake News? The Roles of Bullshit Receptivity, Overclaiming, Familiarity, and Analytic Thinking. *Journal of Personality, 88*(2), 185–200. https://doi.org/10.1111/jopy.12476

Pennycook, G., & Rand, D. G. (2021). The Psychology of Fake News. *Trends in Cognitive Sciences, 25*(5), 388–402. https://doi.org/10.1016/j.tics.2021.02.007

Pennycook, G., & Rand, D. G. (2022). Accuracy Prompts Are a Replicable and Generalizable Approach for Reducing the Spread of Misinformation. *Nature Communications, 13*, 2333. https://doi.org/10.1038/s41467-022-30073-5

Pereira, A., Harris, E. A., & Van Bavel, J. J. (2021). Identity Concerns Drive Belief: The Impact of Partisan Identity on the Belief and Dissemination of

True and False News. *Group Processes & Intergroup Relations.* https://doi .org/10.1177/13684302211103000

Peter, C., & Koch, T. (2015). When Debunking Scientific Myths Fails (and When It Does Not): The Backfire Effect in the Context of Journalistic Coverage and Immediate Judgments as Prevention Strategy. *Science Communication, 38*(1), 3–25. https://doi.org/10.1177/1075547015613523

Peter, L. (2022). How Ukraine's "Ghost of Kyiv" Legendary Pilot Was Born. BBC News. www.bbc.co.uk/news/world-europe-61285833

Petersen, M. B., Osmundsen, M., & Tooby, J. (2022). The Evolutionary Psychology of Conflict and the Functions of Falsehood. In D. C. Barker & E. Suhay (Eds.), *The Politics of Truth in Polarized America. Concepts, Causes and Correctives.* Oxford University Press. https://doi.org/10.31234/osf.io/kaby9

Pew Research Center. (2017). *Religious Belief and National Belonging in Central and Eastern Europe: Social Views and Morality.* www.pewresearch.org/ religion/2017/05/10/social-views-and-morality/

Pfau, M. (1995). Designing Messages for Behavioral Inoculation. In E. Maybach & R. Louiselle Parrott (Eds.), *Designing Health Messages: Approaches from Communication Theory and Public Health Practice* (pp. 99–113). SAGE Publications, Inc. https://doi.org/10.4135/9781452233451

Pfau, M., & Burgoon, M. (1988). Inoculation in Political Campaign Communication. *Human Communication Research, 15*(1), 91–111. https://doi.org/10.1111/j.1468-2958 .1988.tb00172.x

Phartiyal, S., Patnaik, S., & Ingram, D. (2018, June 25). When a Text Can Trigger a Lynching: WhatsApp Struggles with Incendiary Messages in India. Reuters UK.

Piltch-Loeb, R., Su, M., Testa, M., Goldberg, B., Braddock, K., Miller-Idriss, C., Maturo, V., & Savoia, E. (2022). Testing the Efficacy of Attitudinal Inoculation Videos to Enhance COVID-19 Vaccine Acceptance: A Quasi-Experimental Intervention Trial. *JMIR Public Health and Surveillance, 8*(6). https://doi .org/10.2196/34615

Piskorski, J., Stefanovitch, N., Nikolaidis, N., Da San Martino, G., & Nakov, P. (2023). Multilingual Multifaceted Understanding of Online News in Terms of Genre, Framing and Persuasion Techniques. *Proceedings of the 61st Annual Meeting of the Association for Computational Linguistics, 3001–3022.* https://aclanthology .org/2023.acl-long.169.pdf

Pooley, J., & Socolow, M. J. (2013). The Myth of the War of the Worlds Panic. *Slate.* https://slate.com/culture/2013/10/orson-welles-war-of-the-worlds-panic-myth- the-infamous-radio-broadcast-did-not-cause-a-nationwide-hysteria.html

Pornpitakpan, C. (2006). The Persuasiveness of Source Credibility: A Critical Review of Five Decades' Evidence. *Journal of Applied Social Psychology, 34*(2), 243–281. https://doi.org/10.1111/j.1559-1816.2004.tb02547.x

Porter, E., & Wood, T. J. (2021). The Global Effectiveness of Fact-checking: Evidence from Simultaneous Experiments in Argentina, Nigeria, South Africa, and the United Kingdom. *Proceedings of the National Academy of Sciences, 118*(37), e2104235118. https://doi.org/10.1073/pnas.2104235118

Posetti, J., & Matthews, A. (2018). *A Short Guide to the History of "Fake News" and Disinformation.*

Potter, W. J. (2020). *Media Literacy.* SAGE Publications Inc.

Potter, W. J., & Thai, C. L. (2016). Conceptual Challenges in Designing Measures for Media Literacy Studies. *International Journal of Media and Information Literacy*, *1*(1), 27–42.

Prendergast, S. (2019, March). It Must be True, I Read it on the Internet: Regulating Fake News in the Digital Age. Michigan Technology Law Review. https://mttlr.org/2019/03/it-must-be-true-i-read-it-on-the-internet-regulating-fake-news-in-the-digital-age/

Pretus, C., Van Bavel, J. J., Brady, W. J., Harris, E. A., Vilarroya, O., & Servin, C. (2021). The Role of Political Devotion in Sharing Partisan Misinformation. PsyArxiv Preprints. https://doi.org/10.31234/osf.io/7k9gx

Price, V., & Hsu, M. L. (1992). Public Opinion about AIDS Policies. The Role of Misinformation and Attitudes Toward Homosexuals. *Public Opinion Quarterly*, *56*(1), 29–52. https://doi.org/10.1086/269294

Putin, V. (2022). *Address by the President of the Russian Federation.* en.kremlin.ru. http://en.kremlin.ru/events/president/news/67843

Quinn, M. (2023, May 18). Supreme Court Sides with Social Media Companies in Suits by Families of Terror Victims. *CBS News*.

Quiring, O., Ziegele, M., Schemer, C., Jackob, N., Jakobs, I., & Schultz, T. (2021). Constructive Skepticism, Dysfunctional Cynicism? Skepticism and Cynicism Differently Determine Generalized Media Trust. *International Journal of Communication*, *15*, 3497–3518.

Rao, T. S. S., & Andrade, C. (2011). The MMR Vaccine and Autism: Sensation, Refutation, Retraction, and Fraud. *Indian Journal of Psychiatry*, *53*(2), 95–96. https://doi.org/10.4103/0019-5545.82529

Rasmussen, J., Lindekilde, L., & Petersen, M. B. (2022). Public Health Communication Decreases False Headline Sharing by Boosting Self-efficacy. *PsyArxiv Preprints*.

Rathje, S., He, J., Roozenbeek, J., Van Bavel, J. J., & van der Linden, S. (2022). Social Media Behavior Is Associated with Vaccine Hesitancy. *PNAS Nexus*, *1*(4), 1–11. https://doi.org/10.1093/pnasnexus/pgac207

Rathje, S., Roozenbeek, J., Van Bavel, J. J., & van der Linden, S. (2023). Accuracy and Social Motivations Shape Judgements of (mis)information. *Nature Human Behaviour*. https://doi.org/10.1038/s41562-023-01540-w

Rathje, S., Van Bavel, J. J., & van der Linden, S. (2021). Outgroup Animosity Drives Engagement on Social Media. *Proceedings of the National Academy of Sciences*, *118*(26), e2024292118. https://doi.org/10.1073/pnas.2024292118

Reddy, P., Sharma, B., & Chaudhary, K. (2022). Digital Literacy: A Review in the South Pacific. *Journal of Computing in Higher Education*, *34*, 83–108. https://doi.org/10.1007/s12528-021-09280-4

Repnikova, M. (2018, September 6). China's Lessons for Fighting Fake News. Foreign Policy. https://foreignpolicy.com/2018/09/06/chinas-lessons-for-fighting-fake-news/

Reporters Without Borders. (2020, April 1). *Orbán's Orwellian Law Paves Way for "Information Police State" in Hungary.* https://rsf.org/en/orb%C3%A1n-s-orwellian-law-paves-way-information-police-state-hungary

Reporters Without Borders. (2021, January 28). *Poland's New Social Media Law Puts Freedom of Expression at Risk, RSF warns.* https://rsf.org/en/poland-s-new-social-media-law-puts-freedom-expression-risk-rsf-warns

Reuters. (2023, January 18). India Considers Banning News Identified as "Fake" by Govt on Social Media. www.reuters.com/world/india/india-considers-banning-news-identified-fake-by-govt-on-social-media-2023-01-18/

Richards, A. S., & Banas, J. A. (2018). The Opposing Mediational Effects of Apprehensive Threat and Motivational Threat When Inoculating against Reactance to Health Promotion. *Southern Communication Journal*, *83*(4), 245–255. https://doi.org/10.1080/1041794X.2018.1498909

Robbe, J. R. (2010). De literaire aspecten van de Costerlegende: Mythologie in de vorm van een klassieke pleitrede. *Internationale Neerlandistiek*, *48*(3), 17–29.

Robertson, R. E., Green, J., Ruck, D. J., Ognyanova, K., Wilson, C., & Lazer, D. (2023). Users Choose to Engage with more Partisan News than they Are Exposed to on Google Search. *Nature*. https://doi.org/10.1038/s41586-023-06078-5

Roozenbeek, J. (2020a). Identity Discourse in Local Newspapers Before, During and after Military Conflict: A Case Study of Kramatorsk. *Demokratizatsiya: The Journal of Post-Soviet Democratization*, *28*(3), 419–459.

Roozenbeek, J. (2020b). Media and Identity in Wartime Donbas, 2014–2017 [PhD thesis, University of Cambridge]. www.cam.ac.uk/sites/www.cam.ac.uk/files/jon_roozenbeek_-_media_and_identity_in_wartime_donbas_2014-2017.pdf

Roozenbeek, J. (2022). *The Failure of Russian Propaganda*. www.cam.ac.uk/stories/donbaspropaganda

Roozenbeek, J. (2024). *Propaganda and Ideology in the Russian-Ukrainian War*. Cambridge: Cambridge University Press.

Roozenbeek, J., Culloty, E., & Suiter, J. (2023). Countering Misinformation: Evidence, Knowledge Gaps, and Implications of Current Interventions. *European Psychologist*, *28*(3), 189–205. https://doi.org/10.31234/osf.io/b52um

Roozenbeek, J., Freeman, A. L. J., & van der Linden, S. (2021). How Accurate Are Accuracy Nudges? A pre-registered Direct Replication of Pennycook et al. (2020). *Psychological Science*, *32*(7), 1–10. https://doi.org/10.1177/09567976211024535

Roozenbeek, J., Lasser, J., Garcia, D., Goldberg, B., van der Linden, S., & Lewandowsky, S. (2023). How Do Inoculation Interventions Impact Twitter Sharing Behavior? Results from Two Pre-registered Studies. *Under Review*.

Roozenbeek, J., Maertens, R., Herzog, S., Geers, M., Kurvers, R., Sultan, M., & van der Linden, S. (2022). Susceptibility to Misinformation Is Consistent Across Question Framings and Response Modes and Better Explained by Myside Bias and Partisanship than Analytical Thinking. *Judgment and Decision Making*, *17*(3), 547–573. https://doi.org/10.1017/S1930297500003570

Roozenbeek, J., Maertens, R., McClanahan, W., & van der Linden, S. (2021). Disentangling Item and Testing Effects in Inoculation Research on Online Misinformation. *Educational and Psychological Measurement*, *81*(2), 340–362. https://doi.org/10.1177/0013164420940378

Roozenbeek, J., Schneider, C. R., Dryhurst, S., Kerr, J., Freeman, A. L. J., Recchia, G., van der Bles, A. M., & van der Linden, S. (2020). Susceptibility to Misinformation about COVID-19 around the World. *Royal Society Open Science*, *7*(201199). https://doi.org/10.1098/rsos.201199

Roozenbeek, J., Traberg, C. S., & van der Linden, S. (2022). Technique-based Inoculation against Real-world Misinformation. *Royal Society Open Science*, *9*(211719). https://doi.org/10.1098/rsos.211719

Roozenbeek, J., & van der Linden, S. (2018). The Fake News Game: Actively Inoculating against the Risk of Misinformation. *Journal of Risk Research*, 22(5), 570–580. https://doi.org/10.1080/13669877.2018.1443491

Roozenbeek, J., & van der Linden, S. (2019). Fake News Game Confers Psychological Resistance against Online Misinformation. *Humanities and Social Sciences Communications*, 5(65), 1–10. https://doi.org/10.1057/s41599-019-0279-9

Roozenbeek, J., & van der Linden, S. (2020). Breaking Harmony Square: A Game that "inoculates" against Political Misinformation. *The Harvard Kennedy School (HKS) Misinformation Review*, 1(8). https://doi.org/10.37016/mr-2020-47

Roozenbeek, J., & van der Linden, S. (2022). How to Combat Health Misinformation: A Psychological Approach. *American Journal of Health Promotion*, 36(3), 569–575. https://doi.org/10.1177/08901171211070958

Roozenbeek, J., van der Linden, S., Goldberg, B., Rathje, S., & Lewandowsky, S. (2022). Psychological Inoculation Improves Resilience against Misinformation on Social Media. *Science Advances*, 8(34). https://doi.org/10.1126/sciadv.abo6254

Roozenbeek, J., van der Linden, S., & Nygren, T. (2020). Prebunking Interventions Based on "inoculation" Theory Can Reduce Susceptibility to Misinformation across Cultures. *The Harvard Kennedy School (HKS) Misinformation Review*, 1(2). https://doi.org/10.37016//mr-2020-008

Roozenbeek, J., & Zollo, F. (2022). Democratize Social-media Research – With Access and Funding. *Nature*, 612(7940), 404. https://doi.org/10.1038/d41586-022-04407-8

Ross Arguedas, A., Robertson, C. T., Fletcher, R., & Kleis Nielsen, R. (2022). *Echo Chambers, Filter Bubbles, and Polarisation: A Literature Review.*

Rozado, D., Hughes, R., & Halberstadt, J. (2022). Longitudinal Analysis of Sentiment and Emotion in News Media Headlines Using Automated Labelling with Transformer Language Models. *PLOS ONE*, 17(10), e0276367. https://doi.org/10.1371/journal.pone.0276367

RTÉ News. (2022). Elderly Ukrainian Woman Berates Occupying Russian Soldiers. *YouTube*. www.youtube.com/watch?v=oQFGwkOWtKo

Ruane, K. A. (2010). Fairness Doctrine: History and Constitutional Issues. *Journal of Current Issues in Crime, Law and Law Enforcement*, 2(1), 75–89.

Saleh, N., Makki, F., van der Linden, S., & Roozenbeek, J. (2023). Inoculating against Extremist Persuasion Techniques – Results from a Randomised Controlled Trial in Post-Conflict Areas in Iraq. *Advances in Psychology*, 1(1), 1–21. https://doi.org/10.56296/aip00005

Saleh, N., Roozenbeek, J., Makki, F., McClanahan, W., & van der Linden, S. (2021). Active Inoculation Boosts Attitudinal Resistance against Extremist Persuasion Techniques – A Novel Approach Towards the Prevention of Violent Extremism. *Behavioural Public Policy*, 1–24. https://doi.org/10.1017/bpp.2020.60

Saltor, J., Barberia, I., & Rodríguez-Ferreiro, J. (2023). Thinking Disposition, Thinking Style, and Susceptibility to Causal Illusion Predict Fake News Discriminability. *Applied Cognitive Psychology*, 37(2), 360–368. https://doi.org/10.1002/acp.4008

Saltz, E., Barari, S., Leibowicz, C., & Wardle, C. (2021). Misinformation Interventions Are Common, Divisive, and Poorly Understood. *Harvard Kennedy School Misinformation Review*. https://doi.org/10.37016/mr-2020-81

San Martino, A., & Perramon, X. (2010). Phishing Secrets: History, Effects, and Countermeasures. *International Journal of Network Security*, 11(3), 163–171.

Sasaki, S., Kurokawa, H., & Ohtake, F. (2021). Effective but Fragile? Responses to Repeated Nudge-based Messages for Preventing the Spread of COVID-19 Infection. *The Japanese Economic Review*, 62, 371–408. https://doi.org/10.1007/s42973-021-00076-w

Sasse, G. (2019). Most People in Separatist-held areas of Donbas Prefer Reintegration with Ukraine – New Survey. The Conversation. https://theconversation.com/most-people-in-separatist-held-areas-of-donbas-prefer-reintegration-with-ukraine-new-survey-124849

Sasse, G., & Lackner, A. (2019). *Attitudes and Identities across the Donbas Front line: What has Changed from 2016 to 2019?* Zentrum für Osteuropa- und internationale Studien, No. 3 (August 2019). www.zois-berlin.de/en/publications/attitudes-and-identities-across-the-donbas-front-line-what-has-changed-from-2016-to-2019

Schimmack, U. (2020, December 30). A Meta-Scientific Perspective on "Thinking: Fast and Slow." Replication Index. https://replicationindex.com/category/implicit-priming/

Schimmack, U., Heene, M., & Kesavan, K. (2017, February 2). Reconstruction of a Train Wreck: How Priming Research Went off the Rails. Replication Index. https://replicationindex.com/2017/02/02/reconstruction-of-a-train-wreck-how-priming-research-went-of-the-rails/

Schlichtkrull, M., Ousidhoum, N., & Vlachos, A. (2023). The Intended Uses of Automated Fact-Checking Artefacts: Why, How and Who. *Arxiv Preprints*. https://doi.org/10.48550/arXiv.2304.14238

Schmid, P., Altay, S., & Scherer, L. (2023). The Psychological Impacts and Message Features of Health Misinformation: A Systematic Review of Randomized Controlled Trials. *European Psychologist*, 28(3), 162–172. https://doi.org/10.1027/1016-9040/a000494

Schmid-Petri, H., & Bürger, M. (2021). The Effect of Misinformation and Inoculation: Replication of an Experiment on the Effect of False Experts in the Context of Climate Change Communication. *Public Understanding of Science*, 31(2), 152–167. https://doi.org/10.1177/09636625211024550

Schreiber, M. (2022). "Bot Holiday": Covid Disinformation Down as Social Media Pivot to Ukraine. *The Guardian*. www.theguardian.com/media/2022/mar/04/bot-holiday-covid-misinformation-ukraine-social-media

Schwartz, A. B. (2015). *Broadcast Hysteria: Orson Welles's War of the Worlds and the Art of Fake News*. Hill & Wang.

Scott, M., & Dickson, A. (2023, February 28). How UK's Online Safety Bill fell victim to never-ending political crisis. *Politico*. www.politico.eu/article/online-safety-bill-uk-westminster-politics/

Shi, W. (2023). Efficacy of Educational Misinformation Games. *ArXiv Preprints*. doi: 10.48550/arXiv.2305.09429

Sifuentes, J. (2019, November 20). La propaganda de la guerra civil entre Octaviano y Marco Antonio. World History Encyclopedia. www.worldhistory.org/trans/es/2-1474/la-propaganda-de-la-guerra-civil-entre-octaviano-y/

Silva, M., Giovanini, L., Fernandes, J., Oliveira, D., & Silva, C. S. (2023). What Makes Disinformation Ads Engaging? A Case Study of Facebook Ads from the Russian Active Measures Campaign. *Journal of Interactive Advertising*. https://doi.org/10 .1080/15252019.2023.2173991

Snopes. (2016). *Protests Seek to #EndFathersDay?* www.snopes.com/fact-check/ fathers-day-protest-photo/

Snopes. (2023). *tHis Is a Big troLl.* www.snopes.com/lisa-birgit-holst/

Social Science Research Council. (2022). *Building a Better Toolkit (for Fighting Misinformation): Large Collaborative Project to Compare Misinformation Interventions.* www.ssrc.org.

Soll, J. (2016). The Long and Brutal History of Fake News. *Politico.* www.politico.com/ magazine/story/2016/12/fake-news-history-long-violent-214535/

Soniak, M. (2023, March 6). When Corn Flakes Were Part of an Anti-Masturbation Crusade. *Mental Floss.* www.mentalfloss.com/article/32042/ corn-flakes-were-invented-part-anti-masturbation-crusade

Stamouli, N. (2022, August 8). How Greece became Europe's Worst Place for Press Freedom. *Politico.* www.politico.eu/article/greece-became-europe-worst-place-press-freedom/

Stanford Research into the Impact of Tobacco Advertising. (2021). More Doctors Smoke Camels. Tobacco.Stanford.Edu. https://tobacco.stanford.edu/cigarette/ img0074/d

Stanovich, K. E., & Toplak, M. E. (2023). Actively Open-Minded Thinking and Its Measurement. *Journal of Intelligence, 11*(2), 27. https://doi.org/10.3390/ jintelligence11020027

Stanovich, K. E., West, R. F., & Toplak, M. E. (2013). Myside Bias, Rational Thinking, and Intelligence. *Current Directions in Psychological Science, 22*(4), 259–264. https://doi.org/10.1177/0963721413480174

Starbird, K. (2019). Disinformation's Spread: Bots, Trolls and All of Us. *Nature, 571*(449). https://doi.org/10.1038/d41586-019-02235-x

Starmans, B. J. (2019). 10 Examples of Fake News from History. The Social Historian. www.thesocialhistorian.com/fake-news/

Steele, E. J., Gorczynski, R. M., Lindley, R. A., Tokoro, G., Temple, R., & Wickramasinghe, N. C. (2020). Origin of New Emergent Coronavirus and Candida Fungal Diseases-Terrestrial or Cosmic? *Advances in Genetics, 106*, 75–100. https://doi.org/10.1016/bs.adgen.2020.04.002

Steele, M. A., Halkin, S. L., Smallwood, P. D., McKenna, T. J., Mitsopoulos, K., & Beam, M. (2008). Cache Protection Strategies of a Scatter-hoarding Rodent: Do Tree Squirrels Engage in Behavioural Deception? *Animal Behaviour, 75*(2), 705–714. https://doi.org/10.1016/j.anbehav.2007.07.026

Sunstein, C. R. (2001). *Republic.com.* Princeton University Press.

Sunstein, C. R. (2007). *Republic.com 2.0.* Princeton University Press.

Sunstein, C. R. (2017). *#republic: Divided Democracy in the Age of Social Media.* Princeton University Press.

Sunstein, C. R. (2023). Conspiracy Theory: On Certain Misconceptions about the Uses of Behavioral Science in Government. *SSRN Electronic Journal.* https://doi .org/10.2139/ssrn.4320348

Supreme Court of the United States. *(2023, May 18). TWITTER, INC. v. TAAMNEH ET AL. CERTIORARI TO THE UNITED STATES COURT OF APPEALS FOR THE NINTH CIRCUIT.* www.supremecourt.gov/opinions/22pdf/21-1496_d18f.pdf

Sussman, G. (2021). Propaganda and the Cold War. *Journalism & Communication Monographs, 23*(1), 70–75. https://doi.org/10.1177/1522637920983768

Swift, J. (1710). The Art of Political Lying. *The Examiner.*

Swift, J. (1726). *Travels Into Several Remote Nations of the World. In Four Parts. By Lemuel Gulliver, First a Surgeon, and then a Captain of Several Ships.* Benjamin Motte.

Swift, J. (1729). A Modest Proposal for Preventing the Children of Poor People From being a Burthen to Their Parents or Country, and For Making them Beneficial to the Publick. *Project Gutenberg.* www.gutenberg.org/files/1080/1080-h/1080-h.htm

Swire-Thompson, B., DeGutis, J., & Lazer, D. (2020). Searching for the Backfire Effect: Measurement and Design Considerations. *Journal of Applied Research in Memory and Cognition, 9*(3), 286–299. https://doi.org/10.1016/j.jarmac.2020.06.006

Swire-Thompson, B., Miklaucic, N., Wihbey, J., Lazer, D., & DeGutis, J. (2022). Backfire Effects after Correcting Misinformation Are Strongly Associated with Reliability. *Journal of Experimental Psychology: General, 151*(7), 1655–1665. https://doi.org/10.1037/xge0001131

Szebeni, Z., Lönnqvist, J.-E., & Jasinskaja-Lahti, I. (2021). Social Psychological Predictors of Belief in Fake News in the Run-Up to the 2019 Hungarian Elections: The Importance of Conspiracy Mentality Supports the Notion of Ideological Symmetry in Fake News Belief. *Frontiers in Psychology, 12.* https://doi.org/10.3389/fpsyg.2021.790848

Szostek, J. (2017). The Power and Limits of Russia's Strategic Narrative in Ukraine: The Role of Linkage. *Perspectives on Politics, 15*(2), 379–395. https://doi.org/10.1017/S153759271700007X

Tandoc, E. C., Lim, Z. W., & Ling, R. (2018). Defining "Fake News." *Digital Journalism, 6*(2), 137–153. https://doi.org/10.1080/21670811.2017.1360143

Tappin, B. M., Pennycook, G., & Rand, D. G. (2020). Bayesian or Biased? Analytic Thinking and Political Belief Updating. *Cognition, 204,* 104375. https://doi.org/10.1016/j.cognition.2020.104375

Tay, L. Q., Hurlstone, M. J., Kurz, T., & Ecker, U. K. H. (2021). A Comparison of Prebunking and Debunking Interventions for Implied Versus Explicit Misinformation. *British Journal of Psychology.* https://doi.org/10.1111/bjop.12551

Tearle, O. (2021). *Who Said, "A Lie Is Halfway Round the World Before the Truth Has Got Its Boots On"? Interesting Literature.* https://interestingliterature.com/2021/06/lie-halfway-round-world-before-truth-boots-on-quote-origin-meaning/

Terrell, M. C. (1904). Lynching from a Negro's Point of View. *The North American Review, 178*(571), 853–868. www.jstor.org/stable/25150991

Terren, L., & Borge-Bravo, R. (2021). Echo Chambers on Social Media: A Systematic Review of the Literature. *Review of Communication Research, 9,* 99–118. https://doi.org/10.12840/ISSN.2255-4165.028

Teter, M. (2020). *Blood Libel: On the Trail of an Antisemitic Myth.* Harvard University Press.

Thakur, P., & Ward, A. L. (2019, March 3). Nuclear Crisis Communication in an Era of Fake News and Media Overload – 19414. *WM2019: 45. Annual Waste Management Conference.* www.osti.gov/biblio/23005317

Thaler, R., & Sunstein, C. R. (2008). *Nudge: Improving Decisions about Health, Wealth, and Happiness.* Yale University Press.

The Onion. (2012). Kim Jong-Un Named The Onion's Sexiest Man Alive For 2012. *The Onion.* www.theonion.com/kim-jong-un-named-the-onions-sexiest-man-alive-for-2012-1819574194

The Oxford Essential Dictionary of the U.S. Military. (2002). *Information Warfare.* www.oxfordreference.com/display/10.1093/acref/9780199891580.001.0001/acref-9780199891580-e-3994?rskey=sortth&result=3843

Thomas, C. L. I. (1994). *Global Alert for All: Jesus Is Coming Soon.* https://groups.google.com/g/sci.stat.edu/c/q1Ng7bvtmOg/m/CawblLbmsIwJ?pli=1

Thorne, J., & Vlachos, A. (2018). Automated Fact Checking: Task Formulations, Methods and Future Directions. *Proceedings of the 27th International Conference on Computational Linguistics,* 3346–3359. https://aclanthology.org/C18-1283

Timberg, C., & Romm, T. (2018, December 17). *New Report on Russian Disinformation, Prepared for the Senate, Shows the Operation's Scale and Sweep.* Washington Post.

Todd, C., & O'Brien, K. J. (2016). Teaching Anthropogenic Climate Change Through Interdisciplinary Collaboration: Helping Students Think Critically about Science and Ethics in Dialogue. *Journal of Geoscience Education, 64*(1), 52–59. https://doi.org/10.5408/12-331.1

Tolz, V., & Teper, Y. (2018). Broadcasting Agitainment: A New Media Strategy of Putin's Third Residency. *Post-Soviet Affairs, 34*(4), 213–227. https://doi.org/10.1080/1060586X.2018.1459023

Tomlinson, N., & Redwood, S. (2013). Health Beliefs about Pre-school Immunisation: An Exploration of Views of Somali Women Resident in the UK. *Diversity and Equality in Health and Care, 10*(2), 101–113.

Törnberg, P. (2018). Echo Chambers and Viral Misinformation: Modeling Fake News as Complex Contagion. *PLOS ONE, 13*(9), e0203958. https://doi.org/10.1371/journal.pone.0203958

Traberg, C. S., Harjani, T., Roozenbeek, J., & van der Linden, S. (2023). The Socio-cognitive Factors That Underpin Misinformation Susceptibility. *Under Review.*

Traberg, C. S., Roozenbeek, J., & van der Linden, S. (2022). Psychological Inoculation against Misinformation: Current Evidence and Future Directions. *The ANNALS of the American Academy of Political and Social Science, 700*(1), 136–151. https://doi.org/10.1177/00027162221087936

Traberg, C. S., & van der Linden, S. (2022). Birds of a Feather Are Persuaded Together: Perceived Source Credibility Mediates the Effect of Political Bias on Misinformation Susceptibility. *Personality and Individual Differences, 185*(111269). https://doi.org/10.1016/j.paid.2021.111269

Tully, M., Vraga, E. K., & Bode, L. (2020). Designing and Testing News Literacy Messages for Social Media. *Mass Communication and Society, 23*(1), 22–46. https://doi.org/10.1080/15205436.2019.1604970

UK Government. (2022, December 16). *A Guide to the Online Safety Bill.* www.gov.uk/guidance/a-guide-to-the-online-safety-bill

UK Parliament. (2021, December 14). *No Longer the Land of the Lawless: Joint Committee Reports.* Committees.Parliament.Uk. https://committees.parliament.uk/committee/534/draft-online-safety-bill-joint-committee/news/159784/no-longer-the-land-of-the-lawless-joint-committee-reports/

UK Parliament. (2023, May 10). *Online Safety Bill*. Bills.Parliament.UK. https://bills.parliament.uk/bills/3137

UNESCO. (2021). *Media and Information Literate Citizens: Think Critically, Click Wisely!* https://unesdoc.unesco.org/ark:/48223/pf0000377068

University of Cambridge. (2019). *'Trickster God' Used Fake News in Babylonian Noah Story*. www.cam.ac.uk/research/news/trickster-god-used-fake-news-in-babylonian-noah-story

U.S. Department of State. (2023, May 1). *Disarming Disinformation: Our Shared Responsibility*. www.state.gov/disarming-disinformation/

Vahedi, Z., Sibalis, A., & Sutherland, J. E. (2018). Are Media Literacy Interventions Effective at Changing Attitudes and Intentions Towards Risky Health Behaviors in Adolescents? A Meta-analytic Review. *Journal of Adolescence, 67*, 140–152. https://doi.org/10.1016/j.adolescence.2018.06.007

Van Bavel, J. J., Harris, E. A., Pärnamets, P., Rathje, S., Doell, K. C., & Tucker, J. A. (2021). Political Psychology in the Digital (mis)Information age: A Model of News Belief and Sharing. *Social Issues and Policy Review, 15*(1), 84–113. https://doi.org/10.1111/sipr.12077

Van Bavel, J. J., & Pereira, A. (2018). The Partisan Brain: An Identity-Based Model of Political Belief. *Trends in Cognitive Sciences, 22*(3), 213–224. https://doi.org/j.tics.2018.01.004

van der Linde, A. (1870). *De Costerlegende*. Martinus Nijhoff.

van der Linden, S. (2022). Misinformation: Susceptibility, Spread, and Interventions to Immunize the Public. *Nature Medicine, 28*(3), 460–467. https://doi.org/10.1038/s41591-022-01713-6

Van der Linden, S. (2023). *Foolproof: Why Misinformation Infects Our Minds and How to Build Immunity*. W. W. Norton & Company.

van der Linden, S., Leiserowitz, A., Rosenthal, S., & Maibach, E. (2017). Inoculating the Public against Misinformation about Climate Change. *Global Challenges, 1*(2), 1600008. https://doi.org/10.1002/gch2.201600008

van der Linden, S., Maibach, E., Cook, J., Leiserowitz, A., & Lewandowsky, S. (2017). Inoculating against Misinformation. *Science, 358*(6367), 1141–1142. https://doi.org/10.1126/science.aar4533

van der Linden, S., Panagopoulos, C., Azevedo, F., & Jost, J. T. (2020). The Paranoid Style in American Politics Revisited: Evidence of an Ideological Asymmetry in Conspiratorial Thinking. *Political Psychology, 42*(1), 23–51. https://doi.org/10.1111/pops.12681

van der Linden, S., & Roozenbeek, J. (2020). Psychological Inoculation against Fake News. In R. Greifeneder, M. Jaffé, E. Newman, & N. Schwarz (Eds.), *The Psychology of Fake News: Accepting, Sharing, and Correcting Misinformation* (pp. 147–170). Psychology Press. https://doi.org/10.4324/9780429295379-11

van der Meer, T. G. L. A., Hameleers, M., & Ohme, J. (2023). Can Fighting Misinformation Have a Negative Spillover Effect? How Warnings for the Threat of Misinformation Can Decrease General News Credibility. *Journalism Studies*. https://doi.org/10.1080/1461670X.2023.2187652

Van Niekerk, B. (2015). Information Warfare in the 2013–2014 Ukraine crisis. In *Cybersecurity Policies and Strategies for Cyberwarfare Prevention*. https://doi.org/10.4018/978-1-4666-8456-0.ch012

van Prooijen, J.-W., Ligthart, J., Rosema, S., & Xu, Y. (2022). The Entertainment Value of Conspiracy Theories. *British Journal of Psychology*, 113, 25–48. https://doi.org/10.1111/bjop.12522

Varol, O., Ferrara, E., Davis, C. A., Menczer, F., & Flammini, A. (2017). Online Human-Bot Interactions: Detection, Estimation, and Characterization. *Proceedings of the Eleventh International AAAI Conference on Web and Social Media (ICWSM 2017), abs/1703.0.*

Vellani, V., Zheng, S., Ercelik, D., & Sharot, T. (2023). The Illusory Truth effect Leads to the Spread of Misinformation. *Cognition*, 236, 105421. https://doi.org/10.1016/j.cognition.2023.105421

Voigtländer, N., & Voth, H.-J. (2015). Nazi Indoctrination and Anti-Semitic Beliefs in Germany. *Proceedings of the National Academy of Sciences*, 112(26), 7931–7936. https://doi.org/10.1073/pnas.1414822112

Volkov, D., & Kolesnikov, A. (2022). *My Country, Right or Wrong: Russian Public Opinion on Ukraine.*

Vosoughi, S., Roy, D., & Aral, S. (2018). The Spread of True and False News online. *Science*, 359(6380), 1146–1151. https://doi.org/10.1126/science.aap9559

Vraga, E. K., & Bode, L. (2017). Using Expert Sources to Correct Health Misinformation in Social Media. *Science Communication*, 39(5), 621–645. https://doi.org/10.1177/1075547017731776

Vraga, E. K., & Bode, L. (2020). Defining Misinformation and Understanding its Bounded Nature: Using Expertise and Evidence for Describing Misinformation. *Political Communication*, 37(1), 136–144. https://doi.org/10.1080/10584609.2020.1716500

Vraga, E. K., Kim, S. C., & Cook, J. (2019). Testing Logic-based and Humor-based Corrections for Science, Health, and Political Misinformation on Social Media. *Journal of Broadcasting & Electronic Media*, 63(3), 393–414. https://doi.org/10.1080/08838151.2019.1653102

Vuorre, M., Orben, A., & Przybylski, A. K. (2021). There Is No Evidence That Associations Between Adolescents' Digital Technology Engagement and Mental Health Problems Have Increased. *Clinical Psychological Science*, 9(5), 823–835. https://doi.org/10.1177/2167702621994549

Wagner, M. (2021). Affective Polarization in Multiparty Systems. *Electoral Studies*, 69, 102199. https://doi.org/10.1016/j.electstud.2020.102199

Waits, T. (1973, March 6). *Step Right Up.* Asylum Records.

Walter, N., Cohen, J., Holbert, R. L., & Morag, Y. (2020). Fact-Checking: A Meta-Analysis of What Works and for Whom. *Political Communication*, 37(3), 350–375. https://doi.org/10.1080/10584609.2019.1668894

Walter, N., & Murphy, S. T. (2018). How to Unring the Bell: A Meta-analytic Approach to Correction of Misinformation. *Communication Monographs*, 85(3), 423–441. https://doi.org/10.1080/03637751.2018.1467564

Walter, N., & Tukachinsky, R. (2020). A Meta-analytic Examination of the Continued Influence of Misinformation in the Face of Correction: How Powerful Is It, Why Does It Happen, and How to Stop It? *Communication Research*, 47(2), 155–177. https://doi.org/10.1177/0093650219854600

Wardle, C., & Derakhshan, H. (2017). *Information Disorder: Toward an Interdisciplinary Framework for Research and Policymaking.* https://rm.coe

.int/information-disorder-toward-an-interdisciplinary-framework-for-researc/168076277c

Wasserman, I. M. (1998). Media Rhetoric and Images of Lynching in the Nineteenth and Twentieth Centuries. *Michigan Sociological Review*, 12, 68–94. www.jstor.org/stable/40969023

Whitehead, H. S., French, C. E., Caldwell, D. M., Letley, L., & Mounier-Jack, S. (2023). A Systematic Review of Communication Interventions for Countering Vaccine Misinformation. *Vaccine*, 41(5), 1018–1034. https://doi.org/10.1016/j.vaccine.2022.12.059

Whitfield, S. (2020). Why the 'Protocols of the Elders of Zion' Is Still Pushed by Anti-Semites More than a Century after Hoax First Circulated. *The Conversation*. https://theconversation.com/why-the-protocols-of-the-elders-of-zion-is-still-pushed-by-anti-semites-more-than-a-century-after-hoax-first-circulated-145220

Wiggins, R. (2000). Al Gore and the Creation of the Internet. *First Monday*, 5(10).

Williams, M. N., & Bond, C. M. C. (2020). A Preregistered Replication of "Inoculating the Public against Misinformation about Climate Change." *Journal of Environmental Psychology*, 70, 101456. https://doi.org/10.1016/j.jenvp.2020.101456

Wilson, A. (2014). *Ukraine Crisis: What It Means for the West*. Yale University Press.

Wilson, S. L., & Wiysonge, C. (2020). Social Media and Vaccine Hesitancy. *BMJ Global Health*, 5(e004206). https://doi.org/10.1136/bmjgh-2020-004206

Wilton Park. (2017). #Fake News: Innocuous or Intolerable? MixCloud. www.mixcloud.com/wiltonpark/fake-news-innocuous-or-intolerable/

Wineburg, S., Breakstone, J., McGrew, S., Smith, M., & Ortega, T. (2022). Lateral Reading on the Open Internet: A District-wide Field Study in High School Government Classes. *Journal of Educational Psychology*, 114(5), 893–909. https://doi.org/10.1037/edu0000740

Wojcieszak, M., Casas, A., Yu, X., Nagler, J., & Tucker, J. A. (2022). Most Users Do Not Follow Political Elites on Twitter; Those Who Do Show Overwhelming Preferences for Ideological Congruity. *Science Advances*, 8(39). https://doi.org/10.1126/sciadv.abn9418

Wood, T., & Porter, E. (2019). The Elusive Backfire Effect: Mass Attitudes' Steadfast Factual Adherence. *Political Behavior*, 41(1), 135–163. https://doi.org/10.1007/s11109-018-9443-y

WorldPublicOpinion.org. (2008). *International Poll: No Consensus On Who Was Behind 9/11*. https://worldpublicopinion.net/international-poll-no-consensus-on-who-was-behind-911/

Worobey, M., Levy, J. I., Serrano, L. M., Crits-Christoph, A., Pekar, J. E., Goldstein, S. A., Rasmussen, A. L., Kraemer, M. U. G., Newman, C., Koopmans, M. P. G., Suchard, M. A., Wertheim, J. O., Lemey, P., Robertson, D. L., Garry, R. F., Holmes, E. C., Rambaut, A., & Andersen, K. G. (2022). The Huanan Seafood Wholesale Market in Wuhan Was the Early Epicenter of the COVID-19 Pandemic. *Science*, 377(6609), 951–959. https://doi.org/10.1126/science.abp8715

Worthington, M. (2019). *Ea's Duplicity in the Gilgamesh Flood Story*. Routledge.

Yablokov, I. (2015). Conspiracy Theories as a Russian Public Diplomacy Tool: The Case of Russia Today (RT). *Politics*, 35(3–4), 301–315. https://doi.org/10.1111/1467-9256.12097

Young, Z. (2018, July 4). French Parliament Passes Law against "Fake News." *Politico.* www.politico.eu/article/french-parliament-passes-law-against-fake-news/

Zarocostas, J. (2020). How to Fight an Infodemic. *The Lancet, 395*(10225), 676. https://doi.org/10.1016/S0140-6736(20)30461-X

Zerback, T., Töpfl, F., & Knöpfle, M. (2021). The Disconcerting Potential of online Disinformation: Persuasive Effects of Astroturfing Comments and Three Strategies for Inoculation against Them. *New Media & Society, 23*(5), 1080–1093. https://doi.org/10.1177/1461444820908530

Zielinski, S. (2015). The Great Moon Hoax Was Simply a Sign of Its Time. Smithsonian Magazine. www.smithsonianmag.com/smithsonian-institution/great-moon-hoax-was-simply-sign-its-time-180955761/

Ziemer, C.-T., & Rothmund, T. (2022). Psychological Underpinnings of Disinformation Countermeasures: A Systematic Scoping Review. *PsyArxiv Preprints.* doi: 10.31234/osf.io/scq5v

Zollo, F., Bessi, A., Del Vicario, M., Scala, A., Caldarelli, G., Shekhtman, L., Havlin, S., & Quattrociocchi, W. (2017). Debunking in a World of Tribes. *PLOS ONE, 12*(7), 1–27. https://doi.org/10.1371/journal.pone.0181821

Zurth, P. (2021). The German NetzDG as Role Model or Cautionary Tale? Implications for the Debate on Social Media Liability: Implications for the Debate on Social Media Liability. *Fordham Intellectual Property, Media and Entertainment Law Journal, 31*(4). https://ir.lawnet.fordham.edu/iplj/vol31/iss4/4

INDEX